Divine Manifestations: Angels and Theophanies in Biblical Studies

Antonio M. Palmer

Divine Manifestations:
Angels and Theophanies in Biblical Studies

Published by:
Kingdom Publishing, LLC
1350 Blair Drive, Suite F
Odenton, MD 21113

Printed in the United States of America

Copyright ©2005 by Antonio Palmer

ISBN: 978-1-967006-02-1

TABLE OF CONTENTS

Introduction

Throughout the biblical narrative, divine encounters play a pivotal role in revealing God's nature, purposes, and relationship with humanity. These manifestations take various forms, most notably through angelic messengers and direct theophanies where God appears in perceivable ways to human recipients. This study explores the rich tapestry of divine manifestations woven throughout scripture, examining their theological significance, literary function, and historical development.

Angels, derived from the Hebrew *mal'ak* and Greek *angelos* (both meaning "messenger"), serve as divine intermediaries who execute God's will, deliver messages, and intervene in human affairs. As Michael S. Heiser notes, "The word 'angel' is not a description of what these beings are (their ontology); it is a description of what they do (their function)."[1] These celestial beings appear at critical junctures in the biblical narrative, particularly in moments of covenant establishment, divine intervention, and prophetic revelation.

Theophanies—from the Greek theos (God) and phainein (to appear)—represent direct manifestations of God's presence in forms perceivable to human senses. As Benjamin D. Sommer observes, "God appears in the Bible in ways that seem to compromise divine transcendence yet preserve divine freedom."[2] These appearances challenge simplistic understandings of divine incorporeality while affirming God's willingness to enter into human experience.

The study of angels and theophanies requires a multifaceted methodological approach. Textual analysis examines the literary presentation and vocabulary of divine manifestations across biblical

---

1   Michael S. Heiser, *The Unseen Realm: Recovering the Supernatural Worldview of the Bible* (Bellingham, WA: Lexham Press, 2015), 23.
2   Benjamin D. Sommer, *The Bodies of God and the World of Ancient Israel* (Cambridge: Cambridge University Press, 2009), 1.

genres. Historical-critical methods situate these accounts within their Ancient Near Eastern context, comparing biblical presentations with contemporaneous understandings of divine manifestation. Theological interpretation considers how these appearances reveal divine character and purposes within the larger canonical framework.

This work aims to provide a comprehensive biblical theology of divine manifestation, tracing developmental patterns from the Hebrew Bible through the New Testament while maintaining sensitivity to the distinct voices and perspectives within the biblical canon. By examining how God appears and acts through both angelic messengers and direct theophanies, we gain deeper insight into the biblical understanding of divine-human communication and relationship.

Part I
Foundational Concepts

Chapter 1

Angels in Biblical Theology

Etymology and Terminology

The primary Hebrew term for angel, *mal'ak,* appears approximately 213 times in the Hebrew Bible.[1] As Carol A. Newsom observes, "The basic meaning of the word is 'messenger,' whether human or divine, and thus the meaning must be determined from context."[2] The Septuagint consistently translates *mal'ak* as *angelos,* which carries the same semantic range and forms the basis for English "angel."

Other significant Hebrew terms associated with celestial beings include:

- *benê hā'ĕlōhîm* ("sons of God") – appears in Genesis 6:2, Job 1:6, 2:1, 38:7, and Psalm 29:1, referring to divine beings who comprise God's heavenly court.[3]
- *qĕdōšîm* ("holy ones") – used in passages like Psalm 89:5-7 and Daniel 8:13 to denote heavenly beings in God's presen
- *şĕbā'ōt* ("hosts") – frequently used in the divine title "YHWH of hosts," referring to God's command over heavenly armies.[4]
- *śārîm* ("princes") – used primarily in Daniel to denote high-ranking angelic beings with specific territorial jurisdictions.

---

1   David Noel Freedman and Michael E. O'Connor, *"Mal'āk,"* in *Theological Dictionary of the Old Testament,* ed. G. Johannes Botterweck, Helmer Ringgren, and Heinz-Josef Fabry, trans. David E. Green (Grand Rapids: Eerdmans, 1997), 8:308-25.

2   Carol A. Newsom, *"Angels,"* in *The Anchor Bible Dictionary,* ed. David Noel Freedman (New York: Doubleday, 1992), 1:248.

3   Michael S. Heiser, *"The Divine Council in Late Canonical and Non-Canonical Second Temple Jewish Literature"* (PhD diss., University of Wisconsin-Madison, 2004), 37-42.

4   Patrick D. Miller Jr., *The Divine Warrior in Early Israel* (Atlanta: Society of Biblical Literature, 2006), 64-67.

In the New Testament, *angelos* appears approximately 175 times, maintaining the dual meaning of human and divine messengers, though predominantly referring to the latter.[5] Additional terms include:

- *pneumata* ("spirits") – Hebrews 1:14 describes angels as "ministering spirits."
- *dynameis* ("powers") – listed among celestial beings in Romans 8:38 and elsewhere.
- *archē* and *exousia* ("rulers" and "authorities") – used in Colossians 1:16 and Ephesians 6:12 to denote spiritual powers.

This terminological variety reflects the complex and multifaceted understanding of celestial beings within biblical literature.

Categories and Hierarchies

While the Bible does not present a systematic angelology with clearly defined ranks, several categories of celestial beings emerge through careful textual analysis. As Darrell D. Hannah notes, "The Hebrew Bible contains no elaborate hierarchies of angels, though it does know of different types of angels with various functions."[6]

The cherubim *(kĕrûbîm)* first appear in Genesis 3:24 as guardians of Eden and feature prominently in tabernacle and temple imagery (Exodus 25:18-22; 1 Kings 6:23-28). Ezekiel's elaborate vision (Ezekiel 1, 10) portrays cherubim as composite beings with multiple faces and wings, supporting the divine throne. As Othmar Keel argues, "The cherubim serve primarily as throne bearers, emphasizing both God's mobility and sovereignty."[7]

---

5   Werner Foerster, *"Angelos,"* in *Theological Dictionary of the New Testament,* ed. Gerhard Kittel, trans. Geoffrey W. Bromiley (Grand Rapids: Eerdmans, 1964), 1:74-87.

6   Darrell D. Hannah, *Michael and Christ: Michael Traditions and Angel Christology in Early Christianity* (Tübingen: Mohr Siebeck, 1999), 15.

7   Othmar Keel, *The Symbolism of the Biblical World: Ancient Near Eastern Iconography and the Book of Psalms,* trans. Timothy J. Hallett (New York: Seabury Press, 1978), 169.

The seraphim *(śĕrāpîm)* appear only in Isaiah's temple vision (Isaiah 6:2-6), described as six-winged beings who proclaim God's holiness and facilitate Isaiah's purification. The etymology suggests a connection to fiery serpents, possibly reflecting their role as boundary guardians of sacred space.[8]

The four living creatures *(zōa)* in Revelation 4:6-8 combine elements of both cherubim and seraphim, demonstrating the New Testament's synthesis of earlier traditions.

Named angels appear primarily in later biblical texts. Michael *(mîkā'ēl,* "Who is like God?") features in Daniel as Israel's protective prince (Daniel 10:13, 21; 12:1) and in Revelation 12:7 leading heavenly forces against the dragon. Gabriel *(gabrî'ēl,* "God's strong one") appears as an interpretive angel in Daniel 8:16 and 9:21, and as the annunciation angel in Luke 1:19, 26. *Raphael* ("God heals") appears only in the deuterocanonical book of Tobit.

The New Testament references archangels (1 Thessalonians 4:16; Jude 9), suggesting some conception of angelic hierarchy, though details remain sparse. Pseudo-Dionysius would later systematize these various references into the elaborate medieval hierarchy of nine angelic orders, but such detailed organization exceeds the biblical evidence.[9]

Functions and Roles

Angels in biblical narrative serve diverse functions reflecting their fundamental role as agents of divine activity. As messengers, they deliver divine communication, particularly announcements of births (Genesis 16:7-12; Judges 13:3-5; Luke 1:11-20, 26-38), guidance in crisis (Genesis 31:11-13; 1 Kings 19:5-7), and prophetic revelation (Zechariah 1-6; Revelation 1:1).

---

8   Karen Randolph Joines, "Winged Serpents in Isaiah's Inaugural Vision," *Journal of Biblical Literature* 86, no. 4 (1967): 410-15.

9   David Lyle Jeffrey, ed., *A Dictionary of Biblical Tradition in English Literature* (Grand Rapids: Eerdmans, 1992), 39-43.

Angels frequently function as protectors and deliverers. The psalmist declares that "the angel of the LORD encamps around those who fear him, and delivers them" (Psalm 34:7), a theme exemplified in narratives like Daniel in the lions' den (Daniel 6:22) and Peter's prison escape (Acts 12:7-11). As Michael Heiler observes, "Angels demonstrate God's protective presence mediated through created beings who function as extensions of divine power."[10]

In military contexts, angels lead divine armies. Joshua encounters the "commander of the army of the LORD" before Jericho (Joshua 5:13-15), and Elisha's servant witnesses mountains "full of horses and chariots of fire" surrounding Dothan (2 Kings 6:17). This warrior aspect culminates in Revelation's cosmic battle led by Michael against draconic forces (Revelation 12:7-9).

Angels also serve liturgical functions, particularly in worship contexts. Isaiah witnesses seraphim proclaiming God's holiness (Isaiah 6:3), and John envisions countless angels worshiping the Lamb (Revelation 5:11-12). This portrayal creates what Matthew Thiessen calls a "liturgical template that connects earthly worship with heavenly reality."[11]

As interpreters and guides, angels help humans understand divine revelation. Daniel's visions are explained by Gabriel (Daniel 8:16-17, 9:21-23), and Revelation features numerous interpretive angels who guide John through complex visions. Zechariah's night visions consistently include an interpreting angel who explains symbolic elements (Zechariah 1:9, 13, 14, 19; 2:3; 4:1, 4-5; 5:5, 10; 6:4-5).

Finally, angels execute divine judgment. The destroying angel strikes Egypt's firstborn (Exodus 12:23), an angel brings pestilence upon Israel after David's census (2 Samuel 24:16-17), and Revelation portrays angels pouring out divine wrath through cosmic plagues (Revelation 16:1-21).

---

10   Michael Heiler, *Angels: Messengers of God* (New York: Crossroad, 1994), 28.

11   Matthew Thiessen, "The Form and Function of the Song of Moses (Deuteronomy 32:1-43)," *Journal of Biblical Literature* 123, no. 3 (2004): 415.

This judging function highlights the dual nature of divine presence—both salvific and potentially destructive.

Development from Hebrew Bible to New Testament

Angelology undergoes significant development across the biblical canon. Early texts present angels in relatively simple terms, primarily as manifestations of divine presence without elaborate descriptions or names. As Peter Schäfer notes, "In the earliest stratum of biblical literature, angels appear as momentary embodiments of divine activity rather than as independent beings with continuing existence."[12]

During and after the Babylonian exile, angelic portrayals become more complex. Daniel introduces named angels, celestial conflicts, and territorial jurisdiction, reflecting what John J. Collins identifies as increased interest in "cosmic dualism and heavenly mediation" during the Second Temple period.[13] Zechariah features the "angel of the LORD" as a distinct interpretive figure rather than a direct manifestation of YHWH, suggesting theological refinement regarding divine transcendence.

Intertestamental literature significantly expanded angelology beyond biblical parameters. The Book of Watchers (1 Enoch 1-36) elaborates on Genesis 6:1-4, developing complex traditions about fallen angels. Texts like Jubilees and the Songs of the Sabbath Sacrifice present detailed hierarchies and specialized angelic functions. The Qumran community emphasized angelic companionship with the righteous, particularly in liturgical contexts.[14]

The New Testament reflects awareness of these developments while maintaining focus on Christ's supremacy. Hebrews explicitly subordinates angels to Christ (Hebrews 1:4-14), addressing what Larry Hurtado calls "a

---

12   Peter Schäfer, *Rivalität zwischen Engeln und Menschen: Untersuchungen zur rabbinischen Engelvorstellung* (Berlin: De Gruyter, 1975), 8.

13   John J. Collins, *Daniel: A Commentary on the Book of Daniel* (Minneapolis: Fortress Press, 1993), 318.

14   Carol A. Newsom, *Songs of the Sabbath Sacrifice: A Critical Edition* (Atlanta: Scholars Press, 1985), 17-38.

tendency in some Jewish circles to elevate angelic veneration to problematic levels."[15] Paul similarly warns against angel worship (Colossians 2:18) while acknowledging angels as part of the cosmic order created through and for Christ (Colossians 1:16).

Revelation presents the most elaborate New Testament angelology, featuring numerous specialized angels who control natural elements, guide John's visionary experience, and participate in eschatological judgment. Yet even here, angels consistently deflect worship (Revelation 19:10, 22:8-9), reinforcing proper theological boundaries.

Throughout this development, angels maintain their fundamental character as servants of God's purposes, messengers of divine communication, and expressions of God's engagement with creation. As Kevin Sullivan observes, "Despite significant development in form and function, biblical angels consistently serve as mediating figures who facilitate divine-human interaction without becoming objects of devotion themselves."[16]

---

15   Larry W. Hurtado, *One God, One Lord: Early Christian Devotion and Ancient Jewish Monotheism* (Philadelphia: Fortress Press, 1988), 93.
16   Kevin P. Sullivan, *Wrestling with Angels: A Study of the Relationship Between Angels and Humans in Ancient Jewish Literature and the New Testament* (Leiden: Brill, 2004), 224.

Chapter 2
Understanding Theophanies

Definition and Distinguishing Characteristics

A theophany—from the Greek *theos* (God) and *phainein* (to appear)—refers to a visible manifestation of God perceptible to human senses. Unlike general divine activity or providential guidance, theophanies involve God's presence taking perceivable form within the created order. As Terence E. Fretheim notes, "The God who transcends the world enters into the life of the world in order to reveal something of the divine nature and purpose."[1]

Theophanies typically exhibit several distinguishing characteristics. First, they feature divine initiative—God chooses to appear rather than being summoned through ritual or magical means. Jörg Jeremias observes that "unlike Ancient Near Eastern parallels, biblical theophanies emphasize divine freedom rather than cultic compulsion."[2] This characteristic underscores theological emphases on divine sovereignty and grace.

Second, theophanies often include sensory elements that mediate divine presence. Natural phenomena like fire (Exodus 3:2), clouds (Exodus 19:9), storms (Psalm 18:7-15), or wind (1 Kings 19:11-13) frequently accompany divine manifestations. These elements simultaneously reveal and conceal, as George W. Savran explains: "The physical manifestations both make divine presence perceptible and protect the human recipient from the potentially lethal effects of unmediated divine glory."[3]

---

1   Terence E. Fretheim, *The Suffering of God: An Old Testament Perspective* (Philadelphia: Fortress Press, 1984), 79.
2   Jörg Jeremias, *Theophanie: Die Geschichte einer alttestamentlichen Gattung* (Neukirchen-Vluyn: Neukirchener Verlag, 1977), 142.
3   George W. Savran, *Encountering the Divine: Theophany in Biblical Narrative* (London: T&T Clark, 2005), 6.

Third, theophanies typically evoke powerful human responses—fear, awe, and prostration being most common. Isaiah cries, "Woe is me! For I am lost" (Isaiah 6:5) when encountering divine presence, while Ezekiel falls on his face (Ezekiel 1:28). This pattern reflects what Rudolf Otto termed the "mysterium tremendum et fascinans"—the awe-inspiring and fascinating mystery that characterizes encounters with the holy.[4]

Fourth, theophanies serve revelatory purposes, conveying divine messages, commissioning prophets, establishing covenants, or delivering promises. Claus Westermann identifies this purposive aspect as essential: "God does not simply appear; God appears in order to speak and act in ways that advance the divine-human relationship."[5]

Finally, theophanies maintain divine transcendence even amid immanence. As Samuel Terrien argues, "Biblical theophanies paradoxically preserve divine freedom and otherness precisely in the moment of intimate presence."[6] This dialectic prevents theophanic accounts from reducing God to the manifestation itself—God appears in the burning bush but is not identical to it.

Types of Theophanies in Scripture

Biblical theophanies take diverse forms, reflecting different theological emphases and narrative contexts. Among the most significant types are:

Anthropomorphic theophanies depict God in human-like form. Genesis 18 portrays God visiting Abraham at Mamre in the guise of three men, while Genesis 32:24-30 describes Jacob wrestling with a divine figure. Moses speaks with God "face to face, as a man speaks to his friend" (Exodus 33:11), though the full divine glory remains veiled (Exodus 33:20-23). These accounts, as James Barr notes, "use anthropomorphic language

---

4   Rudolf Otto, *The Idea of the Holy*, trans. John W. Harvey (Oxford: Oxford University Press, 1923), 12-40.

5   Claus Westermann, *Theologie des Alten Testaments in Grundzügen* (Göttingen: Vandenhoeck & Ruprecht, 1978), 24.

6   Samuel Terrien, *The Elusive Presence: Toward a New Biblical Theology* (San Francisco: Harper & Row, 1978), 63.

without embarrassment or apology, suggesting early Israelite theology had fewer concerns about divine corporeality than later traditions."[7]

Glory theophanies focus on the *kabod YHWH* (glory of the LORD), a luminous manifestation of divine presence. Exodus describes the divine glory as "like a devouring fire" (Exodus 24:17) and filling the tabernacle (Exodus 40:34-35). Ezekiel's elaborate throne vision depicts the glory as brilliant, fiery radiance surrounding a human-like figure (Ezekiel 1:26-28). As Tryggve Mettinger observes, "The *kabod* tradition emphasizes visual perception of divine presence while maintaining appropriate theological distance."[8]

Name theophanies connect divine manifestation with God's name (shem). Deuteronomy repeatedly refers to the sanctuary as the place where God "causes his name to dwell" (Deuteronomy 12:5, 11; 14:23), suggesting divine presence mediated through name rather than form. When Solomon dedicates the temple, he acknowledges that even heaven cannot contain God, yet prays toward the house where God's name dwells (1 Kings 8:27-29). According to Sandra Richter, "The name theology allows for genuine divine presence while avoiding crude localization of the deity."[9]

Angel theophanies feature the enigmatic "angel of the LORD" *(mal'ak YHWH),* who sometimes speaks as God's representative and other times as God directly. Hagar encounters this figure in the wilderness (Genesis 16:7-13), Jacob receives blessing from him (Genesis 48:15-16), and Moses receives his commission through him at the burning bush (Exodus 3:2-6). This ambiguous figure, as Camilla Hélena von Heijne argues, "navigates

---

7   James Barr, *"Theophany and Anthropomorphism in the Old Testament,"* in Congress Volume: Oxford 1959, Supplements to Vetus Testamentum 7 (Leiden: Brill, 1960), 31-38.

8   Tryggve N.D. Mettinger, *The Dethronement of Sabaoth: Studies in the Shem and Kabod Theologies* (Lund: Gleerup, 1982), 80-115.

9   Sandra L. Richter, *The Deuteronomistic History and the Name Theology: "lešakkēn šemô šām" in the Bible and the Ancient Near East* (Berlin: de Gruyter, 2002), 37.

the theological tension between divine transcendence and immanence through a figure both distinct from and identified with YHWH."[10]

Dream and vision theophanies occur during altered states of consciousness. Jacob sees God at the top of a heavenly ladder (Genesis 28:12-13), Isaiah beholds the divine throne (Isaiah 6:1-5), and Ezekiel witnesses the divine chariot (Ezekiel 1). These accounts, according to Susan Niditch, "use the dream-vision format to mediate encounters that might otherwise transgress boundaries between divine and human realms."[11]

Nature theophanies associate divine appearance with cosmic phenomena. The Sinai theophany features thunder, lightning, thick cloud, trumpet blast, fire, and smoke (Exodus 19:16-19). Elijah experiences divine presence not in wind, earthquake, or fire, but in "a sound of sheer silence" (1 Kings 19:11-12). Psalms frequently depict God appearing in storms (Psalm 18:7-15; 29:3-9; 97:2-5). As Theodore Hiebert notes, "Natural theophanies connect divine power with creation while distinguishing Israelite conceptions from nature deities of surrounding cultures."[12]

Christophanies refer to manifestations of Christ, either pre-incarnate appearances in the Hebrew Bible (as some interpret the "angel of the LORD") or post-resurrection appearances in the New Testament. The disciples encounter the risen Jesus despite locked doors (John 20:19, 26), and Paul meets Christ in blinding light on the Damascus road (Acts 9:3-6). The transfiguration (Matthew 17:1-8; Mark 9:2-8; Luke 9:28-36) reveals Christ's divine glory to select disciples. As Larry Hurtado observes, "Christophanies form part of early Christian conviction that Jesus shares in divine identity and manifests divine presence."[13]

---

10   Camilla Hélena von Heijne, *The Messenger of the Lord in Early Jewish Interpretations of Genesis* (Berlin: Walter de Gruyter, 2010), 94.

11   Susan Niditch, *The Symbolic Vision in Biblical Tradition* (Chico, CA: Scholars Press, 1983), 175.

12   Theodore Hiebert, *The Yahwist's Landscape: Nature and Religion in Early Israel* (New York: Oxford University Press, 1996), 143.

13   Larry W. Hurtado, *Lord Jesus Christ: Devotion to Jesus in Earliest Christianity* (Grand Rapids: Eerdmans, 2003), 179.

Theological Significance of Divine Self-Disclosure

Theophanies carry profound theological implications regarding divine nature and divine-human relationship. First, they affirm divine freedom and initiative in revelation. Unlike various Ancient Near Eastern traditions where deities could be manipulated through ritual, biblical theophanies emphasize God's sovereign choice to appear. As Walter Brueggemann notes, "YHWH is not available on command but comes in freedom according to divine purpose."[14]

Second, theophanies demonstrate divine accommodation to human limitations. God adapts to human perceptual capacities through visible forms, audible voices, and comprehensible language. As John Calvin famously expressed it, God "lisps with us as nurses are wont to do with little children," adjusting self-disclosure to human capacity.[15] This accommodating quality highlights divine grace and communicative intent.

Third, theophanies affirm divine immanence alongside transcendence. They challenge simplistic understandings of divine remoteness by portraying God's willingness to enter created space and time. Yet they simultaneously preserve divine transcendence through elements like cloud, fire, and overwhelming glory that prevent complete access or comprehension. As Michael Wyschogrod observes, "The biblical God is both infinitely beyond human experience and intimately engaged with human history."[16]

Fourth, theophanies establish and renew covenant relationships. Divine appearances frequently coincide with covenant establishments—with Noah after the flood (Genesis 9:8-17), with Abraham regarding his descendants (Genesis 15, 17), with Israel at Sinai (Exodus 19-24). These appearances, according to Frank Moore Cross, "dramatize the personal

---

14   Walter Brueggemann, *Theology of the Old Testament: Testimony, Dispute, Advocacy* (Minneapolis: Fortress Press, 1997), 570.

15   John Calvin, *Institutes of the Christian Religion,* ed. John T. McNeill, trans. Ford Lewis Battles (Philadelphia: Westminster Press, 1960), 1.13.1.

16   Michael Wyschogrod, *The Body of Faith: God and the People Israel* (New York: Seabury Press, 1983), 36.

nature of covenant commitment, emphasizing that covenant binds persons rather than merely establishing legal conditions."[17]

Fifth, theophanies authenticate prophetic messengers and divine messages. Moses receives his commission through the burning bush theophany (Exodus 3), Isaiah through the temple vision (Isaiah 6), and Ezekiel through the chariot throne (Ezekiel 1). As Gerhard von Rad notes, "The theophany legitimates the prophet as one who has stood in the divine council and been entrusted with authentic divine communication."[18]

Finally, theophanies anticipate eschatological divine presence. Isaiah envisions a future when "the glory of the LORD shall be revealed, and all people shall see it together" (Isaiah 40:5). Ezekiel foresees the divine glory returning to the temple (Ezekiel 43:1-5), and Zechariah describes a day when "the LORD will be king over all the earth" (Zechariah 14:9). Revelation culminates with the declaration that "the dwelling of God is with mortals" (Revelation 21:3). As Richard Bauckham argues, "Biblical theophanies provide partial and temporary glimpses of the full divine presence that constitutes eschatological hope."[19]

Hermeneutical Approaches to Theophanic Texts

Interpreting theophanic texts presents unique challenges due to their extraordinary subject matter and diverse literary forms. Several interpretive approaches have emerged in the history of biblical scholarship.

Literal-historical interpretation treats theophanic accounts as straightforward descriptions of actual events. This approach, advocated by conservative scholars like E.J. Young, maintains that "if Scripture presents an account as historical, it should be received as such rather than reduced

---

17   Frank Moore Cross, *Canaanite Myth and Hebrew Epic: Essays in the History of the Religion of Israel* (Cambridge: Harvard University Press, 1973), 295.
18   Gerhard von Rad, *Old Testament Theology,* trans. D.M.G. Stalker (Louisville: Westminster John Knox, 2001), 1:289.
19   Richard Bauckham, *The Theology of the Book of Revelation* (Cambridge: Cambridge University Press, 1993), 141.

to metaphor or projection."[20] While respecting the text's self-presentation, this approach sometimes struggles with anthropomorphic elements and apparent contradictions with divine incorporeality.

Mythological interpretation views theophanies as expressions of mythic consciousness without necessarily affirming their historicity. Influenced by comparative religion, Rudolf Bultmann and others understood theophanic accounts as reflecting ancient worldviews that modern interpreters must "demythologize."[21] Critics contend this approach imposes modern categories of myth versus history that ancient authors would not have recognized.

Form-critical approaches analyze theophanic accounts according to literary patterns and cultural contexts. Sigmund Mowinckel identified cultic settings for many theophanic texts, especially in Psalms, arguing they originated in temple liturgy.[22] Jörg Jeremias developed a comprehensive form-critical analysis of theophanic texts, identifying standard elements like approach, reaction, and reassurance.[23] Form criticism illuminates literary conventions while sometimes underemphasizing unique theological content.

Canonical interpretation examines theophanies within the larger biblical witness. Brevard Childs argued that "regardless of original settings, theophanic accounts must be interpreted within the final form of scripture and its theological framework."[24] This approach attends to how texts function within the completed canon rather than focusing exclusively on hypothetical original contexts.

---

20   Edward J. Young, *My Servants the Prophets* (Grand Rapids: Eerdmans, 1952), 143.

21   Rudolf Bultmann, *"New Testament and Mythology,"* in *Kerygma and Myth: A Theological Debate,* ed. *Hans Werner Bartsch,* trans. Reginald H. Fuller (London: SPCK, 1953), 1-44.

22   Sigmund Mowinckel, *The Psalms in Israel's Worship,* trans. D.R. Ap-Thomas (Nashville: Abingdon, 1962), 1:106-92.

23   Jörg Jeremias, *Theophanie: Die Geschichte einer alttestamentlichen Gattung,* 2nd ed. (Neukirchen-Vluyn: Neukirchener Verlag, 1977), 34-69.

24   Brevard S. Childs, *Introduction to the Old Testament as Scripture* (Philadelphia: Fortress Press, 1979), 164-66.

Theological interpretation focuses on theophanies' revelatory content within a faith framework. Karl Barth understood theophanies as instances of God's self-revelation, emphasizing that "God remains subject even in revelation; God is not captured by the manifestation but freely present through it."[25] This approach prioritizes theological significance over historical reconstruction.

Narrative analysis examines how theophanies function within biblical storytelling. Robert Alter demonstrated how theophanic accounts use literary techniques like type-scenes, repetition, and strategic ambiguity to engage readers.[26] This approach highlights how narrative presentation shapes theological understanding.

Intertextual reading traces connections between theophanic accounts across the biblical canon. Richard Hays showed how New Testament authors reinterpreted Hebrew Bible theophanies in light of Christ, creating "echoes of scripture" that resonate across both testaments.[27] This approach illuminates how biblical authors themselves interpreted earlier theophanic traditions.

A comprehensive hermeneutic of theophanic texts benefits from multiple interpretive lenses. As J. Richard Middleton observes, "Responsible interpretation addresses historical context, literary form, canonical placement, and theological significance without reducing these multilayered texts to a single dimension."[28] The complex nature of divine self-disclosure requires interpretive humility and methodological flexibility.

Contemporary interpretation increasingly recognizes that theophanic accounts speak not only about God but also about human capacity to

---

25   Karl Barth, *Church Dogmatics,* trans. G.T. Thomson and Harold Knight (Edinburgh: T&T Clark, 1936-1977), II/1:362.

26   Robert Alter, *The Art of Biblical Narrative,* rev. ed. (New York: Basic Books, 2011), 56-78.

27   Richard B. Hays, *Echoes of Scripture in the Letters of Paul* (New Haven: Yale University Press, 1989), 14-33.

28   J. Richard Middleton, *The Liberating Image: The Imago Dei in Genesis 1* (Grand Rapids: Brazos Press, 2005), 25.

perceive and articulate divine presence. As Walter Brueggemann suggests, "Theophanic texts witness to the human struggle to speak about unspeakable encounters with the divine Other using inevitably inadequate language and imagery."[29] This recognition invites interpretive openness while still affirming that these texts communicate genuine divine self-disclosure rather than merely human religious projection.

---

29   Walter Brueggemann, *Theology of the Old Testament: Testimony, Dispute, Advocacy* (Minneapolis: Fortress Press, 1997), 568.

Chapter 3

Historical and Cultural Context

Ancient Near Eastern Parallels and Influences

Understanding biblical angels and theophanies requires situating them within their broader Ancient Near Eastern (ANE) context. While biblical presentations remain distinctive, they emerge from and dialogue with a cultural milieu where divine manifestations and intermediary beings were common theological concepts.

Mesopotamian traditions featured various classes of intermediary beings. The *lamassu* and *shedu* (protective spirits often depicted as human-headed winged bulls) guarded temples and palaces. As Jeremy Black and Anthony Green observe, "These beings mediated between divine and human realms, bringing divine protection into human space."[1] Mesopotamian texts also mention messenger deities who carried communication between gods and between divine and human realms. The *apkallu* (primeval sages) transmitted divine wisdom to humanity, somewhat paralleling biblical angels' revelatory functions.

Egyptian religious texts describe numerous intermediary beings. The *ba* and *ka* aspects of deities could manifest separately from the god's essential nature, allowing for divine presence in multiple locations. Jeremy Naydler notes that "these manifestations enabled divine-human interaction while maintaining divine transcendence."[2] The Egyptian "Instruction of Merikare" mentions protective beings who escort the deceased, conceptually similar to guardian angels in later biblical and post-biblical tradition.

---

1   Jeremy Black and Anthony Green, *Gods, Demons and Symbols of Ancient Mesopotamia: An Illustrated Dictionary* (Austin: University of Texas Press, 1992), 115.

2   Jeremy Naydler, *Temple of the Cosmos: The Ancient Egyptian Experience of the Sacred* (Rochester, VT: Inner Traditions, 1996), 87.

Canaanite religion, particularly as revealed in the Ugaritic texts, provides the closest parallels to biblical angelic concepts. The Ugaritic pantheon included messenger deities who executed divine commands. According to Mark S. Smith, "The Ugaritic messengers exhibit similar functions to biblical *mal'ak,* though biblical tradition radically subordinates these figures to YHWH's exclusive divinity."[3] Canaanite texts also describe divine councils where lesser deities gathered around the high god El, paralleling biblical references to God's heavenly court (1 Kings 22:19-22; Job 1:6-12; Psalm 82).

Regarding theophanies, ANE literature provides significant comparative material. Mesopotamian texts describe divine appearances in dreams, visions, and occasionally physical manifestations. The Epic of Gilgamesh portrays divine beings appearing in dreams to communicate with humans. The "Poem of Erra" describes how the god Marduk "clothed himself with the halo of ten gods" when appearing to humans, suggesting concern with the dangerous power of unmediated divine presence.[4]

Egyptian texts typically associate divine manifestation with cult statues and sacred animals rather than direct appearances. However, New Kingdom royal texts describe divine encounters where gods appeared to pharaohs in dreams or visions. The "Proclamation of Ramesses II" recounts the god Amun-Re appearing to the king during battle, suggesting, as Jan Assmann notes, "the possibility of divine manifestation at crucial historical moments."[5]

Canaanite literature vividly portrays divine manifestations, often associated with storm imagery. Baal appears in "seven lightnings" and "eight storehouses of thunder," imagery closely paralleling biblical storm

---

3   Mark S. Smith, *The Origins of Biblical Monotheism: Israel's Polytheistic Background and the Ugaritic Texts* (Oxford: Oxford University Press, 2001), 54.
4   Luigi Cagni, *The Poem of Erra* (Malibu, CA: Undena Publications, 1977), 30.
5   Jan Assmann, *The Search for God in Ancient Egypt,* trans. David Lorton (Ithaca, NY: Cornell University Press, 2001), 221.

theophanies.[6] As Theodore J. Lewis observes, "Both Canaanite and biblical traditions associate divine appearance with overwhelming natural forces, though biblical texts consistently deny these forces any independent divine status."[7]

Hittite texts describe gods appearing to kings in dreams and visions, particularly in contexts of divine guidance for military campaigns. Royal prayers frequently request divine manifestation through oracular signs, suggesting institutionalized expectation of divine communication.

Several key distinctions emerge when comparing biblical and ANE presentations. First, biblical tradition progressively centralizes divine authority in a single deity rather than distributing it among competing powers. As Patrick D. Miller notes, "While utilizing common ANE imagery, biblical texts subordinate all intermediary beings to YHWH's unrivaled authority."[8]

Second, biblical texts exhibit greater theological restraint regarding divine form. While ANE traditions freely depicted deities in human and animal forms, biblical texts generally avoid concrete descriptions of divine appearance, focusing instead on effects of divine presence like glory, cloud, or fire. Benjamin Sommer suggests this reflects "theological tension between divine presence and transcendence distinctive to biblical thought."[9]

Third, biblical angels, unlike many ANE intermediaries, never become objects of worship themselves. ANE traditions often included cultic veneration of messenger deities, while biblical angels consistently deflect worship toward God alone (Judges 13:16; Revelation 19:10, 22:8-9).

---

6   KTU 1.101:3-4; translation in Dennis Pardee, *Ritual and Cult at Ugarit* (Atlanta: Society of Biblical Literature, 2002), 113.

7   Theodore J. Lewis, "Divine Images and Aniconism in Ancient Israel," *Journal of the American Oriental Society* 118, no. 1 (1998): 36-53.

8   Patrick D. Miller Jr., *The Divine Warrior in Early Israel* (Atlanta: Society of Biblical Literature, 2006), 64-67.

9   Benjamin D. Sommer, *The Bodies of God and the World of Ancient Israel* (Cambridge: Cambridge University Press, 2009), 38.

Despite these distinctions, the ANE background illuminates biblical presentations by demonstrating how biblical authors utilized cultural motifs while transforming them according to Israel's developing monotheistic theology. As Mark S. Smith argues, "Biblical writers did not create ex nihilo but rather adapted existing conceptual frameworks while reconfiguring them according to their distinctive theological commitments."[10]

Greco-Roman Concepts of Divine Manifestations

The Hellenistic world into which Second Temple Judaism and early Christianity emerged provided another significant cultural framework for understanding divine messengers and manifestations. Greek and Roman religious traditions featured various forms of divine appearance and intermediary beings that influenced—and were influenced by—Jewish and Christian concepts.

Greek tradition recognized several categories of divine manifestations. *Epiphaneia* (appearance) described a deity becoming visible to humans, typically in human form. Numerous Greek myths recount gods appearing disguised as mortals, as when Zeus and Hermes visit Baucis and Philemon (Ovid, *Metamorphoses* 8.611-724). According to Robert Parker, "These accounts emphasized the importance of proper hospitality, since divine visitors often tested human responses and rewarded kindness."[11]

Greek literature described divine manifestations in battle contexts, as when Athena appears to strengthen warriors. Homer's *Iliad* portrays gods physically participating in the Trojan War, sometimes visible only to favored mortals. Divine intervention in battles parallels biblical accounts like Joshua's encounter with the "commander of the LORD's army" (Joshua 5:13-15).

The concept of *daimones* in Greek thought provided intermediary figures between gods and humans. For Plato, daimones carried prayers and

---

10   Mark S. Smith, *The Early History of God: Yahweh and the Other Deities in Ancient Israel,* 2nd ed. (Grand Rapids: Eerdmans, 2002), 19.

11   Robert Parker, *On Greek Religion* (Ithaca, NY: Cornell University Press, 2011), 103.

sacrifices to gods and divine blessings to humans (Symposium 202e-203a). While early Greek usage carried neutral or positive connotations, later developments—especially in Jewish and Christian contexts—increasingly viewed daimones as malevolent spirits. As John M. Dillon notes, "The conceptual category remained useful for explaining supernatural intermediaries, even as its moral valuation shifted dramatically."[12]

The Hermetic tradition emphasized divine messengers, particularly Hermes/Mercury as psychopomp and revealer of divine wisdom. Hermetic texts described revelation mediated through divine intermediaries, somewhat paralleling angelic mediation in apocalyptic literature.

Roman religion featured the *genius* (protective spirit) associated with individuals, families, and locations. The emperor's *genius* became particularly significant in imperial cult. Household deities (*lares* and *penates*) protected specific places, conceptually similar to guardian angels in some post-biblical traditions. As Valerie M. Warrior observes, "These intermediary figures bridged cosmic and household spaces, bringing divine protection into daily life."[13]

The philosophical schools, particularly Middle Platonism and Neo-Pythagoreanism, developed sophisticated theories about intermediary beings and divine manifestation. Plutarch described daimons as intermediaries who "transmit things from men to gods and from gods to men" (*On the Obsolescence of Oracles* 416C-417A). Philo of Alexandria synthesized Jewish and Platonic concepts, describing the Logos as supreme intermediary and identifying angels as divine powers manifesting God's activities in the world. As Gregory E. Sterling notes, "Philo's synthesis provided conceptual frameworks that would influence both Jewish angelology and early Christology."[14]

---

12   John M. Dillon, *The Middle Platonists, 80 B.C. to A.D. 220* (Ithaca, NY: Cornell University Press, 1996), 31.

13   Valerie M. Warrior, *Roman Religion* (Cambridge: Cambridge University Press, 2006), 36.

14   Gregory E. Sterling, *"Philo and the Logic of Apologetics: An Analysis of the Hypothetica,"* in Ancient Judaism in its Hellenistic Context, ed. Carol Bakhos (Leiden: Brill, 2005), 135.

Significant interchange occurred between Jewish/Christian and Greco-Roman concepts during the Hellenistic period. The Septuagint translation sometimes reflected Greek theological categories, as when *daimonion* was used for various Hebrew terms. Jewish texts like the Wisdom of Solomon showed engagement with Greek philosophical concepts while maintaining distinctively Jewish theological commitments.

The New Testament's presentation of angels and divine manifestations reflects awareness of Greco-Roman concepts while adapting them to Christian theological frameworks. Acts portrays Paul engaging Athenian philosophical traditions when discussing divine nature (Acts 17:16-34). The author of Hebrews develops sophisticated arguments about Christ's superiority to angels that would be intelligible to audiences familiar with Middle Platonic hierarchies.

Despite these interactions, several distinctive elements appear in biblical and early Christian presentations. First, biblical tradition maintained stricter theological boundaries against worshiping intermediary beings, unlike Greco-Roman traditions where lesser deities received cultic veneration. Second, biblical texts emphasized the moral aspects of divine messengers over metaphysical speculation about their nature, contrasting with philosophical tendencies in Greco-Roman thought. Third, Christian tradition increasingly centered intermediary functions in Christ rather than distributing them among multiple beings, as reflected in Colossians 1:15-20.

Jewish Interpretive Traditions

Between the biblical period and the emergence of rabbinic Judaism, Jewish interpretive traditions significantly developed the concepts of angels and divine manifestation. These elaborations responded to new historical circumstances, engagement with surrounding cultures, and evolving theological concerns.

Apocalyptic literature from the Second Temple period greatly expanded angelology beyond biblical parameters. The Book of Watchers (1 Enoch 1-36) elaborated on Genesis 6:1-4, developing complex traditions about fallen angels. As George W.E. Nickelsburg observes, "Enochic traditions explained evil as originating from rebellious angels who taught forbidden knowledge to humanity, creating a cosmic drama of divine judgment and ultimate restoration."[15] The Astronomical Book (1 Enoch 72-82) described angels governing celestial bodies and natural phenomena, reflecting increased interest in angels' cosmic functions.

The Book of Jubilees introduced the concept of angels present at creation, with specific angels created on the first day: "On the first day He created the heavens which are above and the earth and the waters and all the spirits which serve before Him" (Jubilees 2:2). Jubilees also developed the idea of angels associated with particular nations: "But He appointed a spirit to rule over all the nations, but over Israel He did not appoint any angel or spirit" (Jubilees 15:31-32). As James C. VanderKam notes, "Jubilees reflects growing concern to protect Israel's unique relationship with God while explaining the religious diversity of the Hellenistic world."[16]

Qumran texts reflect extensive angelological development. The War Scroll (1QM) describes angelic participation in eschatological battle between the "sons of light" and "sons of darkness." The Songs of the Sabbath Sacrifice detail elaborate angelic liturgies in the heavenly temple. According to Carol Newsom, "These texts demonstrate how angelic worship provided a template for human liturgical practice, connecting earthly and heavenly realms through parallel ritual actions."[17]

Philo of Alexandria, working within the Hellenistic Jewish tradition, interpreted angels as divine powers (*dynameis*) that manifest God's activities in the world. He identified the Logos as the supreme intermediary between God and creation, with angels serving as subordinate manifestations of divine activities. As David Winston notes, "Philo's synthesis of biblical

---

15   George W.E. Nickelsburg, *1 Enoch 1: A Commentary on the Book of 1 Enoch, Chapters 1-36; 81-108* (Minneapolis: Fortress Press, 2001), 46.

16   James C. VanderKam, *The Book of Jubilees* (Sheffield: Sheffield Academic Press, 2001), 128.

17   Carol A. Newsom, *Songs of the Sabbath Sacrifice: A Critical Edition* (Atlanta: Scholars Press, 1985), 17-38.

and Platonic concepts created a sophisticated philosophical framework for understanding divine mediation without compromising divine unity."[18]

Regarding theophanies, Jewish interpretation increasingly emphasized their mediated nature. The Targums (Aramaic translations/interpretations of Hebrew Scripture) frequently replaced direct divine appearance with references to God's Word *(Memra)*, Glory *(Yekara)*, or Presence *(Shekhinah)*. For example, Targum Onqelos renders Genesis 3:8 ("they heard the sound of the LORD God walking in the garden") as "they heard the voice of the Memra of the LORD God walking in the garden," inserting the intermediary concept of divine Word between God and creation. According to Bruce D. Chilton, "These interpretive moves reflect growing theological concern to protect divine transcendence while affirming genuine divine-human interaction."[19]

The Aramaic Targums particularly developed the concept of the Shekhinah as divine presence manifested in Israel's midst. Targum Pseudo-Jonathan to Exodus 33:14-15 elaborates: "My Shekhinah will go among you and will prepare a resting place for you... If your Shekhinah does not go among us, do not bring us up from here." This concept provided conceptual continuity between biblical theophanies and post-temple Jewish understanding of divine presence. As Gershom Scholem observes, "The Shekhinah concept bridged biblical theophanic language and later Jewish mysticism's concern with divine immanence."[20]

Rabbinic literature continued these interpretive developments. The Talmud and midrashic collections present numerous angelological elaborations, including hierarchies, specific functions, and associations with particular biblical figures. Genesis Rabbah 68:12 interprets Jacob's ladder vision as revealing "the princes of the nations" ascending and descending,

---

18   David Winston, *Logos and Mystical Theology in Philo of Alexandria* (Cincinnati: Hebrew Union College Press, 1985), 42.

19   Bruce D. Chilton, *The Glory of Israel: The Theology and Provenience of the Isaiah Targum* (Sheffield: JSOT Press, 1983), 66.

20   Gershom Scholem, *On the Mystical Shape of the Godhead: Basic Concepts in the Kabbalah,* trans. Joachim Neugroschel (New York: Schocken Books, 1991), 140-96.

suggesting angelic representatives of earthly kingdoms. Exodus Rabbah 32:9 describes Moses ascending to heaven during the Sinai revelation and conversing with angels who oppose giving Torah to humans, portraying angelic involvement in revelation.

Regarding divine manifestation, rabbinic sources typically emphasize mediation through Shekhinah, divine voice *(bat qol),* or angelic representatives. As Alan F. Segal notes, "Rabbinic discussions of theophanic texts carefully balanced affirmation of divine presence with theological caution regarding God's incorporeality and transcendence."[21] This balance appears in rabbinic treatment of anthropomorphic passages, which were often interpreted metaphorically or as accommodations to human understanding.

Jewish mystical traditions further developed concepts of divine manifestation. Merkabah mysticism, drawing on Ezekiel's throne vision, elaborated practices for contemplating divine glory. Hekhalot literature described mystical ascent through heavenly palaces guarded by angels. According to Peter Schäfer, "These traditions transformed biblical theophanic accounts into templates for mystical experience, where visionary encounter with divine glory became the pinnacle of religious aspiration."[22]

Later kabbalastic tradition developed sophisticated theories about divine attributes *(sefirot)* as aspects of God's nature that could be perceived by humans. These developments, while beyond biblical parameters, demonstrate the enduring influence of biblical theophanic and angelic concepts on Jewish theological imagination.

Early Christian Developments

Early Christianity inherited Jewish traditions regarding angels and divine manifestation while radically reconfiguring them around Christ. This

---

21   Alan F. Segal, *Two Powers in Heaven: Early Rabbinic Reports about Christianity and Gnosticism* (Leiden: Brill, 1977), 33-59.

22   Peter Schäfer, *The Hidden and Manifest God: Some Major Themes in Early Jewish Mysticism,* trans. Aubrey Pomerance (Albany: State University of New York Press, 1992), 150.

distinctive christological focus transformed how Christians understood both angelic intermediaries and divine presence.

The New Testament presents angels primarily as servants of Christ and witnesses to his significance. Angels announce Jesus's birth (Luke 1:26-38; 2:8-15), minister to him after his temptation (Matthew 4:11; Mark 1:13), strengthen him in Gethsemane (Luke 22:43), proclaim his resurrection (Matthew 28:5-7; Mark 16:5-7; Luke 24:4-7; John 20:12-13), and will accompany his return (Matthew 16:27; 25:31; Mark 8:38; Luke 9:26; 2 Thessalonians 1:7). As Darrell D. Hannah observes, "Angels in the Gospels function primarily to authenticate Jesus's identity and mission rather than operating as independent agents."[23]

Hebrews explicitly subordinates angels to Christ: "Having become as much superior to angels as the name he has inherited is more excellent than theirs" (Hebrews 1:4). The author marshals seven scriptural citations to establish Christ's superiority over angels (Hebrews 1:5-14), reflecting what David Hay calls "concern to address lingering questions about Christ's status relative to other heavenly beings."[24] This emphasis countered tendencies in some Jewish apocalyptic circles to elevate angelic mediation to problematic levels.

Paul likewise subordinates angels to Christ, identifying Christ as the agent of creation "whether thrones or dominions or rulers or powers" (Colossians 1:16). He warns against angel worship (Colossians 2:18) while acknowledging angels as part of the cosmic order. As Clinton E. Arnold notes, "Paul's christological focus redirected attention from elaborate angelologies toward Christ's cosmic supremacy."[25]

Revelation presents the most elaborate New Testament angelology, featuring numerous specialized angels who control natural elements, guide

---

23   Darrell D. Hannah, *Michael and Christ: Michael Traditions and Angel Christology in Early Christianity* (Tübingen: Mohr Siebeck, 1999), 150.

24   David M. Hay, *Glory at the Right Hand: Psalm 110 in Early Christianity* (Nashville: Abingdon Press, 1973), 46-47.

25   Clinton E. Arnold, *The Colossian Syncretism: The Interface Between Christianity and Folk Belief at Colossae* (Tübingen: Mohr Siebeck, 1995), 32-33.

John's visionary experience, and participate in eschatological judgment. Yet even here, angels consistently deflect worship (Revelation 19:10; 22:8-9), reinforcing proper theological boundaries. According to David Aune, "Revelation uses elaborate angelology to emphasize cosmic scope while maintaining christological focus through angels' subordination to the Lamb."[26]

Regarding divine manifestation, early Christianity presented Christ as the definitive theophany. John's Gospel declares that "the Word became flesh and lived among us, and we have seen his glory" (John 1:14), explicitly connecting incarnation with theophanic glory language. The prologue further states that "No one has ever seen God. It is God the only Son, who is close to the Father's heart, who has made him known" (John 1:18). As Marianne Meye Thompson observes, "John presents Jesus as the ultimate theophany who definitively reveals God's nature and purpose."[27]

Paul describes Christ as "the image of the invisible God" (Colossians 1:15) and the one in whom "the whole fullness of deity dwells bodily" (Colossians 2:9). In 2 Corinthians 4:6, Paul connects creation light with the glory of God revealed "in the face of Jesus Christ," drawing on theophanic imagery to express Christ's revelatory significance. According to N.T. Wright, "Paul reconceives theophany christologically, identifying Jesus not merely as a divine manifestation but as the definitive revelation of God's glory and character."[28]

The transfiguration narratives (Matthew 17:1-8; Mark 9:2-8; Luke 9:28-36) present Jesus temporarily manifesting divine glory, connecting him with biblical theophanic traditions. Peter's confession in the Matthean account ("You are the Messiah, the Son of the living God," Matthew 16:16) immediately precedes this revelation, suggesting the transfiguration confirms Jesus's divine identity. As Joel Marcus notes, "The transfiguration

---

26   David E. Aune, *Revelation 1-5, Word Biblical Commentary 52A* (Dallas: Word Books, 1997), 52.

27   Marianne Meye Thompson, *The God of the Gospel of John* (Grand Rapids: Eerdmans, 2001), 123.

28   N.T. Wright, *Paul and the Faithfulness of God* (Minneapolis: Fortress Press, 2013), 665-66.

narratives draw on Sinai theophany traditions to present Jesus as the new and greater revealer of divine glory."[29]

Post-resurrection appearances in the Gospels combine elements of both human recognition and supernatural manifestation. Jesus appears despite locked doors (John 20:19, 26), appears and disappears suddenly (Luke 24:31, 36), and is sometimes initially unrecognized (Luke 24:16; John 20:14; 21:4). These accounts present what Luke Timothy Johnson calls "a transformed embodiment that transcends normal physical limitations while maintaining genuine bodily presence."[30]

Early Christian theological reflection increasingly identified Christ as the definitive mediator between God and humanity, absorbing functions previously attributed to angels, Torah, and temple. The Epistle to the Hebrews particularly develops this theme, presenting Christ as superior high priest who provides direct access to God's presence (Hebrews 4:14-16; 10:19-22). As David deSilva notes, "Hebrews reconceives divine presence in terms of access through Christ rather than through sacred space or angelic mediation."[31]

Patristic development continued these trajectories while addressing new questions. The Council of Nicaea (325 CE) affirmed Christ as "begotten, not made," distinguishing him ontologically from created angels. John of Damascus (*On the Orthodox Faith* 2.3) systematized angelic doctrine, describing them as "secondary intelligent lights derived from the first Light which is without beginning."[32] The Pseudo-Dionysian corpus elaborated

---

29   Joel Marcus, *The Way of the Lord: Christological Exegesis of the Old Testament in the Gospel of Mark* (Louisville: Westminster John Knox, 1992), 80-93.

30   Luke Timothy Johnson, *The Writings of the New Testament: An Interpretation,* rev. ed. (Minneapolis: Fortress Press, 1999), 183.

31   David A. deSilva, *Perseverance in Gratitude: A Socio-Rhetorical Commentary on the Epistle "to the Hebrews"* (Grand Rapids: Eerdmans, 2000), 187.

32   John of Damascus, *On the Orthodox Faith, in Writings,* trans. Frederic H. Chase Jr., The Fathers of the Church 37 (Washington, DC: Catholic University of America Press, 1958), 208.

sophisticated angelological hierarchies that would influence medieval theology.

Regarding theophanies, patristic writers typically interpreted Hebrew Bible theophanic accounts as appearances of the pre-incarnate Logos. Justin Martyr (*Dialogue with Trypho* 56-62) identified the Angel of the LORD as the pre-incarnate Christ, establishing what would become the dominant Christian interpretation of these enigmatic passages. As Jean Daniélou observes, "This interpretive move created christological continuity across both testaments while addressing theological concerns about divine visibility."[33]

These early Christian developments simultaneously maintained continuity with Jewish traditions regarding angels and divine manifestation while radically reconfiguring them around Christ. The resulting synthesis would profoundly shape subsequent Christian theological reflection on divine presence and mediation.

---

33   Jean Daniélou, *The Theology of Jewish Christianity*, trans. John A. Baker (London: Darton, Longman & Todd, 1964), 146.

Part II
Angels in Biblical Narrative

Chapter 4

Angels in the Torah/Pentateuch

The Cherubim in Genesis

The first angelic beings mentioned in scripture are the cherubim *(kĕrûbîm)* who appear in Genesis 3:24 following humanity's expulsion from Eden: "He drove out the man; and at the east of the garden of Eden he placed the cherubim, and a sword flaming and turning to guard the way to the tree of life." This brief reference establishes several significant aspects of angelic function in biblical narrative.

First, the cherubim serve as guardians of sacred space, preventing unauthorized access to the divine presence symbolized by the tree of life. As Gordon J. Wenham notes, "The cherubim establish a boundary between fallen humanity and divine presence, initiating a pattern of mediated access to God that will characterize much of the biblical narrative."[1] This guardian function anticipates later appearances of cherubim in tabernacle and temple contexts.

Second, the cherubim are associated with divine judgment and the execution of divine decrees. Their appearance marks the implementation of God's sentence of expulsion, suggesting what Umberto Cassuto calls "angelic participation in the divine judicial process."[2] This judicial aspect recurs in later angelic appearances, particularly in contexts of divine intervention.

Third, the association of cherubim with "a sword flaming and turning" introduces a connection between angelic presence and numinous phenomena. The Hebrew term *miṯhappeḵeṯ* (turning) suggests continuous motion, creating what Victor P. Hamilton describes as "a dynamic barrier

---

1   Gordon J. Wenham, *Genesis 1-15, Word Biblical Commentary 1* (Waco, TX: Word Books, 1987), 86.
2   Umberto Cassuto, *A Commentary on the Book of Genesis: Part I, From Adam to Noah,* trans. Israel Abrahams (Jerusalem: Magnes Press, 1961), 174.

of divine power made visible through flame."[3] This combination of angelic beings and luminous manifestation anticipates later theophanic appearances.

While Genesis provides no physical description of the cherubim, Ancient Near Eastern parallels suggest composite beings combining human and animal features. Archaeological discoveries from Mesopotamia and Syria-Palestine reveal guardian figures with human faces, animal bodies, and wings, often positioned at entrances to sacred spaces. These parallels help explain why later biblical references assume readers already understand the cherubim's appearance.

The Eden narrative's presentation of cherubim establishes a pattern that will be developed throughout the Pentateuch: angelic beings mediate divine presence, both revealing and concealing God's power, executing divine judgment while marking boundaries between sacred and profane space.

Angel Encounters with the Patriarchs

The patriarchal narratives feature numerous angelic appearances, with particular concentration in the Abraham and Jacob cycles. These accounts establish foundational patterns for understanding divine-human communication through angelic mediation.

The first explicit angelic appearance occurs in Genesis 16, where "the angel of the LORD" (*mal'ak YHWH*) encounters Hagar in the wilderness. This enigmatic figure speaks with divine authority—"I will so greatly multiply your offspring that they cannot be counted" (Genesis 16:10)— yet remains distinct from God. Hagar's response, naming God "El-roi" (God of seeing) after the encounter, indicates she understood it as genuine divine communication. As David Noel Freedman observes, "This narrative introduces the theological ambiguity that characterizes many angel of the LORD appearances, where the messenger simultaneously represents God

---

3   Victor P. Hamilton, *The Book of Genesis: Chapters 1-17, New International Commentary on the Old Testament* (Grand Rapids: Eerdmans, 1990), 210.

and speaks as God."[4]

Genesis 18-19 presents a complex account of divine manifestation involving three "men" who visit Abraham. The narrative shifts between plural and singular address, with one figure increasingly identified with the LORD while the other two are later explicitly called "angels" (mal'āḵîm) when they visit Lot in Sodom (Genesis 19:1). According to Nahum M. Sarna, "This account deliberately maintains ambiguity about the relationship between divine presence and angelic mediation, suggesting both distinction and identification."[5] The narrative emphasizes divine accommodation to human interaction—the visitors appear as men, accept hospitality, and engage in conversation—while simultaneously revealing superhuman knowledge and power.

The significance of this Mamre theophany is emphasized by its placement immediately before the destruction of Sodom and Gomorrah, linking divine manifestation with both judgment and the opportunity for intercession. The angels who visit Lot explicitly state their task: "we are about to destroy this place" (Genesis 19:13), demonstrating angelic involvement in executing divine judgment.

Jacob's encounters with angels form another significant cluster. Genesis 28 describes his dream at Bethel, where he sees "a ladder set up on the earth, the top of it reaching to heaven; and the angels of God were ascending and descending on it" (Genesis 28:12). This vision establishes connection between earthly and heavenly realms through angelic mediation. As Jon D. Levenson argues, "The Bethel vision portrays angels as cosmic commuters traversing the boundary between divine and human spheres, visualizing ongoing communication between realms."[6]

---

4   David Noel Freedman, "The Name of the God of Moses," *Journal of Biblical Literature 79*, no. 2 (1960): 151-56.
5   Nahum M. Sarna, *Genesis, JPS Torah Commentary* (Philadelphia: Jewish Publication Society, 1989), 128.
6   Jon D. Levenson, *Sinai and Zion: An Entry into the Jewish Bible* (Minneapolis: Winston Press, 1985), 138.

Genesis 32 narrates Jacob's mysterious nighttime wrestling match with an unnamed figure who eventually blesses him, leading Jacob to declare, "I have seen God face to face" (Genesis 32:30). While the text never explicitly identifies this figure as an angel, Hosea 12:4 retrospectively describes Jacob's opponent as both God and an angel: "He strove with the angel and prevailed." This interpretive tradition highlights the theological complexity regarding divine appearance through angelic mediation. According to Esther J. Hamori, "The wrestling narrative intentionally preserves ambiguity about whether Jacob's opponent is God, an angel, or God appearing through angelic mediation."[7]

Perhaps most significantly, Jacob's deathbed blessing in Genesis 48:15-16 brings together multiple angelic traditions: "The God before whom my ancestors Abraham and Isaac walked, the God who has been my shepherd all my life to this day, the angel who has redeemed me from all harm, bless the boys." The parallel structure treats "God" and "the angel" as nearly interchangeable, suggesting what Michael S. Heiser calls "theological fluidity between divine presence and angelic agency in patriarchal experience."[8]

These patriarchal encounters establish several enduring patterns in biblical angelology. First, they demonstrate integration of divine and angelic agency, often blurring distinctions between God's direct action and action through intermediaries. Second, they establish angels as boundary-crossing figures who connect heaven and earth, facilitating divine-human communication. Third, they present angels as active participants in the covenant relationship, delivering promises, providing protection, and executing judgment. As R.W.L. Moberly notes, "Angels in the patriarchal narratives function primarily as manifestations of God's covenantal engagement with chosen individuals and their families."[9]

---

7   Esther J. Hamori, *"When Gods Were Men": The Embodied God in Biblical and Near Eastern Literature* (Berlin: de Gruyter, 2008), 103-27.

8   Michael S. Heiser, *The Unseen Realm: Recovering the Supernatural Worldview of the Bible* (Bellingham, WA: Lexham Press, 2015), 42.

9   R.W.L. Moberly, *The Theology of the Book of Genesis* (Cambridge: Cambridge University Press, 2009), 96.

The Angel of the Lord in Exodus

The book of Exodus features several significant appearances of "the angel of the LORD" *(mal'ak YHWH)*, particularly at pivotal moments in Israel's national formation. These appearances maintain the pattern of ambiguity between divine presence and angelic mediation established in Genesis while adapting it to contexts of corporate deliverance and covenant establishment.

The burning bush theophany (Exodus 3:1-4:17) exemplifies this ambiguity: "The angel of the LORD appeared to him in a flame of fire out of a bush" (Exodus 3:2), yet immediately afterward "God called to him out of the bush" (Exodus 3:4). The narrative shifts seamlessly between references to the angel and to God, suggesting what Brevard Childs describes as "theological intent to simultaneously affirm divine presence while acknowledging mediation."[10] The bush itself—burning yet not consumed—provides a powerful visual metaphor for the paradox of mediated divine presence: God genuinely appears yet remains transcendent.

This theophany initiates Moses's prophetic commission and introduces the divine name YHWH, linking angelic appearance with revelation of divine identity. According to Thomas B. Dozeman, "The angel of the LORD serves as revelatory agent through whom God's character and purposes are disclosed to Moses, establishing a pattern of mediated revelation that will continue throughout Israel's history."[11]

The exodus from Egypt incorporates angelic guidance: "The angel of God who was going before the Israelite army moved and went behind them; and the pillar of cloud moved from in front of them and took its place behind them" (Exodus 14:19). This text explicitly identifies the angel with the cloud/fire pillar, connecting angelic presence with the visible manifestation of divine guidance. William H.C. Propp observes that "the angel and pillar together communicate both divine transcendence and

---

10   Brevard S. Childs, *The Book of Exodus: A Critical, Theological Commentary* (Philadelphia: Westminster Press, 1974), 72.

11   Thomas B. Dozeman, *Commentary on Exodus* (Grand Rapids: Eerdmans, 2009), 128.

immanence, suggesting divine presence mediated through perceptible phenomena."[12]

The preparation for the Sinai covenant includes God's promise: "I am going to send an angel in front of you, to guard you on the way and to bring you to the place that I have prepared" (Exodus 23:20). This angel carries divine authority—"my name is in him" (Exodus 23:21)—yet remains distinct from God. The warning against provoking this angel suggests both the angel's exalted status and the danger associated with divine presence mediated through the angel.

After Israel's idolatry with the golden calf, God declares, "I will send an angel before you" (Exodus 33:2), but this now appears as a reduction of divine presence, prompting Moses to intercede for direct divine accompaniment: "If your presence will not go, do not carry us up from here" (Exodus 33:15). According to Carol Meyers, "This narrative sequence contrasts angelic mediation with direct divine presence, suggesting that while angels represent genuine divine involvement, they nevertheless signify distance in the divine-human relationship."[13]

Throughout Exodus, the angel of the LORD serves multiple functions: revealing divine identity and purpose (burning bush), providing guidance and protection (exodus and wilderness), enforcing covenant boundaries (warnings in Exodus 23), and signifying divine presence while maintaining appropriate separation after sin (Exodus 33). These appearances establish patterns that will recur throughout biblical presentations of angelic mediation.

Angels in the Wilderness Narratives

The wilderness narratives of Numbers and Deuteronomy contain fewer explicit angelic appearances than Genesis and Exodus, yet they continue

---

12   William H.C. Propp, *Exodus 1-18: A New Translation with Introduction and Commentary, Anchor Bible 2* (New York: Doubleday, 1999), 476.

13   Carol Meyers, *Exodus, New Cambridge Bible Commentary* (Cambridge: Cambridge University Press, 2005), 258.

developing the theological significance of angelic mediation in Israel's formative experiences.

Numbers 20:16 retrospectively interprets the exodus through angelic agency: "We cried to the LORD... he heard our voice and sent an angel and brought us out of Egypt." This summary statement suggests ongoing theological reflection that recognized divine deliverance as occurring through angelic mediation, even when earlier narratives emphasized direct divine action.

The mysterious Balaam narrative (Numbers 22-24) features an angel of the LORD who opposes the prophet's journey to curse Israel. Significantly, the angel remains invisible to Balaam while appearing to his donkey, until "the LORD opened the eyes of Balaam, and he saw the angel of the LORD standing in the road, with his drawn sword in his hand" (Numbers 22:31). According to James Kugel, "This account emphasizes that angelic perception requires divine enabling, suggesting that spiritual realities remain invisible without special revelation."[14] The angel's drawn sword recalls the cherubim's flaming sword in Genesis 3:24, connecting this appearance with divine judgment and boundary enforcement.

The Balaam narrative also develops the concept of angelic opposition to those who oppose God's purposes. The angel declares, "I have come out as an adversary, because your way is perverse before me" (Numbers 22:32). This establishes what Jacob Milgrom calls "the obstructive function of angels, who act as divine agents to prevent actions contrary to divine will."[15] This function complements the more familiar protective role of angels toward God's people.

Deuteronomy contains minimal explicit angel references, consistent with its theological emphasis on direct covenant relationship without intermediaries. However, Deuteronomy 33:2 describes God coming "with myriads of holy ones," suggesting divine accompaniment by angelic hosts.

---

14   James L. Kugel, *The God of Old: Inside the Lost World of the Bible* (New York: Free Press, 2003), 34.

15   Jacob Milgrom, Numbers, *JPS Torah Commentary* (Philadelphia: Jewish Publication Society, 1990), 189.

This imagery anticipates later biblical developments regarding divine manifestation with heavenly armies.

Throughout the wilderness narratives, angels function primarily as extensions of divine presence, enforcing covenant boundaries and protecting Israel from both external threats and internal deviation. The relative scarcity of angel appearances in these texts suggests theological emphasis on developing Israel's direct covenant relationship with God, with angels serving supportive rather than central roles in this formative period.

Theological Significance in Pentateuchal Angel Appearances

The Pentateuch's presentation of angels establishes foundational patterns that will influence all subsequent biblical angelology. Several key theological themes emerge from these narratives.

First, angels consistently appear as agents of divine revelation, disclosing God's identity, will, and purposes to humans. From the cherubim marking Eden's boundary to the angel commissioning Moses, angelic beings mediate divine communication. As John Goldingay notes, "Angels in the Pentateuch function primarily as vehicles for divine self-disclosure, making God's presence and purposes perceptible within human experience."[16]

Second, angels serve as boundary figures who navigate the space between divine transcendence and immanence. Their appearances simultaneously affirm God's genuine engagement with creation while preserving appropriate distinction between Creator and creature. According to Benjamin Sommer, "Angelic mediation provides theological solution to the problem of divine presence, allowing for real divine-human interaction without compromising divine freedom and otherness."[17]

Third, angels participate in the establishment and maintenance of covenant relationships. They deliver covenant promises (Genesis 16:10;

---

16   John Goldingay, *Old Testament Theology, Volume 1: Israel's Gospel* (Downers Grove, IL: InterVarsity Press, 2003), 243.
17   Benjamin D. Sommer, *The Bodies of God and the World of Ancient Israel* (Cambridge: Cambridge University Press, 2009), 40.

22:15-18), guide covenant people (Exodus 14:19), protect them from harm (Genesis 19:1-22), and enforce covenant boundaries (Numbers 22:22-35). This covenantal function, as David Clines observes, "integrates angelic activity into the central theological framework of the Pentateuch—God's covenant commitment to Abraham's family and the nation emerging from it."[18]

Fourth, angels manifest divine authority while consistently deflecting worship toward God alone. Unlike parallel Ancient Near Eastern traditions where messenger deities received cultic veneration, biblical angels never become objects of worship themselves. This theological restraint, according to Patrick Miller, "reflects developing monotheistic emphasis that would become central to Israelite religion."[19]

Fifth, the ambiguous relationship between "the angel of the LORD" and God proper establishes a pattern of divine self-revelation through intermediary figures that will find ultimate expression in later biblical christology. As N.T. Wright argues, "The angel of the LORD traditions created conceptual space within monotheism for understanding divine presence manifested through a distinct figure who both is and is not identifiable with God."[20]

The Pentateuch's angelology thus establishes theological foundations that will be developed throughout the biblical canon: divine presence genuinely available yet appropriately mediated, divine communication occurring through created intermediaries, and divine activity extending through agents while maintaining divine sovereignty. These concepts provide essential framework for understanding subsequent biblical presentations of angels and divine manifestation.

---

18   David J.A. Clines, *The Theme of the Pentateuch*, 2nd ed. (Sheffield: Sheffield Academic Press, 1997), 32.

19   Patrick D. Miller Jr., *The Divine Warrior in Early Israel* (Atlanta: Society of Biblical Literature, 2006), 67.

20   N.T. Wright, *Paul and the Faithfulness of God* (Minneapolis: Fortress Press, 2013), 651.

Chapter 5

Angels in Historical and Prophetic Literature

Angelic Appearances in Joshua, Judges, and Samuel

The historical narratives of Joshua, Judges, and Samuel continue developing angelic presentations established in the Pentateuch while introducing new elements that reflect Israel's changing circumstances. These accounts particularly emphasize angelic involvement in military contexts, covenant maintenance, and prophetic commissioning.

Joshua 5:13-15 presents a pivotal encounter immediately before the conquest of Jericho: "Now when Joshua was near Jericho, he looked up and saw a man standing before him with a drawn sword in his hand." When Joshua asks whose side he represents, the figure responds, "Neither; but as commander of the army of the LORD I have now come" (Joshua 5:14). This enigmatic figure demands reverence—"Remove the sandals from your feet, for the place where you stand is holy" (Joshua 5:15)—echoing God's command to Moses at the burning bush (Exodus 3:5).

While never explicitly called an angel, most scholars identify this figure as an angelic manifestation, possibly the angel of the LORD. As Robert G. Boling notes, "The commander's drawn sword connects him with the angel who opposed Balaam (Numbers 22:23) and anticipates later angelic warrior figures."[1] This appearance serves several functions: it validates Joshua's leadership succession from Moses through similar theophanic experience, it places the subsequent conquest under divine authority, and it emphasizes that the forthcoming battles serve God's purposes rather than merely human territorial ambitions.

The commander's refusal to align with either Israel or its enemies reveals what L. Daniel Hawk calls "the theological priority of divine purposes over

---

1   Robert G. Boling, *Joshua: A New Translation with Notes and Commentary,* *Anchor Bible 6* (Garden City, NY: Doubleday, 1982), 197.

national interests."[2] This appearance establishes a pattern where angelic manifestations challenge simplistic identification of God with human causes, even those of the covenant people.

The book of Judges features several significant angelic appearances, particularly at moments of covenant renewal and leadership commissioning. Judges 2:1-5 describes the angel of the LORD confronting Israel at Bochim regarding covenant violations: "I brought you up from Egypt... I will never break my covenant with you. For your part, do not make a covenant with the inhabitants of this land" (Judges 2:1-2). This judicial function reflects what Susan Niditch identifies as "angelic enforcement of covenant boundaries, particularly addressing the threat of religious syncretism."[3]

The commissioning of Gideon (Judges 6:11-24) presents another complex angel of the LORD encounter. The narrative begins with "the angel of the LORD" appearing under a tree (Judges 6:11) but shifts to "the LORD" directly addressing Gideon (Judges 6:14), then returns to "the angel of God" (Judges 6:20). This fluidity between divine and angelic designation maintains the theological ambiguity established in Pentateuchal theophanies. When Gideon realizes he has seen "the angel of the LORD face to face," he fears death, but receives reassurance: "Peace be to you; do not fear, you shall not die" (Judges 6:22-23). According to Robert Alter, "This interchange maintains tension between divine accessibility and dangerous divine otherness that characterizes many biblical theophanies."[4]

Similar patterns appear in the annunciation to Manoah and his wife regarding Samson's birth (Judges 13:2-23). The angel appears with human appearance but demonstrates superhuman knowledge. When Manoah asks the visitor's name, he receives the enigmatic response, "Why do you ask my name? It is too wonderful" (Judges 13:18), suggesting the figure's identity transcends human categorization. The couple's eventual realization—

---

2   L. Daniel Hawk, *Joshua*, Berit Olam (Collegeville, MN: Liturgical Press, 2000), 83.

3   Susan Niditch, *Judges: A Commentary*, Old Testament Library (Louisville: Westminster John Knox, 2008), 41.

4   Robert Alter, *Ancient Israel: The Former Prophets: Joshua, Judges, Samuel, and Kings* (New York: W.W. Norton, 2013), 173.

"We have seen God" (Judges 13:22)—further emphasizes the theological significance of this angelic encounter as genuine divine manifestation.

The Samuel narratives contain fewer explicit angel references, though 2 Samuel 24:16-17 describes "the angel who was bringing destruction" during David's census plague. This destroying angel becomes visible to David: "David looked up and saw the angel of the LORD standing between earth and heaven, and in his hand a drawn sword stretched out over Jerusalem" (1 Chronicles 21:16, which parallels the Samuel account). This vision prompts David's intercessory prayer that leads to the plague's end. As P. Kyle McCarter observes, "This account explicitly connects angelic agency with divine judgment while creating opportunity for prophetic intercession, demonstrating complex interplay between divine sovereignty, angelic action, and human response."[5]

These historical narratives develop several significant angelological themes. First, they increasingly associate angels with warfare, presenting them as divine warriors who lead heavenly armies. Second, they emphasize angels as covenant enforcers who hold Israel accountable to its commitments. Third, they connect angelic appearances with leadership commissionings, particularly in transitional moments of Israel's history. Fourth, they maintain theological tension between divine presence and divine transcendence through deliberately ambiguous presentation of angelic figures who simultaneously represent and embody divine presence.

Angels in the Davidic Narratives

The historical accounts focusing on David and his dynasty contain relatively few explicit angel references compared to earlier narrative cycles. However, those that appear are theologically significant, particularly in establishing divine protection of the Davidic covenant and Jerusalem as sacred space.

---

5   P. Kyle McCarter Jr., *II Samuel: A New Translation with Introduction, Notes, and Commentary, Anchor Bible 9* (Garden City, NY: Doubleday, 1984), 512.

As noted above, 2 Samuel 24:16-17 (paralleled in 1 Chronicles 21:15-17) presents David's vision of the destroying angel standing over Jerusalem with drawn sword. This angelic appearance connects to the establishment of the temple site: "Then the angel of the LORD ordered Gad to tell David that David should go up and erect an altar to the LORD on the threshing floor of Araunah the Jebusite" (2 Samuel 24:18). According to Sara Japhet, "This account links angelic manifestation with temple establishment, creating theological foundation for Jerusalem's sacred status."[6]

The Chronicler's version emphasizes this connection even more explicitly, describing fire descending from heaven to consume David's sacrifice at this location, followed by the angel sheathing his sword at divine command (1 Chronicles 21:26-27). The narrative concludes with David declaring, "Here shall be the house of the LORD God and here the altar of burnt offering for Israel" (1 Chronicles 22:1). This sequence creates what John Barton calls "theological legitimation for the temple through angelic activity, establishing continuity between divine presence in angelic form and the later institutionalized presence in the temple."[7]

The Davidic promise of 2 Samuel 7 lacks explicit angelic references, instead presenting divine communication through the prophet Nathan. However, later biblical tradition would connect angelic activity with the preservation of David's dynasty. Psalm 91:11-12 declares that God "will command his angels concerning you to guard you in all your ways" and "they will bear you up," promises that post-biblical tradition would associate specifically with Davidic protection. According to Frank Moore Cross, "While not explicit in the original narrative, angelic guardianship became a significant theological framework for understanding divine preservation of the Davidic covenant."[8]

---

6   Sara Japhet, *I & II Chronicles: A Commentary, Old Testament Library* (Louisville: Westminster John Knox, 1993), 384.

7   John Barton, *The Theology of the Book of Amos, Old Testament Theology* (Cambridge: Cambridge University Press, 2012), 74.

8   Frank Moore Cross, *Canaanite Myth and Hebrew Epic: Essays in the History of the Religion of Israel* (Cambridge: Harvard University Press, 1973), 241.

The relative scarcity of angel appearances in the core Davidic narratives may reflect theological emphasis on the king's direct relationship with YHWH without need for intermediaries. As J.J.M. Roberts observes, "Royal ideology typically emphasized the king's unique access to divine presence, potentially reducing the narrative significance of angelic mediation in these contexts."[9] The David-focused narratives instead emphasize prophetic mediation through figures like Nathan, Samuel, and Gad, establishing patterns that would become central to subsequent Israelite religion.

Angelic Visions in Major Prophets

The major prophetic books—Isaiah, Jeremiah, and Ezekiel—contain significant angelic visions that develop biblical angelology in new directions. These texts particularly emphasize angelic participation in divine council, mediation of prophetic calls, and execution of divine judgment.

Isaiah's inaugural vision (Isaiah 6:1-13) introduces the seraphim *(šĕrāpîm)*, fiery six-winged beings who surround God's throne proclaiming divine holiness. Unlike previous angel appearances in narrative contexts, these beings primarily function liturgically, engaged in perpetual worship: "Holy, holy, holy is the LORD of hosts; the whole earth is full of his glory" (Isaiah 6:3). One seraph performs purification for Isaiah, touching his lips with a burning coal to cleanse him for prophetic service (Isaiah 6:6-7).

The term *šĕrāpîm* appears elsewhere only in association with fiery serpents (Numbers 21:6; Deuteronomy 8:15), suggesting what John Oswalt calls "dangerous numinous quality appropriate to beings in direct divine presence."[10] Their six wings—two covering the face, two covering the feet, and two for flying—emphasize both mobility to perform divine service and appropriate reverence in divine presence.

This inaugural vision establishes several significant angelological developments. First, it presents angels engaged in perpetual worship rather

---

9   J.J.M. Roberts, "The Davidic Origin of the Zion Tradition," *Journal of Biblical Literature 92*, no. 3 (1973): 329-44.

10   John N. Oswalt, *The Book of Isaiah: Chapters 1-39, New International Commentary on the Old Testament* (Grand Rapids: Eerdmans, 1986), 180.

than merely delivering occasional messages, suggesting ongoing heavenly liturgy parallel to earthly temple service. Second, it portrays angels as models of appropriate response to divine holiness, demonstrating reverence while maintaining ability to function in divine presence. Third, it connects angelic activity with prophetic commissioning, establishing pattern where heavenly beings prepare humans for divine service. According to R.E. Clements, "The seraphim provide an interpretive bridge between divine transcendence and prophetic calling, making Isaiah's commission possible while emphasizing the holiness that necessitates mediation."[11]

The book of Jeremiah contains minimal explicit references to angels, though Jeremiah 23:18 refers to standing "in the council of the LORD," suggesting conceptual awareness of divine heavenly assembly attended by angelic beings. This relative absence of angelic mediation may reflect Jeremiah's emphasis on direct divine communication: "Is not my word like fire, says the LORD, and like a hammer that breaks a rock in pieces?" (Jeremiah 23:29).

Ezekiel's elaborate throne vision (Ezekiel 1-3) presents complex angelic beings identified as living creatures *(ḥayyôṯ)* and later explicitly as cherubim (Ezekiel 10:15). These composite beings feature four faces (human, lion, ox, and eagle), human hands under their wings, and wheels within wheels that enable multidirectional movement. Their primary function is bearing the divine throne-chariot, creating mobile base for God's glory *(kaḇôḏ YHWH)*.

These cherubim demonstrate what Daniel I. Block identifies as "perfect integration of diverse cosmic elements—human, animal, avian—in service of divine presence, suggesting comprehensive divine sovereignty over all creation."[12] Their ability to move in any direction without turning represents divine omnipresence, while their multiple faces suggest divine omniscience. According to Moshe Greenberg, "Ezekiel's cherubim synthesize Israelite

---

11   R.E. Clements, *Isaiah 1-39, New Century Bible Commentary* (Grand Rapids: Eerdmans, 1980), 74.

12   Daniel I. Block, *The Book of Ezekiel: Chapters 1-24, New International Commentary on the Old Testament* (Grand Rapids: Eerdmans, 1997), 96.

temple imagery with Mesopotamian throne guardians, creating theological statement about God's transcendent glory being simultaneously present with exiled community."[13]

Ezekiel's vision also includes angelic figures in human form. Ezekiel 9-10 describes six executioners led by one clothed in linen who carries a writing case. These figures carry out judgment on idolatrous Jerusalem, marking the faithful for preservation while slaying the unfaithful. Chapter 40 introduces "a man whose appearance shone like bronze" who guides Ezekiel through the visionary temple, measuring its dimensions and explaining its significance. Margaret S. Odell suggests these human-form angels represent "gradations of divine presence, allowing for divine communication and action while maintaining appropriate theological distance."[14]

The major prophets thus develop biblical angelology in several important directions. They elaborate heavenly worship around God's throne, present more complex descriptions of angelic beings, emphasize angelic participation in both judgment and preservation, and establish connections between heavenly realities and earthly prophetic service. These developments would significantly influence subsequent apocalyptic literature and New Testament angelology.

Angels in Apocalyptic Literature (Daniel)

The book of Daniel represents the most elaborate development of angelology within the Hebrew Bible, introducing named angels, cosmic conflicts, and extensive angelically mediated revelation. These developments respond to Israel's experience of imperial domination, providing theological framework for understanding history as arena for cosmic conflict between divine and anti-divine forces.

---

13   Moshe Greenberg, *Ezekiel 1-20: A New Translation with Introduction and Commentary, Anchor Bible 22* (Garden City, NY: Doubleday, 1983), 53.

14   Margaret S. Odell, *Ezekiel, Smyth & Helwys Bible Commentary* (Macon, GA: Smyth & Helwys, 2005), 110.

Daniel 7 presents "one like a human being" *(kəḇar 'ĕnāš)* who approaches the Ancient of Days to receive universal dominion (Daniel 7:13-14). While interpretations vary regarding this figure's identity—messianic human, angelic being, corporate symbol for Israel, or divine manifestation—the vision establishes heavenly court context where exalted beings participate in divine judgment and dominion. According to John J. Collins, "This heavenly being introduces ambiguous mediatorial figure who transcends normal angelic categories while participating in divine authority."[15]

Daniel 8:15-17 and 9:20-23 introduce Gabriel *(gaḇrî'ēl,* "God's mighty one"), the first named angel in canonical Jewish scripture. Gabriel appears "like a man" to interpret Daniel's visions, identifying himself by name and claiming to have been "sent" to provide understanding. This naming represents significant development in biblical angelology, suggesting individual identity and specific function for this heavenly being. As Carol A. Newsom observes, "Named angels reflect increased interest in heavenly hierarchy and specialized angelic roles, developments that would become central to later apocalyptic and mystical traditions."[16]

Daniel 10-12 presents another elaborate angelic encounter, describing "a man clothed in linen, with a belt of gold from Uphaz around his waist" (Daniel 10:5) whose appearance includes luminous body, fiery eyes, burnished limbs, and thunderous voice. This majestic figure—unnamed but given tremendous authority—reveals that he has been engaged in cosmic conflict: "The prince of the kingdom of Persia opposed me twenty-one days. So Michael, one of the chief princes, came to help me" (Daniel 10:13).

This passage introduces Michael *(mîḵā'ēl,* "Who is like God?"), identified as "one of the chief princes" and later as "the great prince, the protector of your people" (Daniel 12:1). These references establish concept of angelic patrons for specific nations, with Michael particularly

---

15   John J. Collins, *Daniel: A Commentary on the Book of Daniel, Hermeneia* (Minneapolis: Fortress Press, 1993), 304.
16   Carol A. Newsom, *"Angels," in The Anchor Bible Dictionary,* ed. David Noel Freedman (New York: Doubleday, 1992), 1:251.

associated with Israel's protection. According to Anathea E. Portier-Young, "This framework allows Daniel to present earthly imperial conflicts as manifestations of deeper spiritual warfare, providing theological meaning for Israel's suffering under foreign domination."[17]

The cosmic conflict portrayed in Daniel significantly expands biblical understanding of angelic activity. Angels are no longer merely messengers or throne attendants but active participants in ongoing struggle that spans both heavenly and earthly realms. This framework presents history as arena for working out divine purposes against spiritual opposition, with angels serving as key agents in this cosmic drama. As Andrew Chester notes, "Daniel's cosmic dualism never becomes absolute, always maintaining divine sovereignty over the conflict while acknowledging genuine opposition from rebellious spiritual powers."[18]

Daniel also develops the interpretive function of angels, who explain visionary symbolism and historical implications. Unlike earlier prophetic literature where prophets directly receive divine communication, Daniel consistently presents revelation as mediated through angelic figures who translate symbolic visions into understandable messages. According to Benjamin D. Sommer, "This increased emphasis on angelic mediation reflects theological concern to maintain divine transcendence while explaining continued revelation during period when direct prophecy was perceived as declining."[19]

Daniel's angelology would exert tremendous influence on subsequent Jewish apocalyptic literature, early Christianity, and rabbinic tradition. Its named angels, cosmic conflict motif, national angelic patrons, and interpretive angelic function established patterns that would be elaborated

---

17   Anathea E. Portier-Young, *Apocalypse Against Empire: Theologies of Resistance in Early Judaism* (Grand Rapids: Eerdmans, 2011), 230.

18   Andrew Chester, *Messiah and Exaltation: Jewish Messianic and Visionary Traditions and New Testament Christology* (Tübingen: Mohr Siebeck, 2007), 113.

19   Benjamin D. Sommer, *"The Babylonian Exile and Beyond,"* in *The Cambridge History of Judaism, Volume 1: The Persian Period,* ed. W.D. Davies and Louis Finkelstein (Cambridge: Cambridge University Press, 1984), 324.

in texts like 1 Enoch, Jubilees, the Dead Sea Scrolls, and ultimately the New Testament, particularly Revelation.

Theological Developments in Historical and Prophetic Angelology

The portrayal of angels across the historical and prophetic literature represents significant theological development from Pentateuchal presentations. Several key trajectories emerge in these texts.

First, angels increasingly function as revealers of cosmic perspective on historical events. While Pentateuchal angels primarily delivered messages to individuals, the angels in historical and prophetic texts interpret broader historical patterns and reveal divine purposes within seemingly chaotic events. According to John J. Collins, "Angels provide heavenly perspective on earthly events, demonstrating divine sovereignty despite apparent triumph of human empires."[20] This cosmic-historical function reaches its fullest expression in Daniel but appears earlier in prophetic throne visions and even military contexts like Joshua's encounter with the divine commander.

Second, angels become more clearly differentiated from God proper, even as they continue to represent divine presence. The theological ambiguity surrounding the angel of the LORD in Pentateuchal narratives gradually gives way to clearer distinction between God enthroned in heaven and angelic servants who perform specific functions. Isaiah's seraphim, Ezekiel's cherubim, and Daniel's named angels all maintain clear distinction from the divine even as they mediate divine presence. As Benjamin D. Sommer observes, "This differentiation reflects theological refinement regarding divine transcendence while maintaining genuine divine engagement through created intermediaries."[21]

Third, angels increasingly appear as part of elaborate heavenly hierarchy rather than as solitary messengers. Isaiah's vision presents multiple seraphim

---

20   John J. Collins, *The Apocalyptic Imagination: An Introduction to Jewish Apocalyptic Literature,* 2nd ed. (Grand Rapids: Eerdmans, 1998), 103.
21   Benjamin D. Sommer, *The Bodies of God and the World of Ancient Israel* (Cambridge: Cambridge University Press, 2009), 42.

surrounding the divine throne; Ezekiel portrays four cherubim bearing God's throne-chariot; Daniel refers to "chief princes" among the angels, suggesting hierarchical organization. According to Darrell D. Hannah, "This development reflects growing interest in heavenly organization that parallels earthly political structures, particularly as Israel experienced incorporation into larger imperial systems."[22]

Fourth, angels become associated with specific nations and territories. Daniel explicitly identifies Michael as Israel's angelic patron while referring to "the prince of Persia" as opposing divine purposes. This development, as Andrew Chester suggests, "provided theological framework for understanding international politics as manifestation of deeper spiritual realities, particularly important during periods when Israel lacked political sovereignty."[23]

Fifth, angels increasingly participate in scenes of judgment, both preserving the faithful and executing divine sentences against the rebellious. Ezekiel's linen-clothed figure marks the faithful for preservation while his companions slay the idolaters; Daniel portrays angelic participation in divine court proceedings. According to Patrick D. Miller, "This judicial function connects angelology with eschatological expectation, where final judgment will reveal and implement divine justice currently obscured by historical circumstances."[24]

Sixth, angels feature more prominently in visionary literature, serving as guides, interpreters, and mediators of increasingly complex symbolic revelation. Daniel's elaborate visions consistently feature angelic interpretation; Ezekiel's temple tour is guided by an angelic figure; Zechariah's night visions (discussed in later chapters) feature interpreting angels who explain symbolic elements. Carol A. Newsom suggests this reflects "growing emphasis on heavenly secrets requiring angelic mediation

---

22   Darrell D. Hannah, *Michael and Christ: Michael Traditions and Angel Christology in Early Christianity* (Tübingen: Mohr Siebeck, 1999), 28.

23   Andrew Chester, *Messiah and Exaltation: Jewish Messianic and Visionary Traditions and New Testament Christology* (Tübingen: Mohr Siebeck, 2007), 118.

24   Patrick D. Miller Jr., *Sin and Judgment in the Prophets: A Stylistic and Theological Analysis* (Chico, CA: Scholars Press, 1982), 123.

to become intelligible, particularly as direct prophetic revelation was perceived as diminishing."[25]

These developments would profoundly influence subsequent Jewish and Christian angelology, particularly in apocalyptic and mystical traditions. While maintaining continuity with Pentateuchal presentations of angels as divine messengers and manifestations, the historical and prophetic literature expanded biblical angelology to address new theological questions arising from Israel's changing historical circumstances. As Israel experienced exile, imperial domination, and challenges to traditional theological frameworks, angels provided conceptual resources for understanding divine activity within history's complexities.

---

25   Carol A. Newsom, *Songs of the Sabbath Sacrifice: A Critical Edition* (Atlanta: Scholars Press, 1985), 17-38.

Chapter 6
Angels in Wisdom and Poetic Literature

Angels in Psalms

The Psalter presents a rich but understated angelology that reflects Israel's worship tradition. Unlike narrative or apocalyptic texts where angels actively participate in dramatic encounters, Psalms typically references angels within broader theological frameworks of divine sovereignty, cosmic order, and appropriate worship.

The Hebrew term *mal'āk* (messenger/angel) appears relatively infrequently in Psalms, but when it does, it often emphasizes protection of the faithful. Psalm 34:7 declares, "The angel of the LORD encamps around those who fear him, and delivers them," establishing what Craig C. Broyles calls "the protective encircling of divine presence through angelic agency."[1] Similarly, Psalm 91:11-12 promises, "For he will command his angels concerning you to guard you in all your ways. On their hands they will bear you up, so that you will not dash your foot against a stone." This protective function, according to Samuel Terrien, "grounds human confidence not in direct divine intervention but in divinely commissioned agents who implement divine care."[2]

More frequently, Psalms references angels using terms like *'ĕlōhîm* (gods/divine beings), *bənê 'ĕlōhîm* (sons of God/divine beings), or *qədōšîm* (holy ones). Psalm 8:5 describes humans as made "a little lower than *'ĕlōhîm*," which the Septuagint renders as "angels" *(angelous)*, reflecting Jewish interpretive tradition that understood this term as referring to heavenly beings rather than God proper in this context. According to Peter C. Craigie, "This comparison establishes angels as standard for measuring

---

1   Craig C. Broyles, *Psalms, New International Biblical Commentary* (Peabody, MA: Hendrickson, 1999), 168.
2   Samuel Terrien, *The Psalms: Strophic Structure and Theological Commentary* (Grand Rapids: Eerdmans, 2003), 645.

human status—below angels but above other creatures—within creation's hierarchy."[3]

Psalm 29:1 calls upon the "sons of God" *(bənê 'ĕlîm)* to "ascribe to the LORD glory and strength," portraying celestial beings leading cosmic worship. Psalm 89:5-7 similarly presents "the holy ones" *(qədōšîm)* praising God's wonders and acknowledges that "in the council of the holy ones" none compares to the LORD. These references, according to Hermann Gunkel, "incorporate Ancient Near Eastern divine assembly motifs while transforming them to emphasize YHWH's incomparable position among heavenly beings who serve rather than rival the supreme God."[4]

Psalm 103:20-21 explicitly commands angelic worship: "Bless the LORD, O you his angels, you mighty ones who do his bidding, obedient to his spoken word. Bless the LORD, all his hosts, his ministers that do his will." This text presents angels as exemplary worshipers characterized by immediate obedience to divine command. According to J. Clinton McCann, "Angels here function rhetorically as model respondents to divine goodness, establishing pattern that human worshipers should emulate."[5]

Psalm 104:4 presents an enigmatic reference that can be translated either "you make the winds your messengers" or "you make your messengers winds." This ambiguity, as noted by Frank-Lothar Hossfeld, "reflects theological understanding of angels as operating through natural phenomena while transcending mere natural forces, embodying divine activity within creation's processes."[6]

---

3   Peter C. Craigie, *Psalms 1-50, Word Biblical Commentary 19* (Waco, TX: Word Books, 1983), 108.

4   Hermann Gunkel, *Introduction to Psalms: The Genres of the Religious Lyric of Israel,* trans. James D. Nogalski (Macon, GA: Mercer University Press, 1998), 94.

5   J. Clinton McCann Jr., *A Theological Introduction to the Book of Psalms: The Psalms as Torah* (Nashville: Abingdon Press, 1993), 58.

6   Frank-Lothar Hossfeld and Erich Zenger, *Psalms 2: A Commentary on Psalms 51-100,* trans. Linda M. Maloney, Hermeneia (Minneapolis: Fortress Press, 2005), 52.

Psalm 148:2 incorporates angels into cosmic praise: "Praise him, all his angels; praise him, all his host!" This command appears within broader call for all creation—celestial bodies, weather phenomena, geographic features, animals, and humans of every status—to praise God. According to Walter Brueggemann, "This universal praise procession establishes angels as leading section in cosmic choir that encompasses all created reality."[7]

The Psalter's angelology emphasizes several significant theological dimensions. First, angels model proper response to God through immediate obedience and praise, establishing worship pattern for human imitation. Second, angels maintain cosmic order by implementing divine governance, particularly in protecting the faithful. Third, angels occupy intermediate position in creation's hierarchy—above humans but infinitely below God, maintaining proper theological distinctions. Fourth, angels participate in divine council, suggesting cosmic governance through deliberative assembly rather than solitary divine action. These themes reflect what William P. Brown calls "theological integration of heavenly beings within broader biblical wisdom regarding cosmic order and human place within it."[8]

Job's Divine Council

The book of Job contains the Hebrew Bible's most extensive treatment of divine council themes, presenting celestial beings who gather before God and participate in cosmic governance. This heavenly assembly provides crucial framework for the book's exploration of suffering, divine justice, and limits of human knowledge.

Job's prologue introduces the divine council in dramatic fashion: "One day the heavenly beings (*bᵊnê hā'ĕlōhîm*, literally "sons of God") came to present themselves before the LORD, and Satan also came among them" (Job 1:6, repeated with slight variation in 2:1). This scene establishes what Marvin H. Pope describes as "celestial court where divine administration

---

7   Walter Brueggemann, *The Message of the Psalms: A Theological Commentary* (Minneapolis: Augsburg, 1984), 129.
8   William P. Brown, *Seeing the Psalms: A Theology of Metaphor* (Louisville: Westminster John Knox, 2002), 184.

occurs through council deliberation rather than solitary divine decision-making."[9]

The term *śāṭān* (adversary/accuser) appears with the definite article, suggesting a role or function rather than proper name. This figure operates within divine council parameters, requiring divine permission before acting against Job. According to Carol A. Newsom, "The accuser functions as prosecutorial figure within divine council, raising legitimate if ultimately misguided concerns about human righteousness while remaining subject to divine authority rather than representing independent evil principle."[10]

The council reappears in Job 15:8, where Eliphaz sarcastically asks Job, "Have you listened in the council of God?" This rhetorical question implies that divine council access would be necessary to possess the knowledge Job claims. Similarly, in Job 38:7, God describes creation's foundation being laid "while the morning stars sang together and all the heavenly beings *(bənê 'ĕlōhîm)* shouted for joy," suggesting angelic witness to primordial divine activity.

Most significantly, Elihu introduces divine revelation through angelic mediation: "For God speaks in one way, and in two, though people do not perceive it... If there is an angel *(mal'āk)* with them, a mediator *(mēlîṣ)*, one of the thousand, to declare to them what is right for them; then he is gracious to them" (Job 33:14, 23-24). This passage, according to Norman C. Habel, "establishes angels as interpretive intermediaries who translate divine purposes into human understanding, providing theological framework for wisdom pursuit through revealed insight rather than merely empirical observation."[11]

Job's divine council portrayal establishes several significant theological principles. First, it presents divine governance as operating through

---

9   Marvin H. Pope, *Job: Introduction, Translation, and Notes, Anchor Bible 15* (Garden City, NY: Doubleday, 1973), 9.

10   Carol A. Newsom, *"The Book of Job,"* in *The New Interpreter's Bible,* vol. 4, ed. Leander E. Keck (Nashville: Abingdon Press, 1996), 347.

11   Norman C. Habel, *The Book of Job: A Commentary, Old Testament Library* (Philadelphia: Westminster Press, 1985), 465.

deliberative assembly rather than isolated divine action, suggesting what Michael S. Heiser calls "participatory administration of cosmic affairs."[12] Second, it locates apparent random suffering within broader unseen reality where human experience connects to cosmic conflicts beyond human perception. Third, it maintains divine sovereignty even while acknowledging genuine agency of council members, who propose actions but require divine authorization. Fourth, it suggests hierarchical arrangement of heavenly beings, with the accuser functioning within council parameters rather than representing independent demonic opposition.

These divine council themes provide crucial theological context for Job's exploration of unexplained suffering and divine justice. As Elaine Phillips notes, "The divine council framework establishes dramatic irony where readers possess cosmic perspective unavailable to Job himself, creating narrative tension between human questioning and divine purposes revealed only in heavenly assembly."[13] The book ultimately affirms limits of human understanding while suggesting cosmic drama extends beyond human perception.

Angels in Wisdom Traditions

Beyond Job, wisdom literature contains relatively few explicit angel references, consistent with its general focus on ordered creation and practical human behavior rather than supernatural intervention. However, several wisdom passages suggest celestial beings operating within creation's structure.

Proverbs 30:4 asks rhetorical questions emphasizing divine uniqueness: "Who has ascended to heaven and come down?... What is his name or his son's name? Surely you know!" While not explicitly mentioning angels, this passage acknowledges heavenly realm beyond human access while hinting at divine "son" in manner reminiscent of divine council traditions. According

---

12   Michael S. Heiser, *The Unseen Realm: Recovering the Supernatural Worldview of the Bible* (Bellingham, WA: Lexham Press, 2015), 87.
13   Elaine Phillips, "Speaking Truthfully: Job's Friends and Job," *Bulletin for Biblical Research 18, no. 1* (2008): 31-43.

to Michael V. Fox, "This passage emphasizes divine transcendence beyond human wisdom while suggesting divine self-extension through mediatorial figure."[14]

Ecclesiastes lacks direct angel references but mentions "watchers" in potential allusion to divine oversight: "Do not say before the messenger (*mal'āk*, potentially referring to temple functionary rather than celestial being) that it was a mistake" (Ecclesiastes 5:6). This ambiguous reference, according to C.L. Seow, "reflects wisdom tradition's general reticence regarding angelology while acknowledging possible divine oversight of human religious activity."[15]

The Wisdom of Solomon, though deuterocanonical, represents significant development in wisdom angelology: "For righteousness is immortal, but injustice brings death, and the ungodly by their words and deeds summoned death; considering him a friend, they pined away and made a covenant with him, because they are fit to belong to his company" (Wisdom 1:15-16). This personification of death anticipates later wisdom developments where angelic and demonic figures embody cosmic forces. According to David Winston, "Wisdom literature increasingly employed angelic and demonic figures to express cosmic moral forces operating within creation, bridging earlier wisdom emphasis on natural consequences with apocalyptic interest in supernatural agents."[16]

The relative scarcity of angels in wisdom literature represents significant theological perspective rather than mere omission. As Roland E. Murphy observes, "Wisdom's focus on creation's inherent order rather than supernatural intervention established complementary theological tradition that balanced prophetic emphasis on divine interruption with appreciation for God's presence in creation's regular patterns."[17] When

---

14   Michael V. Fox, *Proverbs 10-31, Anchor Bible 18B* (New Haven: Yale University Press, 2009), 853.

15   C.L. Seow, *Ecclesiastes: A New Translation with Introduction and Commentary, Anchor Bible 18C* (New York: Doubleday, 1997), 201.

16   David Winston, *The Wisdom of Solomon, Anchor Bible 43* (Garden City, NY: Doubleday, 1979), 121.

17   Roland E. Murphy, *The Tree of Life: An Exploration of Biblical Wisdom*

wisdom traditions did incorporate angels, they typically presented them as cosmic administrators maintaining creation's order rather than disrupting it through miraculous interventions.

The Book of Sirach (Ecclesiasticus), another deuterocanonical wisdom text, provides interesting development: "Then the prophet Elijah arose like a fire, and his word burned like a torch. He brought a famine upon them, and by his zeal he made them few in number. By the word of the Lord he shut up the heavens, and also three times brought down fire. How glorious you were, Elijah, in your wondrous deeds! Whose glory is equal to yours?... who were taken up by a whirlwind of fire, in a chariot with horses of fire; who are ready at the appointed time, it is written, to calm the wrath of God before it breaks out in fury, to turn the heart of the father to the son, and to restore the tribes of Jacob" (Sirach 48:1-10). This passage, according to Alexander A. Di Lella, "integrates prophetic tradition into wisdom framework by presenting Elijah as angelic figure preserved for eschatological function, bridging wisdom's typical focus on present order with apocalyptic interest in future restoration."[18]

Theological Implications of Angels in Poetic Texts

The presentation of angels in biblical poetry and wisdom literature differs significantly from narrative and apocalyptic texts, emphasizing distinct theological dimensions while maintaining fundamental continuity with broader biblical angelology. Several key theological emphases emerge from these literary contexts.

First, poetic texts particularly emphasize angels as worshipers who model appropriate response to divine majesty. Unlike narrative texts where angels primarily deliver messages or execute judgments, psalmic references frequently portray angels praising God (Psalms 29:1; 103:20-21; 148:2) and participating in celestial liturgy. According to Patrick D. Miller, "This worship function establishes angels as exemplary respondents to divine

---

Literature, 3rd ed. (Grand Rapids: Eerdmans, 2002), 33.

18   Alexander A. Di Lella, *The Wisdom of Ben Sira, Anchor Bible 39* (New York: Doubleday, 1987), 438.

glory, connecting human liturgy with cosmic reality beyond immediate perception."[19]

Second, poetic presentations typically integrate angels within creation's ordered structure rather than emphasizing their disruptive interventions. Angels appear as components of cosmic hierarchy (Psalm 8:5), administrators of providential protection (Psalm 91:11-12), and maintainers of creation boundaries. This integration, as Leo G. Perdue notes, "reflects wisdom tradition's emphasis on discerning God's presence in creation's reliable patterns rather than seeking extraordinary manifestations."[20]

Third, poetic texts emphasize angels' role in cosmic governance through divine council participation. Job's prologue presents celestial beings gathering before God for administrative deliberation; Psalm 89:7 acknowledges the "council of the holy ones" where divine decisions occur. According to Walter Brueggemann, "This council imagery provides theological framework for understanding divine rule as both sovereign and deliberative, maintaining divine freedom while acknowledging delegated administration through created agencies."[21]

Fourth, wisdom traditions particularly develop angels as interpreters who translate divine mysteries into human understanding. Elihu's reference to angelic mediators who declare "what is right" for humans (Job 33:23) establishes angels as hermeneutical bridges between divine perspective and human comprehension. Ellen F. Davis suggests this represents "wisdom's distinctive contribution to biblical angelology—angels as interpretive guides who illuminate creation's moral structure rather than merely announcing divine interventions."[22]

---

19   Patrick D. Miller, *They Cried to the Lord: The Form and Theology of Biblical Prayer* (Minneapolis: Fortress Press, 1994), 320.

20   Leo G. Perdue, *Wisdom Literature: A Theological History* (Louisville: Westminster John Knox, 2007), 174.

21   Walter Brueggemann, *Theology of the Old Testament: Testimony, Dispute, Advocacy* (Minneapolis: Fortress Press, 1997), 249.

22   Ellen F. Davis, *Proverbs, Ecclesiastes, and the Song of Songs, Westminster Bible Companion* (Louisville: Westminster John Knox, 2000), 152.

Fifth, poetic texts maintain careful theological boundaries that preserve divine uniqueness while acknowledging genuine angelic significance. Psalm 89:6 asks, "For who in the skies can be compared to the LORD? Who among the heavenly beings is like the LORD?" This rhetorical question, according to J. Clinton McCann, "establishes fundamental theological distinction between Creator and creature while acknowledging real existence of celestial beings who, though exalted, remain infinitely distant from divine status."[23]

These theological emphases complement narrative and apocalyptic presentations while adding distinctive wisdom perspective on angelic function within cosmic order. As Samuel E. Balentine observes, "Wisdom and poetic angelology grounds supernatural agencies within creation's reliable structure, providing theological balance to apocalyptic emphasis on angels as disruptive interventionists and narrative focus on angels as occasional divine messengers."[24] This integration of angels within cosmic order rather than merely beyond it represents wisdom's distinctive contribution to biblical angelology.

---

23   J. Clinton McCann Jr., *"The Book of Psalms,"* in *The New Interpreter's Bible,* vol. 4, ed. Leander E. Keck (Nashville: Abingdon Press, 1996), 1046.
24   Samuel E. Balentine, *Job, Smyth & Helwys Bible Commentary* (Macon, GA: Smyth & Helwys, 2006), 62.

Chapter 7

Angels in the Gospels and Acts

Annunciation Narratives

The New Testament introduces angelic appearances immediately in its narrative, with angels playing crucial roles in announcing the births of both John the Baptist and Jesus. These annunciation accounts establish theological continuity with Hebrew Bible angelic appearances while introducing distinctive features that reflect the Gospels' Christological focus.

Luke's Gospel opens with the angel Gabriel appearing to Zechariah in the temple: "Your prayer has been heard. Your wife Elizabeth will bear you a son, and you will name him John" (Luke 1:13). This appearance contains several significant elements. First, it occurs in sacred space during priestly service, connecting with biblical tradition of temple as meeting place between divine and human realms. Second, it explicitly names the angel—Gabriel—recalling his appearances in Daniel and suggesting interpretive continuity with apocalyptic literature. Third, it emphasizes prophetic fulfillment, with John described as coming "with the spirit and power of Elijah" (Luke 1:17).

According to Raymond E. Brown, "Luke's Gabriel appearance intentionally echoes Daniel's angelophanies, creating literary continuity between prophetic expectations and their fulfillment in the gospel narrative."[1] Gabriel's self-identification—"I stand in the presence of God, and I have been sent to speak to you" (Luke 1:19)—emphasizes his status as divine messenger rather than independent agent, maintaining theological clarity about angelic role.

---

1   Raymond E. Brown, *The Birth of the Messiah: A Commentary on the Infancy Narratives in the Gospels of Matthew and Luke,* updated ed. (New York: Doubleday, 1993), 270.

The annunciation to Mary (Luke 1:26-38) presents the same angel, Gabriel, now appearing to a young woman outside institutional religious contexts. This appearance emphasizes divine initiative crossing social boundaries, as the angel addresses Mary as "favored one" *(kecharitōmenē)* despite her humble status. Gabriel's message introduces complex theological content regarding incarnation: "The Holy Spirit will come upon you, and the power of the Most High will overshadow you; therefore the child to be born will be holy; he will be called Son of God" (Luke 1:35).

Joseph Fitzmyer notes that this annunciation "adapts conventional biblical birth announcement patterns while introducing unprecedented theological content regarding divine conception."[2] The angel serves as messenger of mystery beyond human comprehension, yet requires Mary's consent—"Let it be with me according to your word" (Luke 1:38)—suggesting what Beverly Roberts Gaventa calls "divine respect for human agency even while announcing divine initiative."[3]

Matthew's Gospel presents angelic annunciation to Joseph through dreams rather than waking appearances: "An angel of the Lord appeared to him in a dream and said, 'Joseph, son of David, do not be afraid to take Mary as your wife, for the child conceived in her is from the Holy Spirit'" (Matthew 1:20). This dreamed angelophany, according to Craig S. Keener, "connects with Hebrew Bible tradition of divine guidance through dreams while emphasizing Joseph's Davidic lineage, making the angel messenger of dynastic significance."[4]

These annunciation narratives establish several significant patterns for New Testament angelology. First, they present angels as heralds of divine initiative rather than respondents to human prayer or ritual. Second, they emphasize angels interpreting events within salvation-historical framework, connecting present circumstances to scriptural promises. Third, they

---

2   Joseph A. Fitzmyer, *The Gospel According to Luke I–IX, Anchor Bible 28* (Garden City, NY: Doubleday, 1981), 348.

3   Beverly Roberts Gaventa, *Mary: Glimpses of the Mother of Jesus* (Columbia: University of South Carolina Press, 1995), 56.

4   Craig S. Keener, *The Gospel of Matthew: A Socio-Rhetorical Commentary* (Grand Rapids: Eerdmans, 2009), 98.

present angels addressing human fear with reassurance—"Do not be afraid" (Luke 1:13, 30; Matthew 1:20)—acknowledging the overwhelming nature of divine encounter even through angelic mediation. Fourth, they require human response to angelic messages, suggesting divine respect for human freedom within divine purposes.

Angels at the Birth, Temptation, and Resurrection of Jesus

Angels appear at pivotal moments in Jesus's life, particularly marking transitions between major narrative movements in the gospel accounts. These appearances establish theological framework for understanding Jesus's identity and mission while connecting his story with broader biblical patterns of divine guidance and protection.

The birth narratives feature angelic announcement to shepherds: "An angel of the Lord stood before them, and the glory of the Lord shone around them" (Luke 2:9). This appearance combines individual angelic messenger with divine glory *(doxa)*, creating what Raymond Brown describes as "theophanic quality that exceeds typical angelophany, emphasizing cosmic significance of seemingly humble birth."[5] The subsequent appearance of "a multitude of the heavenly host" praising God (Luke 2:13) presents angels as worshipers who model appropriate response to incarnation.

According to Luke Timothy Johnson, "The angelic announcement to shepherds democratizes divine revelation by addressing marginalized figures rather than religious authorities, establishing pattern where heavenly recognition precedes and contrasts with human rejection."[6] The angels interpret Jesus's significance through combining royal language—"a Savior, who is the Messiah, the Lord" (Luke 2:11)—with humble sign: "a child wrapped in bands of cloth and lying in a manger" (Luke 2:12).

Following Jesus's temptation, angels appear as servants: "Then the devil left him, and suddenly angels came and waited on him" (Matthew 4:11; similarly Mark 1:13). This brief reference, according to Ulrich Luz,

---

5   Raymond E. Brown, *The Birth of the Messiah*, 426.
6   Luke Timothy Johnson, *The Gospel of Luke, Sacra Pagina 3* (Collegeville, MN: Liturgical Press, 1991), 47.

"establishes Jesus's authority over angelic beings who respond to his needs after testing, contrasting with Satan's earlier challenge to command angels for protection."[7] The angels' ministry *(diēkonoun)* suggests restoration following testing, possibly including physical nourishment similar to Elijah's wilderness experience (1 Kings 19:5-8).

The resurrection narratives feature prominent angelic appearances across all four Gospels, though with significant variations. Matthew describes "an angel of the Lord, descending from heaven" who rolls back the stone and sits upon it, with appearance "like lightning" and clothing "white as snow" (Matthew 28:2-3). Mark mentions "a young man, dressed in a white robe, sitting on the right side" (Mark 16:5). Luke reports "two men in dazzling clothes" (Luke 24:4), while John describes "two angels in white, sitting where the body of Jesus had been lying, one at the head and the other at the feet" (John 20:12).

Despite these variations, the angelic figures consistently interpret the empty tomb's significance: "He is not here; for he has been raised, as he said" (Matthew 28:6). According to N.T. Wright, "The angels function as authoritative interpreters who transform potential confusion into revelatory moment, explaining absence as victory rather than loss."[8] Their appearance creates continuity with earlier biblical theophanies while emphasizing new reality of resurrection.

Several theological patterns emerge from these angelic appearances surrounding Jesus's life. First, angels consistently direct attention toward Jesus rather than themselves, serving his mission rather than independent purposes. Second, angels interpret Jesus's significance within scriptural framework, connecting his experiences with divine promises. Third, angels mark boundaries between cosmic realms, appearing at moments where heaven and earth intersect most dramatically—incarnation, testing, and resurrection. Fourth, angels provide supernatural testimony to Jesus's

---

7   Ulrich Luz, *Matthew 1-7: A Commentary,* trans. Wilhelm C. Linss, Hermeneia (Minneapolis: Fortress Press, 2007), 156.
8   N.T. Wright, *The Resurrection of the Son of God* (Minneapolis: Fortress Press, 2003), 611.

identity, offering heavenly perspective on events whose significance might remain hidden from merely human viewpoint.

Angelic Guidance in Acts

The book of Acts presents angels as active agents guiding the early church's mission and protecting its leaders. These appearances demonstrate continuity between Jesus's ministry and the apostolic church while emphasizing divine oversight of mission development beyond Jesus's immediate followers.

Acts 5:19-20 describes an angel releasing the apostles from prison: "During the night an angel of the Lord opened the prison doors, brought them out, and said, 'Go, stand in the temple and tell the people the whole message about this life.'" This angelic rescue, according to F. Scott Spencer, "establishes pattern where divine intervention liberates gospel proclamation from human constraint, demonstrating heavenly authorization for apostolic preaching despite official opposition."[9]

A similar prison release occurs for Peter in Acts 12:7-11, where "an angel of the Lord" awakens him, removes his chains, and guides him out of prison. The narrative emphasizes Peter's initial confusion—"He did not know that what was happening with the angel's help was real; he thought he was seeing a vision" (Acts 12:9)—suggesting what C.K. Barrett calls "phenomenological complexity of angelic experience that transcends simple distinctions between vision and physical manifestation."[10]

Acts 8:26 attributes Philip's mission direction to angelic guidance: "Then an angel of the Lord said to Philip, 'Get up and go toward the south.'" This guidance leads to Philip's encounter with the Ethiopian eunuch, establishing what Luke Timothy Johnson describes as "angelic participation in mission

---

9   F. Scott Spencer, *Acts, Sheffield New Testament Guides* (Sheffield: Sheffield Academic Press, 1997), 58.

10   C.K. Barrett, *A Critical and Exegetical Commentary on the Acts of the Apostles, International Critical Commentary* (Edinburgh: T&T Clark, 1994), 1:580.

expansion across cultural boundaries, demonstrating divine initiative in gospel movement beyond Jewish communities."[11]

Cornelius's vision (Acts 10:3-6) features "an angel of God" who directs him to send for Peter, initiating pivotal narrative sequence leading to Gentile incorporation into the church. According to Beverly Roberts Gaventa, "The angel serves as divine catalyst for cross-cultural encounter that neither Peter nor Cornelius would have initiated independently, demonstrating divine orchestration of mission development."[12]

Paul receives angelic assurance during sea voyage: "For last night an angel of the God to whom I belong and whom I worship stood by me, and said, 'Do not be afraid, Paul; you must stand before the emperor; and indeed, God has granted safety to all those who are sailing with you'" (Acts 27:23-24). This appearance, according to Joseph Fitzmyer, "connects Paul's missionary journey with divine purpose, placing apparent disaster within providential framework while establishing Paul's spiritual authority among his fellow travelers."[13]

These angelic appearances in Acts establish several significant patterns. First, angels consistently advance the gospel mission, removing obstacles and creating connections that extend proclamation to new communities. Second, angels provide protection for key mission leaders, particularly when opposition threatens to terminate their ministry prematurely. Third, angels offer divine interpretation of challenging circumstances, helping disciples perceive God's purposes within apparent setbacks. Fourth, angels initiate cross-cultural connections, suggesting divine orchestration of the church's expansion beyond ethnic and social boundaries.

According to Craig Keener, "Luke's presentation of angels creates narrative continuity between gospel events and church experience,

---

11   Luke Timothy Johnson, *The Acts of the Apostles, Sacra Pagina 5* (Collegeville, MN: Liturgical Press, 1992), 153.
12   Beverly Roberts Gaventa, *Acts, Abingdon New Testament Commentaries* (Nashville: Abingdon Press, 2003), 165.
13   Joseph A. Fitzmyer, *The Acts of the Apostles, Anchor Bible 31* (New York: Doubleday, 1998), 775.

demonstrating that the same divine guidance that directed Jesus's ministry continues directing the apostolic mission."[14] These appearances establish theological framework where the church's expansion occurs through divine initiative rather than merely human planning, with angels serving as agents of divine direction.

Angels as Messengers and Interpreters

Throughout the Gospels and Acts, angels function primarily as messengers (*angeloi* literally means "messengers") who interpret events within divine perspective. This interpretive function appears with notable consistency across various angelic encounters.

The birth narratives particularly emphasize this interpretive role. The angel explains to Joseph that Mary's pregnancy comes "from the Holy Spirit" (Matthew 1:20), providing divine perspective on circumstances that appeared scandalous from merely human viewpoint. The angelic announcement to shepherds interprets Jesus's significance as "a Savior, who is the Messiah, the Lord" (Luke 2:11), providing theological framework for perceiving divine purpose within humble birth.

According to Raymond Brown, "The angelic interpretations provide heavenly hermeneutic that transcends immediate appearances, enabling recipients to perceive divine action within ordinary human circumstances."[15] This interpretive function continues biblical patterns established in Hebrew Bible, particularly Daniel's angelically interpreted visions, while focusing specifically on Christ's identity and significance.

The resurrection narratives similarly feature angelic interpretation of the empty tomb: "He is not here; for he has been raised, as he said" (Matthew 28:6). Without this interpretation, the empty tomb remains ambiguous sign potentially attributable to various causes. According to N.T. Wright, "The angelic message transforms absence into proclamation, interpreting vacant space as victory rather than violation or loss."[16]

---

14   Craig S. Keener, *Acts: An Exegetical Commentary, vol. 1* (Grand Rapids: Baker Academic, 2012), 193.

15   Raymond E. Brown, *The Birth of the Messiah*, 312.

16   N.T. Wright, *The Resurrection of the Son of God*, 611.

In Acts, angels repeatedly interpret circumstances within divine purpose. The angel directing Cornelius explains that his "prayers and alms have ascended as a memorial before God" (Acts 10:4), providing spiritual interpretation of Cornelius's devotion. The angel assuring Paul during storm places apparent disaster within divine plan: "God has granted safety to all those who are sailing with you" (Acts 27:24).

This interpretive function establishes angels as mediators between divine and human perspective, enabling human recipients to perceive transcendent significance within immanent events. According to Luke Timothy Johnson, "Angels bridge epistemological gap between limited human perception and comprehensive divine knowledge, making temporarily available to humans the eternal perspective that angels permanently possess."[17]

Beyond verbal interpretation, angels in the Gospels and Acts sometimes communicate through actions with symbolic significance. The angel at Jesus's tomb rolls away the stone and sits upon it (Matthew 28:2), enacting victory over sealed death. The angel liberating Peter strikes him on the side (Acts 12:7), physically initiating movement from imprisonment to freedom.

These symbolic actions, according to Beverly Roberts Gaventa, "perform visually what verbal interpretation explains conceptually, creating multimedia divine communication that addresses recipients through multiple sensory channels."[18] This combination of verbal and enacted communication characterizes many biblical angelophanies, suggesting divine accommodation to human perceptual needs.

The New Testament presents angels as interpreters who possess heavenly perspective unavailable to humans through natural means. Their interpretations consistently focus attention on Christ and his ongoing work through the Spirit-empowered church, demonstrating what F. Scott Spencer calls "christocentric hermeneutic that perceives all events

---

17   Luke Timothy Johnson, *The Acts of the Apostles*, 153.
18   Beverly Roberts Gaventa, *From Darkness to Light: Aspects of Conversion in the New Testament* (Philadelphia: Fortress Press, 1986), 96.

in relation to Christ's person and mission."[19] This interpretive framework establishes theological continuity while acknowledging the unprecedented nature of incarnation, crucifixion, and resurrection.

Theological Significance of Angels in the Gospels and Acts

The presentation of angels in the Gospels and Acts reflects distinctive theological emphases that both continue and transform Hebrew Bible angelology. Several significant developments emerge in these texts.

First, angels consistently point toward Jesus rather than exercising independent authority. Unlike Hebrew Bible angels who sometimes function as semi-autonomous divine representatives, New Testament angels primarily serve Christ's mission. According to Darrell Bock, "Angels in the Gospels demonstrate new cosmic hierarchy where Christ occupies central position and angels function as his attendants rather than independent divine agents."[20] This christocentric orientation appears even in post-resurrection narratives, where angels interpret Jesus's absence rather than replacing his presence.

Second, angels mark major transitions in salvation history, appearing at pivotal narrative moments—incarnation, resurrection, Pentecost, mission expansion—rather than as regular mediators of divine communication. According to Joel Green, "Angelic appearances in Luke-Acts cluster around salvation-historical boundaries, marking decisive moments in divine plan while remaining relatively absent from ongoing church experience where Spirit guidance predominates."[21] This pattern suggests shifting emphasis from angelic mediation to Spirit-guided community as primary locus of divine presence.

---

19   F. Scott Spencer, *The Gospel of Luke and Acts of the Apostles* (Nashville: Abingdon Press, 2008), 76.

20   Darrell L. Bock, *Luke 1:1–9:50, Baker Exegetical Commentary on the New Testament* (Grand Rapids: Baker Academic, 1994), 215.

21   Joel B. Green, *The Gospel of Luke, New International Commentary on the New Testament* (Grand Rapids: Eerdmans, 1997), 121.

Third, angels demonstrate cosmic recognition of Jesus's significance before and despite human rejection. The angelic birth announcement to shepherds precedes widespread acknowledgment of Jesus's identity; angels at the tomb proclaim resurrection while disciples remain confused. According to Raymond Brown, "Angels provide heavenly testimony that contextualizes human misunderstanding and rejection within broader cosmic drama where Jesus's identity receives supernatural acknowledgment."[22]

Fourth, angels create narrative continuity between Hebrew Bible promises and New Testament fulfillment. Gabriel's announcements explicitly connect with Daniel's prophecies; angels quote scripture to interpret Jesus's empty tomb; angelic guidance in Acts continues patterns established in Israel's history. According to Craig Evans, "Angelic appearances demonstrate that Jesus's story represents fulfillment rather than innovation, connecting gospel events with Israel's sacred traditions through recognizable patterns of divine communication."[23]

Fifth, angels participate in the mission's expansion across social and ethnic boundaries. Angelic direction sends Philip to the Ethiopian eunuch, instructs Peter to visit Cornelius, and guides Paul toward Rome. According to Beverly Roberts Gaventa, "Angels function as divine agents overcoming human resistance to boundary-crossing mission, initiating interactions that human actors might avoid without supernatural prompting."[24]

Sixth, angels model appropriate response to Christ through worship, service, and proclamation. The heavenly host praises God at Jesus's birth; angels minister to Jesus after temptation; angels at the tomb become first resurrection proclaimers. According to Joel Green, "Angels provide paradigmatic examples of proper response to Jesus, modeling for humans the recognition, service, and testimony that Christ deserves."[25]

---

22   Raymond E. Brown, *The Birth of the Messiah*, 426.

23   Craig A. Evans, *Matthew, New Cambridge Bible Commentary* (Cambridge: Cambridge University Press, 2012), 54.

24   Beverly Roberts Gaventa, *Acts*, 165.

25   Joel B. Green, *The Gospel of Luke*, 132.

These theological developments maintain essential continuity with Hebrew Bible angelology while reframing angelic ministry within christological perspective. According to Darrell Hannah, "The Gospels and Acts present angels as central to the story's cosmic dimensions without competing with Christ's supremacy, balancing appreciation for angelic ministry with clear subordination to Jesus's unique status."[26] This balance would prove crucial for subsequent Christian theological reflection on angels, providing framework that acknowledged angelic significance while avoiding their elevation to inappropriate prominence.

---

26   Darrell D. Hannah, *Michael and Christ: Michael Traditions and Angel Christology in Early Christianity* (Tübingen: Mohr Siebeck, 1999), 150.

Chapter 8

Angels in the Epistles and Revelation

Paul's Angelology

Paul's epistles present a complex and multifaceted angelology that integrates traditional Jewish understanding of angels with distinctive Christological perspective. Unlike the narrative presentations in the Gospels and Acts, Paul's references to angels appear primarily within theological arguments addressing specific community concerns.

In Romans 8:38-39, Paul lists angels among cosmic powers that cannot separate believers from God's love in Christ: "For I am convinced that neither death, nor life, nor angels, nor rulers, nor things present, nor things to come, nor powers, nor height, nor depth, nor anything else in all creation, will be able to separate us from the love of God in Christ Jesus our Lord." This comprehensive list, according to James D.G. Dunn, "places angels within broader category of potential spiritual obstacles, suggesting awareness of both benevolent and potentially threatening angelic powers within cosmic hierarchy."[1] The passage emphasizes Christ's supremacy over all spiritual beings, establishing what Michael Wolter calls "Christological relativization of angelic significance."[2]

First Corinthians contains several significant angelic references that address community concerns. Paul warns against improper worship conduct by noting that "the women should have a symbol of authority on their head, because of the angels" (1 Corinthians 11:10). While variously interpreted, this enigmatic reference suggests what Gordon Fee identifies as "awareness of angels as witnesses to worship, reflecting Jewish tradition where angels observe human conduct and participate in liturgical settings."[3]

---

1   James D.G. Dunn, *Romans 1-8, Word Biblical Commentary 38A* (Dallas: Word Books, 1988), 513.
2   Michael Wolter, *Paul: An Outline of His Theology,* trans. Robert L. Brawley (Waco, TX: Baylor University Press, 2015), 124.
3   Gordon D. Fee, *The First Epistle to the Corinthians, New International Commentary on the New Testament* (Grand Rapids: Eerdmans, 1987), 519.

In 1 Corinthians 13:1, Paul uses angelic language as rhetorical superlative: "If I speak in the tongues of mortals and of angels, but do not have love, I am a noisy gong or a clanging cymbal." This hypothetical reference, according to Anthony Thiselton, "acknowledges positive valuation of angelic connection while subordinating it to ethical imperatives, particularly love."[4] The passage suggests awareness of traditions regarding angelic languages while redirecting emphasis toward love as superior spiritual gift.

First Corinthians 6:3 contains the striking claim that believers "will judge angels," introducing eschatological dimension to human-angelic relationship. While not elaborated, this statement suggests what Margaret Mitchell calls "radical reconfiguration of cosmic hierarchy where redeemed humanity receives authority exceeding that of certain angelic beings."[5] This perspective contrasts with typical Second Temple Jewish emphasis on angelic superiority to humans.

Paul's most extended angelological discussions appear in the disputed letter to the Colossians, addressing what many scholars identify as inappropriate veneration of angels within the community. Colossians 2:18 warns against those who insist on "worship of angels," suggesting competing religious practices that emphasized angelic mediation. The letter responds by emphasizing Christ's cosmic supremacy: "He is the image of the invisible God, the firstborn of all creation; for in him all things in heaven and on earth were created, things visible and invisible, whether thrones or dominions or rulers or powers—all things have been created through him and for him" (Colossians 1:15-16).

This Christological framework, according to Clinton Arnold, "subordinates all angelic powers to Christ while acknowledging their genuine existence and cosmic significance."[6] Rather than denying angelic

---

4   Anthony C. Thiselton, *The First Epistle to the Corinthians: A Commentary on the Greek Text, New International Greek Testament Commentary* (Grand Rapids: Eerdmans, 2000), 1036.

5   Margaret M. Mitchell, *Paul and the Rhetoric of Reconciliation: An Exegetical Investigation of the Language and Composition of 1 Corinthians* (Louisville: Westminster John Knox, 1993), 117.

6   Clinton E. Arnold, *The Colossian Syncretism: The Interface Between*

reality, the Colossian Christology incorporates angels within creation's proper order while rejecting their inappropriate veneration. The emphasis on Christ's cosmic reconciliation—"through him God was pleased to reconcile to himself all things, whether on earth or in heaven, by making peace through the blood of his cross" (Colossians 1:20)—suggests what James Dunn calls "comprehensive cosmic scope where Christ's redemptive work affects angelic realms as well as human spheres."[7]

Paul's reference to angels delivering the law at Sinai (Galatians 3:19; cf. Acts 7:53; Hebrews 2:2) represents significant theological development of traditions hinted at in Deuteronomy 33:2 (LXX) and elaborated in Jewish interpretive tradition. According to Hans Dieter Betz, "Paul uses this tradition to emphasize the law's mediated status in contrast to direct promise, establishing theological hierarchy where angelic mediation ranks below direct divine action."[8] This argument distinguishes Sinai covenant (angelically mediated) from Abrahamic promise (directly given), creating an evaluative framework that prioritizes unmediated divine commitment.

Paul occasionally mentions angelic disguise: "Even Satan disguises himself as an angel of light" (2 Corinthians 11:14). This warning, according to Margaret Thrall, "reflects awareness of potential deception through angelic appearances, necessitating discernment regarding spiritual manifestations."[9] The statement suggests both positive associations with "angel of light" as authentic divine messenger and recognition that appearances may prove misleading.

Several theological emphases emerge from Paul's diverse angelological references. First, Paul consistently subordinates angels to Christ, emphasizing their created status relative to Christ's cosmic supremacy.

Christianity and Folk Belief at Colossae (Tübingen: Mohr Siebeck, 1995), 32-33.

7   James D.G. Dunn, The Theology of Paul the Apostle (Grand Rapids: Eerdmans, 1998), 290.

8   Hans Dieter Betz, Galatians: A Commentary on Paul's Letter to the Churches in Galatia, Hermeneia (Philadelphia: Fortress Press, 1979), 169.

9   Margaret E. Thrall, A Critical and Exegetical Commentary on the Second Epistle to the Corinthians, International Critical Commentary (Edinburgh: T&T Clark, 1994), 2:735.

Second, he acknowledges angelic significance within cosmic order while rejecting practices that elevate angels to inappropriate prominence. Third, he recognizes both positive and potentially threatening angelic powers, requiring Christological discernment rather than uncritical acceptance of spiritual manifestations. Fourth, he anticipates eschatological transformation of cosmic hierarchy where redeemed humanity receives authority exceeding certain angelic beings.

According to James Dunn, "Paul's angelology represents creative integration of Jewish apocalyptic traditions within radical Christological framework, maintaining angels' significance while decisively reorienting cosmic hierarchy around Christ's person and work."[10] This integration would prove influential for subsequent Christian theological reflection on angels, establishing patterns that acknowledged angelic reality while preventing their elevation to inappropriate religious prominence.

Angels in Hebrews

The Epistle to the Hebrews presents the New Testament's most extended comparison between Christ and angels, establishing theological framework that both affirms angelic significance and subordinates angels to Christ's superior status. This angelological discussion serves the author's broader purpose of demonstrating Christ's supremacy over all aspects of Jewish religious tradition.

Hebrews opens with seven scriptural citations (Hebrews 1:5-14) demonstrating Christ's superiority to angels. These carefully arranged quotations highlight several contrasts: Christ is Son while angels are servants; Christ receives worship while angels offer worship; Christ sits enthroned while angels are sent forth in service. According to Harold Attridge, "This catena of citations creates comprehensive scriptural argument for Christological supremacy, addressing apparent Jewish Christian overvaluation of angels as mediators between God and humanity."[11]

---

10   James D.G. Dunn, *The Theology of Paul the Apostle* (Grand Rapids: Eerdmans, 1998), 104.

11   Harold W. Attridge, *The Epistle to the Hebrews, Hermeneia* (Philadelphia: Fortress Press, 1989), 50.

The author grounds this superiority claim in Christ's participation in creation: "Through whom he also created the worlds" (Hebrews 1:2). This perspective, according to Luke Timothy Johnson, "connects Christ with creation's origins rather than merely its redemption, establishing ontological rather than merely functional superiority over angels as created beings."[12]

Hebrews explicitly addresses the relationship between salvation and angelic mediation: "For if the message declared through angels was valid, and every transgression or disobedience received a just penalty, how can we escape if we neglect so great a salvation?" (Hebrews 2:2-3). This passage acknowledges the Sinai covenant's angelic mediation (aligning with Paul's perspective in Galatians 3:19) while emphasizing the superior revelation that comes directly through the Son.

The author recognizes humanity's current position as "a little lower than the angels" (Hebrews 2:7, quoting Psalm 8:5 LXX) while anticipating eschatological elevation where the created order becomes subject to redeemed humanity rather than angels (Hebrews 2:5-8). According to David deSilva, "This eschatological perspective reconfigures cosmic hierarchy based on Christ's redemptive work rather than original creation order, anticipating restoration that elevates redeemed humanity above angelic status."[13]

Hebrews contains notable references to positive angelic activity, including hospitality to angels (Hebrews 13:2) and angels as "spirits in the divine service, sent to serve for the sake of those who are to inherit salvation" (Hebrews 1:14). These acknowledgments, according to Craig Koester, "maintain proper appreciation for angelic ministry while contextualizing it within theological framework that prioritizes direct access to God through Christ."[14]

---

12   Luke Timothy Johnson, *Hebrews: A Commentary, New Testament Library* (Louisville: Westminster John Knox, 2006), 68.

13   David A. deSilva, *Perseverance in Gratitude: A Socio-Rhetorical Commentary on the Epistle "to the Hebrews"* (Grand Rapids: Eerdmans, 2000), 108.

14   Craig R. Koester, *Hebrews: A New Translation with Introduction and Commentary, Anchor Bible 36* (New York: Doubleday, 2001), 192.

The author's concern appears directed not against angels themselves but against religious perspectives that elevated angelic mediation at the expense of Christ's direct high priestly ministry. This emphasis on immediate access to God through Christ rather than angelic intermediaries appears throughout the epistle: "Let us therefore approach the throne of grace with boldness" (Hebrews 4:16); "we have confidence to enter the sanctuary by the blood of Jesus" (Hebrews 10:19).

According to L.D. Hurst, "Hebrews represents the most comprehensive New Testament argument against inappropriate angelological developments within early Christianity, providing theological foundation for accepting angels' legitimate ministry while rejecting their elevation to mediatorial status that properly belongs to Christ alone."[15] This balanced perspective would prove influential for subsequent Christian angelology, establishing a Christocentric framework for appreciating angelic ministry without compromising Christ's unique mediatorial role.

Angels in the Epistles and Revelation

The Catholic Epistles contain relatively few explicit angel references, though those present reinforce significant theological themes. First Peter 1:12 states that the gospel reveals mysteries "into which angels long to look," suggesting what Karen Jobes calls "angelic interest in human redemption as transcendent event attracting heaven's attention."[16] This perspective places human salvation at creation's center, with angels as witnesses rather than primary participants.

First Peter 3:22 emphasizes Christ's cosmic authority: "who has gone into heaven and is at the right hand of God, with angels, authorities, and powers made subject to him." This comprehensive subordination, according to Paul Achtemeier, "establishes Christological framework for understanding

---

15   L.D. Hurst, *The Epistle to the Hebrews: Its Background of Thought*, Society *for New Testament Studies Monograph Series 65* (Cambridge: Cambridge University Press, 1990), 45.

16   Karen H. Jobes, *1 Peter, Baker Exegetical Commentary on the New Testament* (Grand Rapids: Baker Academic, 2005), 97.

all spiritual beings within creation's proper order, with Christ occupying supreme position following his resurrection and ascension."[17]

Second Peter 2:4 and Jude 6 reference angelic rebellion and punishment, with fallen angels "kept in chains/darkness until the judgment." These allusions to traditions developed in 1 Enoch and other Second Temple literature, according to Richard Bauckham, "incorporate apocalyptic traditions regarding cosmic rebellion while emphasizing divine sovereignty over all spiritual powers, even rebellious ones."[18] These brief references suggest early Christian acceptance of certain aspects of Jewish angelological tradition while maintaining distinctive Christological emphasis.

Revelation presents the New Testament's most elaborate angelology, featuring numerous specialized angels who control natural elements, guide John's visionary experience, and participate in eschatological judgment. The term "angel" *(angelos)* appears approximately seventy times in the book, making angels the most frequently mentioned beings after God and Christ.

Several distinctive angelological features characterize Revelation. First, angels appear with specific cosmic functions: angels of the seven churches (Revelation 1:20), angels controlling the four winds (Revelation 7:1), the angel with authority over fire (Revelation 14:18), and the angel with authority over water (Revelation 16:5). According to David Aune, "This functional specialization reflects developed angelological tradition familiar from apocalyptic literature while emphasizing divine sovereignty exercised through delegated angelic administration."[19]

Second, angels serve as interpreters guiding John through his visionary experience. "The revelation of Jesus Christ, which God gave him to show his servants what must soon take place; he made it known by sending his angel

---

17   Paul J. Achtemeier, *1 Peter: A Commentary on First Peter, Hermeneia* (Minneapolis: Fortress Press, 1996), 273.

18   Richard J. Bauckham, *Jude, 2 Peter, Word Biblical Commentary 50* (Waco, TX: Word Books, 1983), 52.

19   David E. Aune, *Revelation 1-5, Word Biblical Commentary 52A* (Dallas: Word Books, 1997), 108.

to his servant John" (Revelation 1:1). Similar interpretive angels appear throughout the book, explaining visionary elements and directing John's attention. According to Elisabeth Schüssler Fiorenza, "These interpreting angels maintain apocalyptic convention where heavenly beings bridge cognitive gap between divine realities and human comprehension."[20]

Third, angels consistently deflect worship toward God alone. When John falls down to worship the interpreting angel, he receives immediate correction: "You must not do that! I am a fellow servant with you and your comrades who hold the testimony of Jesus. Worship God!" (Revelation 19:10; similarly 22:8-9). According to Craig Koester, "This explicit rejection of angel worship establishes clear theological boundary distinguishing Christian practice from contemporaneous religious traditions that incorporated veneration of angelic beings."[21]

Fourth, angels participate in cosmic warfare against demonic forces. Revelation 12:7-9 describes Michael and his angels fighting against the dragon and his angels, resulting in Satan's expulsion from heaven. This cosmic conflict, according to Adela Yarbro Collins, "integrates traditional Jewish angelology within distinctively Christian apocalyptic framework where Christ's incarnation, death, and resurrection trigger decisive heavenly battle with ongoing earthly implications."[22]

Fifth, angels function as divine agents executing judgment. Seven angels sound trumpets announcing sequential judgments (Revelation 8-9); seven angels pour out bowls of God's wrath (Revelation 16); an angel casts a millstone into the sea symbolizing Babylon's fall (Revelation 18:21); and angels gather humanity for final judgment (Revelation 14:14-20). According to G.K. Beale, "These angels implement divine decisions rather than determining judgments themselves, maintaining theological

20   Elisabeth Schüssler Fiorenza, *The Book of Revelation: Justice and Judgment,* 2nd ed. (Minneapolis: Fortress Press, 1998), 170.

21   Craig R. Koester, *Revelation: A New Translation with Introduction and Commentary, Anchor Yale Bible 38A* (New Haven: Yale University Press, 2014), 738.

22   Adela Yarbro Collins, *The Combat Myth in the Book of Revelation, Harvard Dissertations in Religion 9* (Missoula, MT: Scholars Press, 1976), 107.

clarity regarding divine sovereignty even while acknowledging angelic participation in eschatological events."[23]

Revelation's complex angelology demonstrates significant continuity with Jewish apocalyptic traditions while introducing distinctive Christian elements, particularly subordination to Christ as "King of kings and Lord of lords" (Revelation 19:16). The book presents angels as numerous and active cosmic agents while maintaining clear theological boundaries that prevent their elevation to inappropriate religious prominence.

Theological Developments in New Testament Angelology

The New Testament's diverse angelological presentations reveal several significant theological developments that both continue and transform Jewish angelological traditions. These developments reflect the early Christian community's effort to integrate traditional understanding of angelic beings within its distinctive Christological framework.

First, New Testament texts consistently subordinate angels to Christ, establishing what Darrell Hannah calls "radical Christological repositioning of cosmic hierarchy."[24] This subordination appears through various theological strategies: Hebrews' extended scriptural argument for Christ's superiority (Hebrews 1-2); Paul's cosmic Christology placing Christ above all creation including "thrones, dominions, rulers, and powers" (Colossians 1:15-20); John's vision of countless angels worshiping the Lamb (Revelation 5:11-12); and Gospel narratives where angels serve Christ and announce his significance.

This Christological reframing, according to Larry Hurtado, "represented significant theological innovation within Jewish monotheistic tradition, creating conceptual space for Christ's divine status while maintaining

---

23   G.K. Beale, *The Book of Revelation: A Commentary on the Greek Text, New International Greek Testament Commentary* (Grand Rapids: Eerdmans, 1999), 809.

24   Darrell D. Hannah, *Michael and Christ: Michael Traditions and Angel Christology in Early Christianity* (Tübingen: Mohr Siebeck, 1999), 149.

fundamental commitment to one God."[25] Rather than rejecting angelology, early Christianity incorporated angels within Christocentric cosmic order that maintained their significance while clarifying their created status relative to Christ's unique position.

Second, New Testament texts emphasize direct access to God through Christ rather than angelic mediation. Hebrews particularly develops this theme through its high priestly Christology: "Since, then, we have a great high priest who has passed through the heavens, Jesus, the Son of God, let us hold fast to our confession" (Hebrews 4:14). This emphasis, according to David deSilva, "directly addressed prevalent Jewish and Greco-Roman concepts of spiritual mediation through various intermediary beings, offering instead immediate access through Christ alone."[26]

This theological emphasis appears even in Revelation, where angels guide John's visionary experience but worship remains directed exclusively toward God and the Lamb. The repeated angelic redirection of John's attempted worship (Revelation 19:10; 22:8-9) establishes clear boundary distinguishing Christian practice from religious traditions incorporating intermediary veneration.

Third, New Testament angelology increasingly connects with eschatological expectation. Angels announce cosmic transformation beginning with Christ's birth; they proclaim his resurrection as world-changing event; they participate in final judgment; and they witness the redemptive mystery "into which angels long to look" (1 Peter 1:12). According to Jürgen Moltmann, "Angels in New Testament perspective function as witnesses to and participants in eschatological transformation already initiated in Christ's resurrection but awaiting final consummation."[27]

---

25   Larry W. Hurtado, *One God, One Lord: Early Christian Devotion and Ancient Jewish Monotheism,* 3rd ed. (London: T&T Clark, 2015), 93.

26   David A. deSilva, *Perseverance in Gratitude: A Socio-Rhetorical Commentary on the Epistle "to the Hebrews"* (Grand Rapids: Eerdmans, 2000), 219.

27   Jürgen Moltmann, *The Coming of God: Christian Eschatology,* trans. Margaret Kohl (Minneapolis: Fortress Press, 1996), 50.

Fourth, New Testament texts recognize angels as cosmic administrators while emphasizing Christ's comprehensive authority over all spiritual powers. Revelation presents specialized angels controlling natural elements; Colossians acknowledges "thrones, dominions, rulers, and powers" within cosmic hierarchy; the Gospels show angels serving Christ and executing divine directives. According to Walter Wink, "Early Christian angelology maintained Jewish apocalyptic awareness of cosmic powers while transforming their significance through Christological reframing."[28]

Fifth, New Testament angelology increasingly incorporates ethical dimensions, particularly regarding worship practices. Paul connects angelological claims with concrete ethical concerns in Corinthian correspondence; Colossians warns against angel worship while emphasizing ethical transformation in Christ; and Revelation presents angels as witnesses to and evaluators of church communities. According to David Aune, "Angels increasingly function as ethical exemplars and observers, connecting celestial realities with concrete community practices."[29]

These theological developments collectively established framework for subsequent Christian angelology that would prove influential throughout church history. Rather than rejecting Jewish angelological traditions, early Christianity creatively reframed them within a Christological perspective that maintained angels' legitimate significance while preventing their elevation to inappropriate religious prominence.

According to Darrell Hannah, "The New Testament's sophisticated integration of Jewish angelology within Christocentric framework represented significant theological achievement, navigating between competing dangers of dismissing angels' genuine cosmic significance and compromising Christ's unique mediatorial status."[30] This balanced perspective would guide subsequent Christian theological reflection on

---

28   Walter Wink, *Naming the Powers: The Language of Power in the New Testament* (Philadelphia: Fortress Press, 1984), 15.

29   David E. Aune, *Revelation 1-5, Word Biblical Commentary, 52A* (Dallas: Word Books, 1997), 88.

30   Darrell D. Hannah, *Michael and Christ: Michael Traditions and Angel Christology in Early Christianity* (Tübingen: Mohr Siebeck, 1999), 164.

angels, even as different historical contexts emphasized varying aspects of biblical angelology.

Part III
Theophanies Across Scripture

Chapter 9

Primeval Theophanies

God Walking in the Garden (Genesis 3)

The first explicit divine appearance in scripture occurs in Genesis 3:8: "They heard the sound of the LORD God walking in the garden at the time of the evening breeze, and the man and his wife hid themselves from the presence of the LORD God among the trees of the garden." This seemingly casual reference to divine manifestation establishes foundational patterns for biblical theophany while raising significant theological questions about divine form and presence.

The text describes God anthropomorphically as "walking" *(mithallekh)* in the garden, suggesting physical movement through space. The Hebrew term implies leisurely strolling rather than purposeful travel, suggesting what Victor Hamilton calls "divine enjoyment of creation rather than merely utilitarian presence."[1] This walking occurs "at the time of the evening breeze" *(leruah hayyom)*, potentially indicating regular divine habit rather than exceptional manifestation.

Adam and Eve's reaction—hiding among trees—presumes divine visibility and spatially localized presence. According to Umberto Cassuto, "The narrative presupposes divine appearance in perceivable form from which concealment might be possible, establishing theological framework where God voluntarily adopts limited manifestation accommodated to human perception."[2] This accommodation represents divine grace even within context of judgment.

---

1   Victor P. Hamilton, *The Book of Genesis: Chapters 1-17, New International Commentary on the Old Testament* (Grand Rapids: Eerdmans, 1990), 192.

2   Umberto Cassuto, *A Commentary on the Book of Genesis: Part I, From Adam to Noah,* trans. Israel Abrahams (Jerusalem: Magnes Press, 1961), 149.

The text emphasizes auditory perception: "they heard the sound/ voice of the LORD God" *(wayyishme'u et-qol YHWH Elohim).* While qol can mean either "sound" or "voice," the narrative immediately transitions to divine speech, suggesting both audible movement and verbal communication. Gordon Wenham notes that "this auditory emphasis balances visual anthropomorphism, creating multisensory divine manifestation that engages human perceptual capacities while maintaining appropriate theological restraint."[3]

The divine question "Where are you?" and subsequent interrogation suggest genuine divine-human dialogue rather than simple pronouncement. This conversational quality, according to Walter Brueggemann, "establishes pattern for divine-human relationship where God engages creation as genuine conversation partner despite human rebellion, maintaining relationship even while confronting sin."[4]

This primeval theophany raises significant theological questions regarding divine form and presence. The casual reference to divine walking without explanatory comment suggests what Terence Fretheim calls "narrative worldview where divine appearance in perceivable form represents expected divine activity rather than exceptional manifestation requiring special explanation."[5] This contrasts with later biblical emphasis on divine invisibility and danger of unmediated divine presence.

While ancient Near Eastern parallels featured gods walking among humans, Genesis establishes distinctive theological framework where divine presence manifests in accommodated form while maintaining essential freedom and transcendence. Unlike Mesopotamian accounts where divine presence typically requires cultic invitation through ritual, Genesis presents God initiating encounter according to divine choice. According to John Walton, "This theological independence from ritual manipulation

---

3   Gordon J. Wenham, *Genesis 1-15, Word Biblical Commentary 1* (Waco, TX: Word Books, 1987), 76.

4   Walter Brueggemann, *Genesis, Interpretation* (Atlanta: John Knox Press, 1982), 49.

5   Terence E. Fretheim, *The Suffering of God: An Old Testament Perspective* (Philadelphia: Fortress Press, 1984), 106.

demonstrates fundamental distinction from contemporaneous religious frameworks, emphasizing divine freedom rather than human cultic control."[6]

The narrative deliberately leaves ambiguous whether this manifestation represents temporary divine appearance or more foundational understanding of divine embodiment. This ambiguity, according to Benjamin Sommer, "initiates theological trajectory within biblical canon where divine presence simultaneously expresses genuine divine embodiment within creation while maintaining divine transcendence beyond creaturely limitation."[7] Later biblical texts would develop both dimensions of this theological paradox.

The Genesis 3 theophany occurs at pivotal narrative moment—immediately following human disobedience but before exile from Eden. This liminal placement, according to David Clines, "establishes theological pattern where divine appearance paradoxically coincides with human sin, revealing both divine judgment and relationship-preserving grace."[8] God appears not despite human rebellion but precisely to address it through personal engagement rather than distant decree.

This foundational theophany establishes several patterns that subsequent biblical appearances will develop: divine initiative in self-revelation, accommodation to human perceptual capacities, genuine relational engagement, and manifestation for theological purpose rather than mere display. While later biblical theology would emphasize divine invisibility and danger of unmediated divine presence, this primeval account provides essential starting point for biblical theophanic tradition.

Divine-Human Encounters Before the Flood

The primeval narratives contain additional references to divine-human

---

6   John H. Walton, *Genesis, NIV Application Commentary* (Grand Rapids: Zondervan, 2001), 224.

7   Benjamin D. Sommer, *The Bodies of God and the World of Ancient Israel* (Cambridge: Cambridge University Press, 2009), 42.

8   David J.A. Clines, *"The Image of God in Man,"* Tyndale Bulletin 19 (1968): 62-69.

encounters before the flood, particularly in Genesis 4-6. These brief accounts develop theophanic themes while raising significant interpretive questions regarding divine presence and interaction with early humanity.

Genesis 4:6-7 records divine speech to Cain following his rejected offering: "The LORD said to Cain, 'Why are you angry, and why has your countenance fallen?'" While lacking explicit description of divine appearance, the direct address implies divine presence similar to Eden's conversational theophany. According to Victor Hamilton, "The narrative assumes continuity in divine-human communication patterns established in Eden, suggesting ongoing divine engagement with humanity despite expanding consequences of sin."[9]

More explicitly, Genesis 4:16 states that "Cain went away from the presence of the LORD" *(millipne YHWH)*, suggesting localized divine presence from which physical departure was possible. This spatial language, according to Umberto Cassuto, "reflects conceptual framework where divine presence manifested particularly in Eden's vicinity while remaining accessible through less immediate forms elsewhere."[10] This creates early biblical geography of divine presence with varying degrees of immediacy.

Genesis 4:26 cryptically notes that during Enosh's time "people began to invoke the name of the LORD" *(huhal liqro' beshem YHWH)*. While not explicitly theophanic, this reference suggests developing patterns of divine-human communication potentially including invocation of divine presence. According to Claus Westermann, "This reference indicates ritual response to perceived divine accessibility, suggesting human recognition of divine availability through proper approach."[11]

Genesis 5:22-24 twice states that "Enoch walked with God" *(yithallek 'et-ha'elohim),* using the same verbal root as God's walking in Eden. This reciprocal language, according to Gordon Wenham, "suggests mutual

---

9   Victor P. Hamilton, *The Book of Genesis: Chapters 1-17,* 230.

10   Umberto Cassuto, *A Commentary on the Book of Genesis: Part I, From Adam to Noah,* 226-27.

11   Claus Westermann, *Genesis 1-11: A Commentary,* trans. John J. Scullion (Minneapolis: Augsburg, 1984), 336.

relationship involving direct divine-human companionship rather than merely metaphorical religious devotion."[12] The account culminates with the cryptic statement that "Enoch walked with God; then he was no more, because God took him," suggesting extraordinary divine-human intimacy resulting in exceptional outcome.

The most complex pre-flood theophanic reference appears in Genesis 6:1-4, where "the sons of God" *(bene ha'elohim)* interact with human women. While variously interpreted throughout interpretive history, many scholars identify these beings as divine or semi-divine entities. According to Michael Heiser, "The ancient audience would have recognized these beings as members of the divine council or second-tier divine beings similar to those in contemporaneous Near Eastern religious texts."[13] The passage suggests boundaries between divine and human realms becoming inappropriately transgressed, leading to divine judgment.

Genesis 6:5-7 presents divine observation of human wickedness followed by decision to destroy humanity. While lacking explicit theophanic language, the anthropomorphic description of God "seeing" human wickedness and being "sorry" for creating humanity continues the primeval narrative's presentation of God's engaged involvement with creation. According to Walter Brueggemann, "These emotional anthropomorphisms communicate genuine divine relationship with creation rather than distant detachment, emphasizing pathos within divine character despite maintaining ultimate divine sovereignty."[14]

The culmination appears in Genesis 6:13-21, where God speaks directly to Noah, providing specific instructions regarding the approaching flood and covenant preservation. While the text does not describe divine appearance, the direct and extended communication suggests theophanic encounter similar to earlier Edenic conversation. According to Gerhard von Rad, "The narrative presents seamless continuation of divine communicative

---

12   Gordon J. Wenham, *Genesis 1-15,* 127.
13   Michael S. Heiser, *The Unseen Realm: Recovering the Supernatural Worldview of the Bible* (Bellingham, WA: Lexham Press, 2015), 93.
14   Walter Brueggemann, *Genesis,* 78.

presence established in earlier primeval accounts, suggesting theophanic manifestation required no special explanation within narrative worldview."[15]

These pre-flood divine-human encounters establish several theological patterns. First, they present divine presence as potentially available through direct communication despite expanding human sin. Second, they suggest geographical differentiation in divine presence, with Eden representing special locale of divine manifestation while allowing divine encounters elsewhere. Third, they establish pattern where divine presence simultaneously judges human sin while providing covenant preservation for the faithful. Fourth, they maintain anthropomorphic divine presentation while introducing boundaries between divine and human realms whose transgression brings judgment.

These accounts provide essential foundation for biblical theophanic tradition, establishing divine self-revelation as fundamental divine characteristic rather than exceptional accommodation. According to Terence Fretheim, "The primeval narratives present God as fundamentally communicative being whose self-disclosure through perceivable manifestation represents divine nature rather than merely occasional divine strategy."[16] This theological understanding would undergo significant development through subsequent biblical revelation while maintaining continuity with these foundational accounts.

God's Covenant with Noah

The flood narrative culminates with divine covenant establishment featuring several significant theophanic elements. Genesis 8:20-22 records Noah's post-flood sacrifice followed by divine response: "And when the LORD smelled the pleasing odor, the LORD said in his heart, 'I will never again curse the ground because of humankind.'" While lacking explicit divine appearance, this anthropomorphic presentation of God "smelling"

---

15   Gerhard von Rad, *Genesis: A Commentary,* rev. ed., trans. John H. Marks (Philadelphia: Westminster Press, 1972), 129.
16   Terence E. Fretheim, *The Suffering of God: An Old Testament Perspective,* 107.

sacrifice and speaking "in his heart" continues the primeval narrative's portrayal of divine responsiveness to human action.

Genesis 9:1-17 presents more extended divine-human interaction establishing covenant parameters. God directly addresses Noah and his sons, pronouncing blessing, establishing dietary regulations, instituting blood prohibition, and formalizing covenant promise never again to destroy earth through flood. The repetition of the phrase "God said" *(wayyomer elohim)* without describing divine appearance maintains the pattern established in earlier primeval narratives, where divine speech occurs without requiring explanation of divine manifestation.

The covenant culminates with divine promise: "I have set my bow in the clouds, and it shall be a sign of the covenant between me and the earth" (Genesis 9:13). This visible sign, according to Gordon Wenham, "represents divine self-limitation made perceptible through natural phenomenon, creating ongoing theophanic witness to divine covenant commitment."[17] Unlike momentary divine appearances, the rainbow provides enduring visible testimony to divine presence and promise.

The Noahic covenant narrative develops biblical theophany in several significant directions. First, it connects divine appearance with covenant establishment, creating pattern where divine self-revelation enables formalized relationship. According to Michael Horton, "This connection between theophany and covenant would become foundational for biblical theology, where divine self-disclosure enables mutual commitment rather than merely conveying information."[18]

Second, it introduces the concept of covenant signs as ongoing visible reminders of divine presence and commitment. Unlike temporary divine manifestations, these signs provide enduring testimony to divine promises. According to O. Palmer Robertson, "Covenant signs function as divinely established theophanic witnesses that extend divine self-revelation beyond momentary appearance into ongoing relationship."[19]

---

17   Gordon J. Wenham, *Genesis 1-15,* 195.

18   Michael S. Horton, *Covenant and Eschatology: The Divine Drama* (Louisville: Westminster John Knox, 2002), 44.

19   O. Palmer Robertson, *The Christ of the Covenants* (Phillipsburg, NJ: Presbyterian & Reformed, 1980), 17.

Third, it establishes pattern where divine presence manifests after judgment to establish new creation order. The post-flood theophany parallels Eden's post-sin divine appearance, suggesting divine commitment to creation despite human rebellion. According to Walter Brueggemann, "These post-judgment theophanies reveal God's fundamental orientation toward restoration rather than abandonment, establishing theological framework where divine presence returns precisely when human expectation might anticipate divine withdrawal."[20]

Fourth, it presents divine commitment extending beyond immediate covenant participants to creation itself: "the covenant between me and the earth" (Genesis 9:13). This cosmic scope, according to William Brown, "expands theophanic significance beyond anthropocentric focus, establishing divine self-revelation as creation-wide reality rather than merely human religious experience."[21]

The Noahic covenant theophany serves as transition between primeval history and patriarchal narratives, establishing patterns that subsequent divine appearances will develop. Its connection between divine manifestation and covenant establishment, its introduction of enduring theophanic signs, and its cosmic scope provide theological foundation for understanding divine self-revelation as relational commitment rather than merely religious phenomenon.

Theological Implications of Primeval Theophanies

The primeval theophanies establish fundamental theological patterns that subsequent biblical revelation will develop while raising enduring interpretive questions regarding divine presence and self-disclosure. Several key theological dimensions emerge from these foundational accounts.

First, the primeval narratives present divine self-revelation as fundamental divine characteristic rather than extraordinary accommodation. God appears walking in the garden, addresses humans directly, establishes

---

20   Walter Brueggemann, *Genesis*, 83.
21   William P. Brown, *The Seven Pillars of Creation: The Bible, Science, and the Ecology of Wonder* (Oxford: Oxford University Press, 2010), 127.

covenant through personal communication, and provides visible testimony to divine commitment. This consistent presentation, according to Terence Fretheim, "establishes theological framework where divine self-disclosure through perceivable manifestation reflects divine nature as inherently communicative and relationally engaged."[22] This relational understanding provides essential foundation for biblical theophanic tradition.

Second, these accounts present theophany as divine initiative rather than human achievement. Unlike contemporaneous religious frameworks where divine presence typically required ritual invocation through established cultic patterns, Genesis presents God initiating engagement according to divine purpose and timing. According to John Walton, "This theological independence demonstrates fundamental distinction from ancient Near Eastern frameworks, emphasizing divine freedom rather than human manipulative control through ritual technique."[23]

Third, primeval theophanies establish pattern where divine appearance paradoxically coincides with human sin and divine judgment. God appears walking in Eden immediately following human disobedience; addresses Cain after his rejected offering; speaks to Noah both before and after the flood. According to David Clines, "This counter-intuitive pattern establishes theological principle where divine presence addresses rather than avoids human rebellion, revealing both divine judgment and relationship-preserving grace."[24]

Fourth, these theophanies present anthropomorphic divine self-disclosure while leaving ambiguous whether such appearances represent temporary divine accommodation or more fundamental divine embodiment. Genesis describes God walking, speaking, smelling sacrifice, and establishing visible covenant testimony without clarifying the theological relationship between

---

22   Terence E. Fretheim, *The Suffering of God: An Old Testament Perspective*, 106.

23   John H. Walton, *Genesis*, 228.

24   David J.A. Clines, "Humanity as the Image of God," in *On the Way to the Postmodern: Old Testament Essays 1967–1998*, vol. 2, Journal for the Study of the Old Testament Supplement Series 293 (Sheffield: Sheffield Academic Press, 1998), 478-80.

divine essence and divine manifestation. This ambiguity, according to Benjamin Sommer, "initiates theological trajectory within biblical canon where divine presence simultaneously expresses genuine divine embodiment within creation while maintaining divine transcendence beyond creaturely limitation."[25]

Fifth, primeval theophanies establish connection between divine self-revelation and covenant relationship. God appears to establish boundaries in Eden, to confront Cain regarding human relationships, and to formalize commitment to creation through Noahic covenant. According to Michael Horton, "This consistent pattern reveals theophany's fundamentally relational purpose, where divine self-disclosure enables covenant relationship rather than merely satisfying religious curiosity or manifesting divine power."[26]

Sixth, these accounts introduce differentiated geography of divine presence, suggesting both special locales of divine manifestation and ongoing divine accessibility beyond particular sacred sites. Eden represents special site of divine walking; Cain departs from divine presence suggesting localized divine manifestation; Noah encounters God through direct communication and ongoing covenant sign. According to Samuel Terrien, "This nuanced presentation balances divine transcendence and immanence, allowing both special sacred space and divine freedom beyond particular locations."[27]

These theological dimensions from primeval theophanies provide foundation for understanding subsequent biblical divine appearances. The narrative simplicity of these accounts—presenting divine manifestation without requiring explanation or expressing surprise—suggests their foundational nature for biblical theology. According to Walter Brueggemann, "These unembellished primeval theophanies establish theological given that divine self-disclosure through perceivable manifestation represents

---

25   Benjamin D. Sommer, *The Bodies of God and the World of Ancient Israel*, 42.
26   Michael S. Horton, Covenant and Eschatology: *The Divine Drama*, 46.
27   Samuel Terrien, *The Elusive Presence: Toward a New Biblical Theology* (San Francisco: Harper & Row, 1978), 70.

divine nature rather than exceptional divine accommodation."[28] This theological foundation would undergo significant development through subsequent biblical tradition while maintaining essential continuity with these primeval divine appearances.

---

28   Walter Brueggemann, *Theology of the Old Testament: Testimony, Dispute, Advocacy* (Minneapolis: Fortress Press, 1997), 573.

Chapter 10

Patriarchal Theophanies

Abraham's Visitors at Mamre

Genesis 18 presents one of the most significant and complex theophanies in biblical literature—the appearance of three visitors to Abraham at Mamre. This narrative combines elements of human hospitality with divine manifestation, creating theological depth that has fascinated interpreters throughout history.

The account begins with straightforward divine appearance: "The LORD appeared to Abraham by the oaks of Mamre, as he sat at the entrance of his tent in the heat of the day" (Genesis 18:1). Immediately following this statement, however, Abraham "looked up and saw three men standing near him" (Genesis 18:2). This juxtaposition creates what Nahum Sarna calls "deliberate narrative tension between divine singularity and visible plurality, establishing theological framework where divine presence manifests through seemingly ordinary human appearance."[1]

Abraham responds with enthusiastic hospitality, addressing the visitors as "my lord" (ʾăḏōnāy, singular) and offering water, rest, and food before hastening to prepare an elaborate meal. Throughout the meal preparation (Genesis 18:6-8), the text refers to the visitors in plural—"they said," "they ate"—suggesting ordinary human encounter. Yet after the meal, the narrative shifts: "They said to him, 'Where is your wife Sarah?' And he said, 'There, in the tent.' Then one said, 'I will surely return to you in due season, and your wife Sarah shall have a son'" (Genesis 18:9-10).

This narrative shift from plural to singular address, according to Victor Hamilton, "creates interpretive ambiguity regarding whether one visitor speaks for all three or whether one visitor represents divine presence

---

1   Nahum M. Sarna, *Genesis, JPS Torah Commentary* (Philadelphia: Jewish Publication Society, 1989), 128.

more directly than the others."[2] The ambiguity intensifies as the promise continues with explicitly divine language: "Is anything too wonderful for the LORD?" (Genesis 18:14). The identity confusion reaches theological climax as "the LORD" debates within himself whether to reveal his plans regarding Sodom to Abraham (Genesis 18:17-19), followed by divine-human dialogue where Abraham intercedes for the city.

The narrative concludes with further ambiguity: "The LORD went his way, when he had finished speaking to Abraham; and Abraham returned to his place" (Genesis 18:33). Yet Genesis 19:1 states, "The two angels came to Sodom in the evening," suggesting the third visitor was distinctly divine while the other two were angelic messengers.

This complex presentation raises significant theological questions. According to Walter Brueggemann, "The narrative deliberately maintains ambiguity between divine presence and human appearance, creating theological space for understanding divine self-disclosure through ordinary human encounter rather than merely supernatural spectacle."[3] The visitors eat and drink like humans yet speak with divine authority and knowledge, simultaneously embodying divine immanence and transcendence.

The Mamre theophany establishes several significant theological patterns. First, it presents divine appearance through seemingly ordinary human encounter that gradually reveals extraordinary characteristics. Second, it combines anthropomorphism with theological restraint, allowing divine embodiment while avoiding simplistic reduction of God to human limitations. Third, it connects theophany with covenant promise, as divine appearance reaffirms the previously established covenant relationship. Fourth, it presents divine self-revelation as invitation to relationship rather than merely passive human reception, as Abraham actively engages through hospitality, conversation, and intercession.

---

2   Victor P. Hamilton, *The Book of Genesis: Chapters 18-50, New International Commentary on the Old Testament* (Grand Rapids: Eerdmans, 1995), 10.

3   Walter Brueggemann, *Genesis, Interpretation* (Atlanta: John Knox Press, 1982), 167.

According to R.W.L. Moberly, "The Mamre theophany establishes theological paradigm where divine presence manifests through mundane human interaction rather than requiring cultic location or ritual invocation, democratizing divine accessibility while maintaining divine freedom."[4] This balance between divine availability and divine sovereignty would become central to biblical theophanic tradition, reaching ultimate expression in New Testament incarnational theology.

The Mamre account has generated diverse interpretations throughout religious history. Early Christian interpretation frequently identified the three visitors as trinitarian manifestation, with Augustine famously suggesting the visitors represented the Trinity while being one in essence. Jewish interpretation traditionally identified the visitors as angels appearing simultaneously with divine presence, maintaining clear distinction between creator and creation. Modern scholarship has emphasized how the narrative navigates theological complexity through deliberate ambiguity, allowing divine manifestation while avoiding simplistic reduction of divine presence to human form.

This interpretive diversity reflects the text's theological sophistication, presenting divine self-disclosure through perceivable manifestation while maintaining divine transcendence beyond full human comprehension. According to Benjamin Sommer, "The Mamre theophany demonstrates biblical comfort with theophanic fluidity, where divine presence genuinely manifests through created forms while maintaining essential divine freedom beyond any particular manifestation."[5] This theological balance would prove foundational for subsequent biblical theophanic presentations.

Jacob's Wrestling at Peniel

Genesis 32:22-32 presents Jacob's mysterious nighttime wrestling match at the Jabbok river, an enigmatic encounter that combines physical

---

4   R.W.L. Moberly, *The Theology of the Book of Genesis* (Cambridge: Cambridge University Press, 2009), 215.

5   Benjamin D. Sommer, *The Bodies of God and the World of Ancient Israel* (Cambridge: Cambridge University Press, 2009), 40.

struggle with divine revelation. This theophany differs significantly from earlier patterns, emphasizing divine-human struggle rather than divine message delivery or covenant establishment.

The account begins with geographical isolation as Jacob remains alone after sending his household across the river. In this solitude, "a man wrestled with him until daybreak" (Genesis 32:24). The Hebrew term ('îš, "man") suggests ordinary human appearance without immediately revealing divine identity. According to Gerhard von Rad, "The narrative initially presents seemingly human encounter that gradually reveals transcendent significance, maintaining theological tension between immanence and transcendence."[6]

The physical struggle continues until dawn when Jacob's opponent says, "Let me go, for the day is breaking." Jacob's response—"I will not let you go, unless you bless me" (Genesis 32:26)—suggests growing recognition of his opponent's more-than-human identity. The subsequent blessing includes name change from Jacob to Israel, signifying transformation through divine encounter: "for you have striven with God and with humans, and have prevailed" (Genesis 32:28).

The climactic moment occurs as Jacob names the place Peniel (Face of God), saying, "For I have seen God face to face, and yet my life is preserved" (Genesis 32:30). This extraordinary claim—seeing God's face and surviving—represents theological high point in patriarchal theophanic experience. According to Terence Fretheim, "Jacob's face-to-face encounter establishes intimate divine-human relationship through struggle rather than merely receptive vision, creating theological paradigm where divine self-disclosure involves genuine engagement rather than passive human observation."[7]

The narrative emphasizes physical impact of divine encounter, as Jacob's hip becomes dislocated during the struggle and he departs limping. This

---

6   Gerhard von Rad, *Genesis: A Commentary,* rev. ed., trans. John H. Marks (Philadelphia: Westminster Press, 1972), 316.
7   Terence E. Fretheim, *The Suffering of God: An Old Testament Perspective* (Philadelphia: Fortress Press, 1984), 92.

enduring bodily mark, according to Walter Brueggemann, "represents permanent transformation through theophanic encounter, where divine presence leaves lasting impact rather than merely momentary religious experience."[8] The subsequent dietary prohibition regarding the sciatic muscle (Genesis 32:32) ritualizes this remembered encounter, transforming personal theophany into communal memory.

This wrestling theophany raises significant interpretive questions regarding the opponent's identity. While Jacob claims to have seen "God face to face," the prophet Hosea later interprets the encounter differently: "He strove with the angel and prevailed" (Hosea 12:4). This interpretive tradition—identifying Jacob's opponent as angelic rather than directly divine—appears in many subsequent Jewish interpretations. According to Michael Fishbane, "This hermeneutical trajectory reflects growing theological concern about anthropomorphic divine presentation, reinterpreting direct divine encounter as mediated angelic manifestation."[9]

The Peniel theophany establishes several distinctive theological patterns. First, it presents divine encounter through struggle rather than harmonious communion, suggesting divine self-disclosure that challenges human identity rather than merely confirming it. Second, it connects theophany with personal transformation, as Jacob emerges with new name, physical mark, and transformed relationship with both God and humans. Third, it emphasizes divine-human intimacy through embodied interaction rather than merely verbal communication, creating theological paradigm for understanding divine presence as genuinely engaged with human physicality.

According to Esther Hamori, "The wrestling theophany establishes divine encounter as transformative confrontation rather than merely instructive revelation, where divine presence addresses human character through engagement rather than proclamation."[10] This participatory

---

8   Walter Brueggemann, *Genesis,* 268.

9   Michael Fishbane, *Biblical Interpretation in Ancient Israel* (Oxford: Clarendon Press, 1985), 375.

10   Esther J. Hamori, *"When Gods Were Men": The Embodied God in Biblical and Near Eastern Literature* (Berlin: de Gruyter, 2008), 109.

understanding of divine self-disclosure would prove influential for subsequent biblical theology, particularly prophetic call narratives where divine presence transforms the human recipient through direct encounter.

The Peniel account also introduces theological tension between divine visibility and invisibility. Jacob claims face-to-face divine vision yet receives no physical description of his opponent beyond "a man." This restraint, according to Samuel Terrien, "maintains theological balance between genuine divine manifestation and divine freedom beyond human perception, allowing real encounter without reducing divine presence to merely visual object."[11] This tension between seeing and not-seeing would become central to biblical theophanic tradition, culminating in New Testament presentations of God revealed yet concealed in Christ.

Moses and the Burning Bush

Exodus 3-4 presents the burning bush theophany, a pivotal encounter that combines natural phenomenon with divine self-revelation. This theophany marks crucial transition from patriarchal to national covenant, establishing Moses as mediator between God and Israel while revealing divine name.

The narrative begins with Moses tending his father-in-law's flock "beyond the wilderness" at "Horeb, the mountain of God" (Exodus 3:1). This geographical setting, according to Thomas Dozeman, "establishes connection between divine manifestation and liminal space, where ordinary human activity intersects with extraordinary divine presence at location already associated with divine encounter."[12]

Moses notices "a flame of fire out of a bush" that burns without being consumed, prompting him to investigate this "great sight" (Exodus 3:2-3). The narrative then shifts perspective: "When the LORD saw that he had turned aside to see, God called to him out of the bush, 'Moses, Moses!'"

---

11   Samuel Terrien, *The Elusive Presence: Toward a New Biblical Theology* (San Francisco: Harper & Row, 1978), 82.

12   Thomas B. Dozeman, *Commentary on Exodus* (Grand Rapids: Eerdmans, 2009), 121.

(Exodus 3:4). This divine initiative, according to Carol Meyers, "establishes theological pattern where human curiosity meets divine intention, creating theophanic encounter through both divine self-disclosure and human receptivity."[13]

The initial divine command—"Come no closer! Remove the sandals from your feet, for the place on which you are standing is holy ground" (Exodus 3:5)—establishes proper response to divine presence. According to Brevard Childs, "This command simultaneously communicates divine accessibility and divine otherness, creating theological framework where divine presence invites approach while requiring appropriate reverence."[14]

The theophany continues with divine self-identification: "I am the God of your father, the God of Abraham, the God of Isaac, and the God of Jacob" (Exodus 3:6). This statement, according to Umberto Cassuto, "establishes continuity between patriarchal covenant relationship and new divine encounter, presenting theophany as development within ongoing relationship rather than merely new religious experience."[15]

Moses responds by hiding his face, "afraid to look at God" (Exodus 3:6). This reaction, according to William Propp, "reflects theological understanding that direct divine vision exceeds appropriate human experience, requiring mediated perception that protects human recipient from overwhelming divine presence."[16] This theme of protected vision recurs throughout biblical theophanic tradition.

The theological climax occurs when Moses asks God's name, receiving the enigmatic response "I AM WHO I AM" (*'ehyeh 'ăšer 'ehyeh*) and the divine name YHWH connected with the God of the ancestors (Exodus

---

13   Carol Meyers, *Exodus, New Cambridge Bible Commentary* (Cambridge: Cambridge University Press, 2005), 54.

14   Brevard S. Childs, *The Book of Exodus: A Critical, Theological Commentary* (Philadelphia: Westminster Press, 1974), 73.

15   Umberto Cassuto, *A Commentary on the Book of Exodus,* trans. Israel Abrahams (Jerusalem: Magnes Press, 1967), 33.

16   William H.C. Propp, *Exodus 1-18: A New Translation with Introduction and Commentary, Anchor Bible 2* (New York: Doubleday, 1999), 200.

3:13-15). This name revelation, according to Thomas Dozeman, "represents unprecedented divine self-disclosure where divine identity becomes available through linguistic formulation while maintaining essential divine freedom beyond human definition."[17] The name simultaneously reveals and conceals, providing addressable divine identity while preserving divine mystery.

The theophany continues through chapter 4 as Moses raises objections and receives divine responses, including miraculous signs demonstrating divine power and provision of Aaron as spokesperson. This extended interaction, according to Walter Brueggemann, "establishes theophany as genuine dialogue rather than merely unilateral divine proclamation, creating space for human questioning within divine self-disclosure."[18]

The burning bush theophany establishes several significant theological patterns. First, it presents divine self-disclosure through natural phenomenon transformed into sacred sign, demonstrating divine presence within creation without reduction to natural forces. Second, it connects theophany with vocational commissioning, where divine appearance leads to human participation in divine purpose. Third, it establishes divine name revelation as central theophanic content, providing linguistic access to divine presence while maintaining divine transcendence. Fourth, it presents theophany as continuation and development of established covenant relationship rather than entirely new religious beginning.

According to Terence Fretheim, "The burning bush theophany establishes theological paradigm where divine presence manifests within ordinary creation while transforming it into extraordinary revelation, creating framework for understanding divine self-disclosure as both immanent within and transcendent beyond created order."[19] This delicate balance would prove foundational for biblical theophanic tradition, providing

---

17   Thomas B. Dozeman, *God on the Mountain: A Study of Redaction, Theology, and Canon in Exodus 19-24* (Atlanta: Scholars Press, 1989), 94.

18   Walter Brueggemann, *Theology of the Old Testament: Testimony, Dispute, Advocacy* (Minneapolis: Fortress Press, 1997), 582.

19   Terence E. Fretheim, *Exodus, Interpretation* (Louisville: John Knox Press, 1991), 56.

theological resources for understanding divine presence as genuinely within yet not limited to creation.

Sinai Theophany

Exodus 19-24 presents the Sinai theophany, the most elaborate and extended divine manifestation in the Hebrew Bible. This complex narrative combines multiple sensory elements, communal and individual divine encounter, and covenant establishment through divine self-disclosure.

The preparation begins with three-day purification, boundary establishment around the mountain, and prohibition against touching the mountain on pain of death (Exodus 19:10-15). These preliminary requirements, according to Jeffrey Niehaus, "create ritual framework distinguishing sacred from profane space and establishing appropriate human preparation for divine encounter."[20] This careful preparation contrasts with previous patriarchal theophanies that occurred without extensive preliminary ritual.

The theophany itself features overwhelming multisensory manifestation: "On the morning of the third day there was thunder and lightning, as well as a thick cloud on the mountain, and a blast of a trumpet so loud that all the people who were in the camp trembled" (Exodus 19:16). Additional elements include smoke "like the smoke of a kiln," intense mountain trembling, and increasingly loud trumpet blast (Exodus 19:18-19). According to George Savran, "This multisensory presentation creates comprehensive theophanic experience engaging entire community through various perceptual channels rather than merely individual visionary encounter."[21]

The divine presence descends specifically upon Sinai: "The LORD came down upon Mount Sinai, to the top of the mountain" (Exodus 19:20). This localization, according to Samuel Terrien, "establishes particular sacred

---

20   Jeffrey J. Niehaus, *God at Sinai: Covenant and Theophany in the Bible and Ancient Near East* (Grand Rapids: Zondervan, 1995), 195.

21   George W. Savran, *Encountering the Divine: Theophany in Biblical Narrative* (London: T&T Clark, 2005), 58.

space for divine manifestation while avoiding permanent confinement of divine presence to single location, creating theological balance between divine accessibility and divine freedom."[22]

The theophany includes both direct communal experience and mediated encounter through Moses. The people remain at the mountain's base while Moses ascends to meet God (Exodus 19:17, 20). After initial divine communication, God announces intention to speak directly to the people "in a dense cloud, in order that the people may hear when I speak with you and so trust you ever after" (Exodus 19:9). This dual approach, according to Thomas Dozeman, "creates theological framework where direct divine self-disclosure authorizes human mediation rather than rendering it unnecessary, establishing pattern for subsequent Israelite prophetic authority."[23]

The people's response reveals theophanic danger: "When all the people witnessed the thunder and lightning, the sound of the trumpet, and the mountain smoking, they were afraid and trembled and stood at a distance, and said to Moses, 'You speak to us, and we will listen; but do not let God speak to us, or we will die'" (Exodus 20:18-19). This reaction, according to Brevard Childs, "demonstrates perceived lethal quality of unmediated divine presence, establishing theological necessity for protected divine encounter through appropriate mediation."[24]

The theophany culminates in covenant establishment, where divine manifestation enables communal commitment. Moses, Aaron, Nadab, Abihu, and seventy elders "went up, and they saw the God of Israel. Under his feet there was something like a pavement of sapphire stone, like the very heaven for clearness. God did not lay his hand on the chief men of the people of Israel; also they beheld God, and they ate and drank" (Exodus

---

22   Samuel Terrien, *The Elusive Presence: Toward a New Biblical Theology*, 107.

23   Thomas B. Dozeman, *God on the Mountain: A Study of Redaction, Theology, and Canon in Exodus 19-24*, 103.

24   Brevard S. Childs, *The Book of Exodus: A Critical, Theological Commentary*, 349.

24:9-11). This remarkable statement—that select representatives "saw the God of Israel" and survived—presents extraordinary divine self-disclosure within covenant establishment context.

The narrative explicitly restricts visual description to what appeared "under his feet," maintaining what Michael Sommer calls "theological restraint regarding divine form while affirming genuine divine visibility."[25] The concluding covenant meal, where leaders "ate and drank" in divine presence, establishes covenant communion as theophanic outcome, creating religious paradigm where divine self-disclosure enables ongoing relationship rather than merely momentary religious experience.

The Sinai theophany establishes several significant theological patterns. First, it presents divine appearance as both dangerous and gracious, requiring appropriate preparation while enabling genuine encounter. Second, it combines direct divine self-disclosure with authorized human mediation, establishing theological framework for subsequent prophetic and priestly roles. Third, it connects theophany with covenant establishment, where divine manifestation enables communal commitment rather than merely individual religious experience. Fourth, it establishes divine revelation as both perceptible manifestation and verbal communication, combining sensory divine presence with specific divine instruction.

According to Walter Brueggemann, "The Sinai theophany establishes paradigmatic religious experience for biblical faith, where divine presence manifests through perceivable phenomena while communicating specific covenant content, combining awe-inspiring manifestation with particular relationship terms."[26] This integration of theophanic experience with covenant content would prove foundational for subsequent biblical theology, where divine self-disclosure consistently enables specific relationship rather than merely general religious awareness.

---

25   Benjamin D. Sommer, *The Bodies of God and the World of Ancient Israel*, 45.

26   Walter Brueggemann, *Theology of the Old Testament: Testimony, Dispute, Advocacy*, 570.

Theological Implications of Patriarchal Theophanies

The patriarchal and Mosaic theophanies collectively establish foundational patterns for biblical understanding of divine self-revelation. Several key theological dimensions emerge from these formative accounts.

First, these theophanies present divine self-disclosure as divine initiative rather than human achievement. Whether appearing to Abraham at Mamre, wrestling with Jacob at Peniel, speaking to Moses from the burning bush, or descending upon Sinai, God initiates encounter according to divine purpose. According to Terence Fretheim, "This consistent divine initiative establishes theological framework where theophany represents divine grace rather than human religious achievement, grounding divine-human relationship in divine character rather than human ritual technique."[27]

Second, patriarchal theophanies integrate divine transcendence and immanence through perceivable divine manifestation that nevertheless preserves divine freedom. God appears in recognizable form to Abraham, engages in physical struggle with Jacob, speaks from within burning bush to Moses, and descends upon Sinai amid natural phenomena, yet in each case maintains essential divine otherness. According to Benjamin Sommer, "These accounts navigate theological tension between divine embodiment and divine transcendence, presenting God as genuinely manifest within creation while never fully captured by any particular manifestation."[28]

Third, these theophanies consistently connect divine appearance with covenant relationship. God appears to Abraham to reaffirm promised offspring, transforms Jacob into covenant namesake Israel through wrestling encounter, commissions Moses to deliver covenant people through burning bush revelation, and establishes formal covenant terms through Sinai manifestation. According to Michael Horton, "This consistent pattern reveals theophany's fundamentally covenantal purpose, where divine self-

---

27   Terence E. Fretheim, *The Suffering of God: An Old Testament Perspective*, 149.

28   Benjamin D. Sommer, *The Bodies of God and the World of Ancient Israel*, 38.

disclosure enables specific relationship rather than merely general religious awareness."[29]

Fourth, patriarchal theophanies present divine revelation as both sensory manifestation and verbal communication. God appears visibly to Abraham while speaking specific promises; wrestles physically with Jacob while pronouncing blessing and new name; appears as flame to Moses while communicating divine name and commission; manifests through environmental phenomena at Sinai while pronouncing covenant commands. According to Walter Brueggemann, "This integration of manifestation and communication establishes theological pattern where divine presence conveys particular content rather than merely numinous experience."[30]

Fifth, these theophanies increasingly emphasize proper preparation and response to divine presence. While Abraham simply offers hospitality to his visitors and Jacob wrestles his opponent without prior ritual, the burning bush requires Moses to remove his sandals on holy ground, and the Sinai theophany demands elaborate community preparation. According to Jeffrey Niehaus, "This developing emphasis establishes theological principle where divine holiness requires appropriate human response while remaining fundamentally gracious divine initiative."[31]

Sixth, patriarchal theophanies present divine appearance as transformative encounter rather than merely informative revelation. Abraham's visitors announce Sarah's miraculous conception; Jacob receives new name, physical mark, and transformed identity; Moses transitions from shepherd to covenant mediator; Israel becomes covenant nation through Sinai encounter. According to Samuel Terrien, "These transformative outcomes

---

29   Michael S. Horton, *Covenant and Eschatology: The Divine Drama* (Louisville: Westminster John Knox, 2002), 42.

30   Walter Brueggemann, *Theology of the Old Testament: Testimony, Dispute, Advocacy,* 574.

31   Jeffrey J. Niehaus, *God at Sinai: Covenant and Theophany in the Bible and Ancient Near East,* 24.

establish theophany as fundamentally relational event that changes human identity rather than merely communicating divine information."[32]

These theological dimensions collectively establish formative paradigm for understanding divine self-disclosure within biblical tradition. Rather than presenting theophany as either crude anthropomorphism requiring later theological refinement or mere literary device without ontological significance, these accounts establish sophisticated theological framework where divine presence genuinely manifests through created forms while maintaining divine transcendence.

According to R.W.L. Moberly, "Patriarchal theophanies provide foundational grammar for biblical understanding of divine self-revelation, where divine freedom and divine accessibility maintain proper theological tension without resolving into either divine absence or simplistic divine reduction to created forms."[33] This theological grammar would undergo significant development through subsequent biblical tradition while maintaining essential continuity with these patriarchal encounters.

---

32   Samuel Terrien, *The Elusive Presence: Toward a New Biblical Theology*, 65.

33   R.W.L. Moberly, *The Old Testament of the Old Testament: Patriarchal Narratives and Mosaic Yahwism* (Minneapolis: Fortress Press, 1992), 89.

Chapter 11

Theophanies in Israel's National Life

Tabernacle and Temple Theophanies

Following the Sinai covenant establishment, divine manifestation becomes increasingly connected with designated sacred spaces—first the tabernacle and later the temple. These localized theophanies establish patterns for understanding institutionalized divine presence within Israel's developing religious tradition.

The tabernacle completion culminates with dramatic divine manifestation: "Then the cloud covered the tent of meeting, and the glory of the LORD filled the tabernacle. Moses was not able to enter the tent of meeting because the cloud settled upon it, and the glory of the LORD filled the tabernacle" (Exodus 40:34-35). This appearance, according to Thomas Dozeman, "transforms portable human construction into genuine divine dwelling place, establishing theological pattern where divine presence inhabits yet transcends human sacred space."[1]

The Hebrew term *kāḇôḏ* (glory) becomes central theological concept for describing divine manifestation in tabernacle and temple contexts. Unlike anthropomorphic appearances to patriarchs, this "glory" suggests luminous divine manifestation that simultaneously reveals and conceals, making divine presence perceivable while avoiding crude visual representation. According to Menahem Haran, "The glory conceptualization allows theological balance between genuine divine presence and appropriate restraint regarding divine form, creating framework for understanding God as truly present yet never fully captured within sacred space."[2]

---

1   Thomas B. Dozeman, *Commentary on Exodus* (Grand Rapids: Eerdmans, 2009), 713.
2   Menahem Haran, *Temples and Temple-Service in Ancient Israel: An Inquiry into Biblical Cult Phenomena and the Historical Setting of the Priestly School* (Winona Lake, IN: Eisenbrauns, 1985), 254.

The cloud and fire manifestation creates visible witness to divine presence: "Throughout all their journeys, whenever the cloud was taken up from the tabernacle, the Israelites would set out; but if the cloud was not taken up, then they did not set out until the day that it was taken up. For the cloud of the LORD was on the tabernacle by day, and fire was in the cloud by night, before the eyes of all the house of Israel at each stage of their journey" (Exodus 40:36-38). This manifestation, according to Samuel Terrien, "provides continuous visible divine presence guiding Israel's wilderness journey while maintaining appropriate theological distance through symbolic rather than anthropomorphic presentation."[3]

Similar theophanic patterns appear at Solomon's temple dedication: "When the priests came out of the holy place, a cloud filled the house of the LORD, so that the priests could not stand to minister because of the cloud; for the glory of the LORD filled the house of the LORD" (1 Kings 8:10-11). This divine manifestation confirms temple legitimacy while demonstrating divine freedom to occupy human construction according to divine choice. According to Jon Levenson, "The glory theophany validates temple construction while simultaneously emphasizing divine sovereignty over sacred space, establishing temple as genuine divine dwelling without suggesting divine confinement."[4]

Solomon's dedication speech recognizes theological tension between localized divine presence and divine transcendence: "But will God indeed dwell on the earth? Even heaven and the highest heaven cannot contain you, much less this house that I have built!" (1 Kings 8:27). This explicit acknowledgment, according to Benjamin Sommer, "demonstrates sophisticated theological understanding where temple houses genuine divine presence while divine being transcends any particular location, creating theological framework later designated as 'name theology.'"[5]

---

3   Samuel Terrien, *The Elusive Presence: Toward a New Biblical Theology* (San Francisco: Harper & Row, 1978), 157.

4   Jon D. Levenson, *Sinai and Zion: An Entry into the Jewish Bible* (Minneapolis: Winston Press, 1985), 143.

5   Benjamin D. Sommer, *The Bodies of God and the World of Ancient Israel* (Cambridge: Cambridge University Press, 2009), 58.

Solomon repeatedly describes the temple as dwelling place for God's name rather than God's essence: "that your name may be forever in this house that I have built" (1 Kings 8:13); "a house built for your name" (1 Kings 8:44). This subtle but significant theological formulation, according to Sandra Richter, "allows genuine divine presence through representative extension without suggesting divine confinement, resolving apparent tension between transcendence and immanence."[6]

Ezekiel's temple vision describes divine glory returning to the restored temple: "The glory of the LORD entered the temple by the gate facing east... and the glory of the LORD filled the temple" (Ezekiel 43:4-5). This restoration theophany, according to Daniel Block, "reverses earlier glory departure [described in Ezekiel 10-11] while maintaining consistent glory manifestation rather than anthropomorphic appearance, emphasizing continuity with pre-exilic temple presence."[7]

The tabernacle and temple theophanies establish several significant theological patterns. First, they institutionalize divine manifestation within particular sacred spaces while maintaining divine freedom beyond those spaces. Second, they shift theophanic emphasis from anthropomorphic appearance to glory manifestation, creating theological vocabulary for divine presence that avoids crude visual representation. Third, they connect divine manifestation with community identity rather than merely individual religious experience, establishing common sacred space as locus for divine-human relationship. Fourth, they incorporate divine manifestation within ritual practice, integrating extraordinary theophanic moments with ongoing worship patterns.

According to Craig Koester, "The tabernacle/temple theophanies create theological framework for understanding divine presence as both genuinely localized and fundamentally transcendent, establishing religious patterns where sacred space provides authentic divine access while avoiding divine

---

6   Sandra L. Richter, *The Deuteronomistic History and the Name Theology: "lešakkēn šemô šām" in the Bible and the Ancient Near East* (Berlin: de Gruyter, 2002), 81.
7   Daniel I. Block, *The Book of Ezekiel: Chapters 25-48, New International Commentary on the Old Testament* (Grand Rapids: Eerdmans, 1998), 580.

domestication."[8] This theological balance would prove crucial for Israel's developing understanding of divine presence, particularly following the eventual temple destruction that necessitated reimagining divine presence beyond particular geographic location.

The Glory of God (kavod YHWH)

The concept of divine glory (*kāḇôḏ* YHWH) represents significant theological development in biblical understanding of divine manifestation. While occasionally appearing in patriarchal contexts, glory language becomes central feature of tabernacle/temple theophanies and prophetic visions, providing theological vocabulary for divine presence that balances immanence and transcendence.

The Hebrew term *kāḇôḏ* derives from root meaning "weight" or "significance," suggesting weighty divine presence that commands appropriate response. According to Tryggve Mettinger, "This terminology shifts emphasis from divine form to divine impact, creating theological category that communicates divine reality while avoiding problematic anthropomorphic specificity."[9] The term appears approximately 200 times in the Hebrew Bible, with concentrated appearances in theophanic contexts.

Exodus first introduces glory manifestation at Sinai: "The glory of the LORD settled on Mount Sinai, and the cloud covered it for six days; on the seventh day he called to Moses out of the cloud. Now the appearance of the glory of the LORD was like a devouring fire on the top of the mountain in the sight of the people of Israel" (Exodus 24:16-17). This description, according to Thomas Dozeman, "establishes glory as perceivable divine manifestation combining both concealment (cloud) and revelation (fire),

---

8   Craig R. Koester, The Dwelling of God: The Tabernacle in the Old Testament, Intertestamental Jewish Literature, and the New Testament (Washington, DC: Catholic Biblical Association of America, 1989), 16.
9   Tryggve N.D. Mettinger, The Dethronement of Sabaoth: Studies in the Shem and Kabod Theologies (Lund: Gleerup, 1982), 81.

creating theological balance between divine accessibility and divine mystery."[10]

The glory concept develops significant connection with tabernacle/temple settings, where divine glory "fills" *(māleʾ)* sacred space (Exodus 40:34-35; 1 Kings 8:10-11; 2 Chronicles 5:13-14, 7:1-2; Ezekiel 43:5, 44:4). This filling language, according to Menahem Haran, "communicates comprehensive divine presence that genuinely occupies physical space while maintaining essential divine nature beyond spatial limitation."[11] The repeated motif of priests unable to minister because of glory's overwhelming presence emphasizes divine independence from human religious management.

Numbers 14:10, 16:19, and 20:6 describe glory appearing at the tent of meeting during community crises, suggesting divine self-disclosure specifically addressing community conflict or rebellion. According to Jacob Milgrom, "These crisis appearances demonstrate glory manifestation as divine responsive presence rather than merely static religious symbol, emphasizing divine engagement with community concerns."[12]

Isaiah's temple vision includes glory language with cosmic scope: "Holy, holy, holy is the LORD of hosts; the whole earth is full of his glory" (Isaiah 6:3). This expansive perspective, according to John Oswalt, "extends glory concept beyond particular sacred space to entire creation, establishing theological framework where specific manifestations represent particular expressions of comprehensive divine presence permeating all reality."[13]

Ezekiel's elaborate vision presents the most detailed glory description in the Hebrew Bible: "Upward from what appeared like the loins I saw something like gleaming amber, something that looked like fire enclosed

---

10   Thomas B. Dozeman, *God on the Mountain: A Study of Redaction, Theology, and Canon in Exodus 19-24* (Atlanta: Scholars Press, 1989), 98.

11   Menahem Haran, *Temples and Temple-Service in Ancient Israel*, 249.

12   Jacob Milgrom, *Numbers, JPS Torah Commentary* (Philadelphia: Jewish Publication Society, 1990), 107.

13   John N. Oswalt, *The Book of Isaiah: Chapters 1-39, New International Commentary on the Old Testament* (Grand Rapids: Eerdmans, 1986), 181.

all around; and downward from what looked like the loins I saw something that looked like fire, and there was a splendor all around. Like the bow in a cloud on a rainy day, such was the appearance of the splendor all around. This was the appearance of the likeness of the glory of the LORD" (Ezekiel 1:27-28). This carefully qualified language—"appearance of the likeness of the glory"—creates what Daniel Block calls "multiple layers of representational distance, communicating genuine divine manifestation while emphasizing its ultimately ineffable quality."[14]

Ezekiel also describes glory mobility as divine presence moves from temple to city threshold (Ezekiel 10:4), from threshold to east gate (Ezekiel 10:18-19), and eventually from city (Ezekiel 11:22-23), creating theological narrative of divine departure from Jerusalem. According to Moshe Greenberg, "This mobility emphasizes divine sovereignty over sacred space, establishing glory as divine presence genuinely connected with yet fundamentally independent from particular locations."[15]

Haggai and Zechariah connect glory with eschatological temple: "I will fill this house with glory, says the LORD of hosts" (Haggai 2:7); "I will be the glory within it" (Zechariah 2:5). These prophetic promises, according to Mark Boda, "transform glory concept from past memory to future hope, establishing theological perspective where divine presence remains fundamentally available despite historical disruptions to sacred space."[16]

The glory concept establishes several significant theological dimensions. First, it creates vocabulary for divine manifestation that avoids anthropomorphic specificity while maintaining genuine divine self-disclosure. Second, it balances divine transcendence and immanence through manifestation that simultaneously reveals and conceals. Third, it connects divine presence with sacred space while maintaining divine freedom beyond spatial confinement. Fourth, it presents divine manifestation as

---

14   Daniel I. Block, *The Book of Ezekiel: Chapters 1-24, New International Commentary on the Old Testament* (Grand Rapids: Eerdmans, 1997), 104.

15   Moshe Greenberg, *Ezekiel 1-20: A New Translation with Introduction and Commentary, Anchor Bible 22* (Garden City, NY: Doubleday, 1983), 196.

16   Mark J. Boda, *Haggai, Zechariah, NIV Application Commentary* (Grand Rapids: Zondervan, 2004), 186.

responsive engagement with community circumstances rather than merely static religious symbol.

According to Samuel Terrien, "The glory tradition represents sophisticated theological development managing tension between divine presence and transcendence, allowing genuine divine manifestation while preserving divine mystery."[17] This conceptualization would prove particularly significant for post-exilic Judaism following temple destruction, providing theological resources for understanding divine presence beyond particular geographic location.

Divine Manifestations to Prophets

Beyond institutionalized sacred spaces, divine manifestation frequently occurs to individual prophets, establishing prophetic authority while revealing divine perspective on contemporary events. These prophetic theophanies feature distinctive elements that both continue and transform earlier theophanic patterns.

Isaiah's inaugural vision (Isaiah 6:1-13) represents classic prophetic throne theophany: "I saw the Lord sitting on a throne, high and lofty; and the hem of his robe filled the temple" (Isaiah 6:1). This temple setting, according to John Oswalt, "connects prophetic experience with established sacred space while transforming typical temple theophany through direct divine vision rather than merely glory manifestation."[18] The prophet sees divine enthronement rather than merely divine effects, suggesting intensified divine self-disclosure.

The vision includes both divine transcendence—throne "high and lofty"—and divine immanence—robe filling temple. According to Christopher Seitz, "This theological balance communicates both divine cosmic sovereignty and genuine divine engagement with particular sacred space, establishing framework for prophetic message addressing both

---

17   Samuel Terrien, *The Elusive Presence: Toward a New Biblical Theology*, 153.

18   John N. Oswalt, *The Book of Isaiah: Chapters 1-39*, 177.

universal ethical standards and particular historical circumstances."[19]

The seraphim's presence and activity—covering faces and feet while proclaiming divine holiness—establishes what Margaret Barker calls "heavenly liturgical context for prophetic commission, where divine manifestation occurs within cosmic worship setting rather than merely isolated prophetic experience."[20] This liturgical dimension connects prophetic authority with temple tradition while transforming it through direct divine encounter.

Isaiah's reaction—"Woe is me! I am lost, for I am a man of unclean lips, and I live among a people of unclean lips; yet my eyes have seen the King, the LORD of hosts!" (Isaiah 6:5)—acknowledges perceived impossibility of human survival following direct divine vision. According to Brevard Childs, "This reaction reflects theological understanding that unmediated divine vision exceeds appropriate human experience, requiring divine grace through purification ritual to enable prophetic function."[21] The subsequent coal ritual transforms potential lethal theophany into prophetic commissioning.

Ezekiel's complex throne-chariot vision (Ezekiel 1) presents the most elaborate prophetic theophany in the Hebrew Bible. The account begins with opened heavens and divine visions (*mar'ôt ĕlōhîm*, Ezekiel 1:1), establishing supernatural visual perception beyond ordinary human capacity. According to Daniel Block, "This visionary language creates cognitive framework for understanding subsequent description as genuine divine self-disclosure mediated through prophetic spiritual perception rather than merely ordinary visual experience."[22]

---

19   Christopher R. Seitz, *Isaiah 1-39, Interpretation* (Louisville: John Knox Press, 1993), 55.

20   Margaret Barker, *The Gate of Heaven: The History and Symbolism of the Temple in Jerusalem* (London: SPCK, 1991), 151.

21   Brevard S. Childs, *Isaiah, Old Testament Library* (Louisville: Westminster John Knox, 2001), 56.

22   Daniel I. Block, *The Book of Ezekiel: Chapters 1-24*, 85.

The vision proceeds through multiple perceptual layers: four living creatures with composite features, wheels within wheels exhibiting independent movement, platform above creatures, throne upon platform, and finally "something that seemed like a human form" with fiery appearance surrounded by rainbow-like brightness, identified as "the appearance of the likeness of the glory of the LORD" (Ezekiel 1:26-28). This carefully qualified language, according to Moshe Greenberg, "creates successive representational distances while affirming genuine divine manifestation, establishing theological balance between divine self-disclosure and divine transcendence."[23]

Jeremiah's initial prophetic experience emphasizes divine word rather than divine vision: "Now the word of the LORD came to me saying..." (Jeremiah 1:4). This verbal emphasis, according to Walter Brueggemann, "represents theological tradition prioritizing divine communication over visual manifestation, establishing prophetic authority through divine speech rather than visionary experience."[24] Even Jeremiah's visual elements—almond branch and boiling pot (Jeremiah 1:11-14)—appear as ordinary objects interpreted through divine speech rather than extraordinary divine manifestations.

Amos similarly emphasizes divine speech—"The words of Amos... which he saw" (Amos 1:1)—creating what James Luther Mays calls "theological paradox where divine communication occurs through both auditory and visual channels, emphasizing prophetic reception of divine message through multiple perceptual dimensions."[25] This speech-oriented prophetic tradition balances more visually-oriented throne theophany tradition.

Micaiah ben Imlah's throne vision (1 Kings 22:19-23) presents divine manifestation within heavenly council context: "I saw the LORD sitting

---

23   Moshe Greenberg, *Ezekiel 1-20: A New Translation with Introduction and Commentary,* 53.

24   Walter Brueggemann, *The Theology of the Book of Jeremiah* (Cambridge: Cambridge University Press, 2007), 35.

25   James Luther Mays, *Amos: A Commentary,* Old Testament Library (Philadelphia: Westminster Press, 1969), 20.

on his throne, with all the host of heaven standing beside him to the right and to the left of him." This council setting, according to H. Wheeler Robinson, "establishes prophetic access to divine deliberative process rather than merely divine decree, creating theological framework where prophetic authority derives from participation in heavenly decision-making rather than merely receiving divine commands."[26]

These prophetic theophanies establish several significant theological patterns. First, they connect divine manifestation with prophetic commissioning, establishing divine self-disclosure as authorization for prophetic ministry rather than merely religious experience. Second, they increasingly emphasize visionary perception rather than ordinary visual experience, creating theological category for divine self-disclosure beyond physical manifestation. Third, they present divine appearance within cosmic context—enthroned amid heavenly beings—rather than merely particular historical situation. Fourth, they maintain tension between divine verbal communication and divine visual manifestation, creating multidimensional understanding of prophetic experience.

According to Walter Zimmerli, "Prophetic theophanies transform earlier theophanic patterns through increased emphasis on cosmic dimensions, heavenly council context, and visionary perception, creating theological framework where divine manifestation authorizes prophetic interpretation of historical events within larger divine purposes."[27] This prophetic transformation would significantly influence subsequent apocalyptic tradition, where divine manifestation increasingly occurs through visionary experience revealing cosmic realities beyond immediate historical circumstances.

---

26   H. Wheeler Robinson, *Inspiration and Revelation in the Old Testament* (Oxford: Clarendon Press, 1946), 167.

27   Walther Zimmerli, *Ezekiel 1: A Commentary on the Book of the Prophet Ezekiel, Chapters 1-24,* trans. Ronald E. Clements, Hermeneia (Philadelphia: Fortress Press, 1979), 98.

Ezekiel's Throne Vision

Ezekiel's inaugural throne-chariot vision (Ezekiel 1) represents the Hebrew Bible's most elaborate and complex theophany, combining multiple perceptual elements while carefully maintaining theological balance between divine self-disclosure and divine transcendence. This vision warrants particular attention for its significant influence on subsequent Jewish mystical tradition and its sophisticated theological presentation.

The account begins with precise historical contextualization—"In the thirtieth year, in the fourth month, on the fifth day of the month, as I was among the exiles by the river Chebar" (Ezekiel 1:1)—grounding extraordinary vision within particular historical moment. According to Daniel Block, "This specific historical framing establishes theological principle where divine transcendent revelation addresses particular human circumstances rather than occurring as abstract religious phenomenon disconnected from historical reality."[28]

The vision proceeds through carefully structured perceptual layers, beginning with storm cloud and fire from the north (Ezekiel 1:4), progressing to four living creatures with composite features (Ezekiel 1:5-14), introducing wheels within wheels exhibiting independent movement (Ezekiel 1:15-21), describing platform above creatures (Ezekiel 1:22-25), and culminating with enthroned "something that seemed like a human form" (Ezekiel 1:26-28).

This hierarchical structure, according to Moshe Greenberg, "creates graduated approach to divine presence, establishing proper theological sequence where direct divine vision occurs only after preparatory perceptual stages."[29] Each element receives detailed description emphasizing both similarity to familiar objects and difference from ordinary experience, creating what Margaret Odell calls "perceptual liminality where vision inhabits conceptual space between ordinary and extraordinary perception."[30]

---

28   Daniel I. Block, *The Book of Ezekiel: Chapters 1-24*, 83.

29   Moshe Greenberg, *Ezekiel 1-20: A New Translation with Introduction and Commentary*, 54.

30   Margaret S. Odell, *Ezekiel, Smyth & Helwys Bible Commentary* (Macon, GA: Smyth & Helwys, 2005), 28.

The vision climaxes with enthroned figure described through multiple qualifications: "something that seemed like a human form... something that looked like gleaming amber... something that looked like fire... the appearance of the likeness of the glory of the LORD" (Ezekiel 1:26-28). This cumulative qualification, according to Benjamin Sommer, "establishes multiple representational distances while affirming genuine divine manifestation, creating sophisticated theological balance between divine self-disclosure and divine transcendence."[31]

The prophet's response—falling on his face—leads immediately to divine commissioning through spirit entering Ezekiel (Ezekiel 2:1-2). This transition, according to Walther Zimmerli, "connects extraordinary vision with prophetic vocation, establishing theophany as authorization for prophetic ministry rather than merely ecstatic religious experience."[32] The extensive divine speech following visionary experience (Ezekiel 2-3) balances visual theophany with verbal commission.

Several distinctive theological elements characterize Ezekiel's throne vision. First, it presents divine mobility through merkabah (chariot-throne) imagery, emphasizing divine sovereignty over geographic location. According to Jon Levenson, "This mobility directly addresses exile's theological crisis regarding divine presence, establishing divine freedom from Jerusalem temple while maintaining genuine divine accessibility to exilic community."[33]

Second, the vision incorporates natural elements—storm, lightning, cloud—while transforming them into supernatural manifestation, creating what Ellen Davis calls "theological continuity between natural order and divine self-disclosure where creation provides vocabulary for divine manifestation without reducing divine presence to natural phenomena."[34]

---

31   Benjamin D. Sommer, *The Bodies of God and the World of Ancient Israel,* 68.

32   Walther Zimmerli, *Ezekiel 1: A Commentary on the Book of the Prophet Ezekiel, Chapters 1-24,* 131.

33   Jon D. Levenson, *Theology of the Program of Restoration of Ezekiel 40-48* (Missoula, MT: Scholars Press, 1976), 10.

34   Ellen F. Davis, *Swallowing the Scroll: Textuality and the Dynamics of*

This integration allows natural elements to become vehicles for divine self-disclosure.

Third, the composite living creatures combine human, lion, ox, and eagle features, suggesting what Jill Middlemas identifies as "comprehensive cosmic representation where various creation aspects participate in divine throne-bearing, establishing theological framework where creation serves rather than contains divine presence."[35] This cosmic integration expands divine manifestation beyond merely human-divine encounter.

Fourth, the vision presents carefully indirect divine representation, avoiding direct description of divine form while affirming genuine divine manifestation. According to Tryggve Mettinger, "This theological restraint maintains divine mystery while affirming divine self-disclosure, creating religious framework where divine presence remains fundamentally available yet never fully comprehended."[36]

Ezekiel's throne vision would exert tremendous influence on subsequent religious tradition. Jewish merkabah mysticism developed elaborate practices for contemplating divine chariot-throne, while apocalyptic literature incorporated throne-room imagery into visionary journeys. Christian tradition connected Ezekiel's living creatures with the four evangelists and incorporated throne imagery into Revelation's heavenly worship scenes.

According to Christopher Rowland, "Ezekiel's vision established theological paradigm integrating divine transcendence and immanence through sophisticated representational strategy, creating framework where divine manifestation remains genuinely accessible while fundamentally mysterious."[37] This theological balance would prove particularly significant

---

Discourse in Ezekiel's Prophecy (Sheffield: Almond Press, 1989), 59.

35   Jill Middlemas, *The Troubles of Templeless Judah* (Oxford: Oxford University Press, 2005), 76.

36   Tryggve N.D. Mettinger, *The Dethronement of Sabaoth: Studies in the Shem and Kabod Theologies,* 106.

37   Christopher Rowland, *The Open Heaven: A Study of Apocalyptic in Judaism and Early Christianity* (New York: Crossroad, 1982), 96.

for religious traditions maintaining divine unknowability while affirming divine self-disclosure.

Theological Developments in National Theophanies

Israel's developing national experience generated significant theological refinement regarding divine manifestation. Several important trajectories emerge through tabernacle/temple theophanies, glory traditions, and prophetic visions.

First, national theophanies increasingly connected divine manifestation with particular sacred spaces while maintaining divine freedom beyond spatial confinement. According to Samuel Terrien, "This institutional localization balanced divine accessibility through established sacred sites with theological awareness of divine transcendence beyond any particular location."[38] This balance created religious framework where divine presence became reliably available through sacred space without suggesting divine limitation to those spaces.

Second, theophanic language shifted from anthropomorphic description toward glory manifestation and visionary perception. According to Benjamin Sommer, "This terminological development reflected theological refinement regarding divine self-disclosure, creating conceptual categories allowing genuine divine manifestation while avoiding crude anthropomorphism."[39] Terms like "glory" *(kābôd)* provided vocabulary for divine presence that simultaneously revealed and concealed.

Third, theophanies increasingly incorporated liturgical dimensions, connecting divine manifestation with community worship rather than merely individual religious experience. Temple theophanies occurred within ritual settings; Isaiah's vision featured seraphic liturgy; prophetic commissions often included ritual elements. According to Frank Moore Cross, "This liturgical integration established divine manifestation within

---

38   Samuel Terrien, *The Elusive Presence: Toward a New Biblical Theology,* 174.

39   Benjamin D. Sommer, *The Bodies of God and the World of Ancient Israel,* 72.

communal religious practice rather than merely exceptional individual experience, creating ongoing theophanic expectation through regular worship."[40]

Fourth, prophetic theophanies presented divine appearance within cosmic context—enthroned amid heavenly beings—rather than merely particular historical situation. According to Walter Brueggemann, "This cosmic framing established theological perspective where historical events represented particular expressions of larger divine purposes discerned through prophetic visionary access to heavenly realities."[41] This perspective would significantly influence apocalyptic tradition.

Fifth, national theophanies increasingly emphasized divine sovereignty through mobility and independence from sacred spaces. The tabernacle's portable design, Solomon's theological nuance regarding divine presence, and especially Ezekiel's mobile throne-chariot vision established what Jon Levenson calls "theological framework where divine presence remained genuinely available while fundamentally free from human containment or manipulation."[42] This theological emphasis proved particularly significant during exile when traditional sacred spaces became inaccessible.

Sixth, theophanies increasingly connected divine manifestation with covenant evaluation rather than merely covenant establishment. While patriarchal theophanies primarily established covenant relationships, national theophanies frequently addressed covenant violations and called for renewed faithfulness. According to Moshe Greenberg, "This evaluative dimension transformed theophany from primarily promissory experience to potentially threatening encounter, where divine presence exposed community failures while maintaining covenant relationship."[43]

---

40   Frank Moore Cross, *Canaanite Myth and Hebrew Epic: Essays in the History of the Religion of Israel* (Cambridge: Harvard University Press, 1973), 169.

41   Walter Brueggemann, *Theology of the Old Testament: Testimony, Dispute, Advocacy* (Minneapolis: Fortress Press, 1997), 145.

42   Jon D. Levenson, *Sinai and Zion: An Entry into the Jewish Bible*, 139.

43   Moshe Greenberg, *Ezekiel 1-20: A New Translation with Introduction and Commentary*, 195.

These theological developments reflected Israel's changing historical circumstances while maintaining fundamental continuity with patriarchal theophanic traditions. According to Terence Fretheim, "National theophanic traditions creatively adapted fundamental theological principle of divine self-disclosure to address new religious questions arising from Israel's developing communal experience, maintaining essential divine character as self-revealing God while refining understanding of how that self-revelation occurs."[44]

This theological refinement would prove particularly significant following temple destruction and exile, when traditional frameworks for understanding divine presence required substantial reconsideration. The developing glory tradition, prophetic visionary experiences, and especially Ezekiel's mobile throne-chariot imagery provided theological resources for understanding divine presence beyond geographic limitation, establishing conceptual foundation for post-exilic religious adaptations.

According to Walter Brueggemann, "National theophanic traditions navigated fundamental theological tension between divine reliable accessibility and divine sovereign freedom, creating religious framework where divine presence remained genuinely available through established channels while maintaining divine transcendence beyond any particular manifestation."[45] This theological balance would continue developing through subsequent Jewish and Christian traditions while maintaining essential connection with biblical theophanic foundations.

---

44   Terence E. Fretheim, *The Suffering of God: An Old Testament Perspective* (Philadelphia: Fortress Press, 1984), 92.
45   Walter Brueggemann, *Theology of the Old Testament: Testimony, Dispute, Advocacy*, 569.

Chapter 12

Christophanies and Incarnation

The relationship between divine manifestations in the Hebrew Bible and the person of Christ represents one of the most significant theological developments in biblical studies. This chapter examines the concept of christophanies—proposed appearances of the pre-incarnate Christ in the Hebrew Bible—alongside the New Testament's presentation of the Incarnation as the definitive divine self-disclosure. The discussion also encompasses Christ's transfiguration and post-resurrection appearances as unique theophanic events that both continue and transform the biblical tradition of divine manifestation.

Pre-incarnate Appearances of Christ

The term "christophany" refers to manifestations of the pre-incarnate Christ in the Hebrew Bible, though the term itself is not found in scripture. This interpretive category emerged primarily through Christian theological reflection on certain theophanic texts, particularly those featuring the enigmatic "Angel of the Lord" figure.

Patristic Origins and Development

The identification of Christ in Hebrew Bible theophanies has deep roots in patristic exegesis. Justin Martyr (c.100-165 CE) was among the first to systematically interpret various divine manifestations as appearances of the pre-incarnate Logos. In his *Dialogue with Trypho,* Justin argues that the God who appeared to Abraham at Mamre, to Jacob at Peniel, and to Moses in the burning bush was not the Father but the Son.[1] As Larry W. Hurtado notes, "This exegetical move allowed Justin to maintain the transcendence

---

1   Justin Martyr, *Dialogue with Trypho,* 56-60.

of God the Father while explaining the anthropomorphic appearances of God in the Hebrew scriptures."[2]

Irenaeus of Lyon (c.130-202 CE) further developed this interpretive approach, writing that "the Son has been from the beginning revealing the Father to all persons in all ways as the Father wills."[3] This patristic reading established a hermeneutical framework that would influence Christian interpretation for centuries.

Key Textual Examples

Several Hebrew Bible passages have been traditionally interpreted as christophanies:

1. Genesis 18: The appearance of three visitors to Abraham at Mamre has been interpreted by many patristic and medieval commentators as a pre-incarnate manifestation of Christ, possibly accompanied by two angels. Augustine's reading sees in this text a foreshadowing of the Trinity, though most contemporary scholars acknowledge this as eisegesis rather than exegesis.[4]

2. Genesis 32:22-32: Jacob's wrestling with a mysterious figure at Peniel has been interpreted as an encounter with the pre-incarnate Christ. The text's ambiguity—referring to the figure as both a "man" and "God"—has invited this Christological reading.

3. Exodus 3:1-15: The burning bush episode, where the Angel of the Lord speaks as God himself, has been read as a christophany by interpreters from Justin Martyr through the Reformation period.

---

2   Larry W. Hurtado, *Lord Jesus Christ: Devotion to Jesus in Earliest Christianity* (Grand Rapids: Eerdmans, 2003), 75.

3   Irenaeus, *Against Heresies*, *4.6.7*, as cited in Gerald O'Collins, *Christology: A Biblical, Historical, and Systematic Study of Jesus*, 2nd ed. (Oxford: Oxford University Press, 2009), 19.

4   Augustine, *De Trinitate*, 2.10.19-20.

4. Joshua 5:13-15: The appearance of the "commander of the Lord's army" before Joshua at Jericho has christophanic elements, particularly in the worship rendered to this figure.

5. Daniel 3:25: The "fourth man" in the fiery furnace, described as "like a son of the gods," has been interpreted in Christian tradition as a pre-incarnate appearance of Christ.

Critical Perspectives

Contemporary biblical scholarship approaches the concept of christophanies with significantly more caution than traditional interpretations. James Dunn argues that "to read these texts as manifestations of the pre-existent Christ is to impose later Christian categories onto Hebrew Bible narratives that functioned in their original context without such Christological significance."[5] Michael S. Heiser, while acknowledging the theological legitimacy of identifying the Angel of the Lord with the second person of the Trinity, cautions against conflating theological conclusions with exegetical observations.[6]

J. Andrew Dearman suggests a more nuanced approach: "While the Hebrew Bible itself does not identify these manifestations as the pre-incarnate Christ, these texts nevertheless created theological space within Second Temple Judaism for conceptualizing divine agency in ways that would prove formative for early Christology."[7]

The Incarnation as Supreme Theophany

If christophanies represent a contested category of divine manifestation, the Incarnation stands as Christianity's central and definitive theophany— God made visible and tangible in human form.

---

5   James D.G. Dunn, *Christology in the Making: A New Testament Inquiry into the Origins of the Doctrine of the Incarnation,* 2nd ed. (Grand Rapids: Eerdmans, 1996), 124.

6   Michael S. Heiser, *The Unseen Realm: Recovering the Supernatural Worldview of the Bible* (Bellingham, WA: Lexham Press, 2015), 40-42.

7   J. Andrew Dearman, *The Book of Hosea, New International Commentary on the Old Testament* (Grand Rapids: Eerdmans, 2010), 178.

Johannine Theology of Divine Manifestation

The Gospel of John provides the most developed theological framework for understanding the Incarnation as theophany. The prologue (John 1:1-18) establishes Jesus as the divine Logos who "became flesh and dwelt among us" (John 1:14). This tabernacling language (ἐσκήνωσεν/ eskēnōsen) deliberately echoes the divine presence in the wilderness tabernacle, establishing the Incarnation as the fulfillment of previous modes of divine presence.[8]

John's Gospel further develops this theme through Jesus' self-declarations. The "I am" (ἐγώ εἰμι/egō eimi) statements not only claim divine identity through echoing Exodus 3:14 but also articulate how Jesus manifests divine reality through accessible metaphors (bread, light, shepherd, vine, etc.).[9] As Marianne Meye Thompson writes, "In John's Gospel, Jesus does not merely speak about God or point to God; Jesus shows God, making the invisible God visible."[10]

The culmination of this theme appears in John 14:8-9, where Philip requests, "Lord, show us the Father," and Jesus responds, "Whoever has seen me has seen the Father." This text establishes the Incarnation as the definitive theophany, superseding all previous divine manifestations.

Pauline Perspectives

Paul's writings contribute significantly to understanding Christ as divine manifestation. Colossians 1:15 describes Christ as "the image of the invisible God," using language (εἰκὼν/eikōn) that connects to Greek philosophical traditions concerning divine representation while also echoing Genesis 1:26-27.[11] This connection suggests that Christ fulfills the representational role originally intended for humanity.

---

8   Marianne Meye Thompson, *The God of the Gospel of John* (Grand Rapids: Eerdmans, 2001), 122-123.

9   Thompson, *The God of the Gospel of John*, 228-232.

10   Thompson, *The God of the Gospel of John*, 101.

11   Gordon D. Fee, *Pauline Christology: An Exegetical-Theological Study* (Peabody, MA: Hendrickson, 2007), 317-325.

Colossians 2:9 further declares that "in him the whole fullness of deity dwells bodily," emphasizing the corporeal nature of divine manifestation in Christ. As Gordon Fee notes, "What Paul asserts here would have been inconceivable to most Greek philosophical traditions, for whom divinity and materiality were incompatible categories."[12]

Philippians 2:6-11, widely recognized as an early Christological hymn, describes Christ's movement from divine form (μορφῇ θεοῦ/morphē theou) to human form (μορφὴν δούλου/morphēn doulou). This text articulates the paradox of divine manifestation through humiliation and exaltation.

Hebrews and the Revelation of God

The Epistle to the Hebrews opens with one of the New Testament's most direct statements concerning Christ as divine manifestation: "He is the radiance of the glory of God and the exact imprint of his nature" (Hebrews 1:3). The language of "radiance" (ἀπαύγασμα/apaugasma) and "exact imprint" (χαρακτὴρ/charaktēr) draws from both Jewish wisdom traditions and Hellenistic philosophy to articulate Christ's revelatory function.[13]

The author of Hebrews establishes a contrast between previous modes of divine communication and the final revelation in Christ: "Long ago, at many times and in many ways, God spoke to our fathers by the prophets, but in these last days he has spoken to us by his Son" (Hebrews 1:1-2). Richard Bauckham observes that this text "establishes the Incarnation not merely as another theophany in a series, but as the culmination and fulfillment of God's self-revelation."[14]

---

12   Fee, *Pauline Christology*, 330.

13   Richard Bauckham, *God Crucified: Monotheism and Christology in the New Testament* (Grand Rapids: Eerdmans, 1999), 43-45.

14   Richard Bauckham, *Jesus and the God of Israel: God Crucified and Other Studies on the New Testament's Christology of Divine Identity* (Grand Rapids: Eerdmans, 2008), 233.

The Transfiguration

The transfiguration narrative (Mark 9:2-8; Matthew 17:1-8; Luke 9:28-36) represents a unique theophanic moment within Jesus' ministry—a temporary unveiling of his divine glory that connects the Incarnation to previous biblical theophanies while anticipating the resurrection.

Textual Features and Allusions

Several features of the transfiguration narratives connect this event to earlier biblical theophanies:

1. **Mountain setting**: Like significant theophanies to Moses and Elijah, the transfiguration occurs on a mountain, establishing continuity with these previous revelatory encounters.

2. **Altered appearance**: Jesus' face shining "like the sun" and his clothes becoming "white as light" (Matthew 17:2) echoes the altered appearance of Moses after his theophanic encounter (Exodus 34:29-35).

3. **Cloud of divine presence**: The "bright cloud" overshadowing the disciples (Matthew 17:5) recalls the cloud of divine presence at Sinai and in the tabernacle/temple.

4. **Divine voice**: The declaration from the cloud, "This is my beloved Son; listen to him" (Mark 9:7), confirms Jesus' identity while establishing his authority over Moses and Elijah, who represent the Law and the Prophets.

Dorothy Lee suggests that these features establish the transfiguration as "a moment of disclosure in which Jesus' true identity is revealed within the hiddenness of his humanity."[15]

Theological Significance

The transfiguration serves multiple theological functions in understanding Christ as divine manifestation:

---

15   Dorothy A. Lee, *Transfiguration*, New Century Theology (London: Continuum, 2004), 24.

1. **Confirmation of identity**: The divine voice affirms Jesus' identity as Son of God, providing divine endorsement of his person and mission.

2. **Anticipation of resurrection glory**: The temporary transformation of Jesus' appearance foreshadows his post-resurrection state. As N.T. Wright observes, "The transfiguration offers a glimpse of the glorified humanity that will characterize Jesus after Easter and, indeed, all humanity in the final resurrection."[16]

3. **Continuity and fulfillment**: The presence of Moses and Elijah places Jesus within Israel's prophetic tradition while also suggesting that he transcends and fulfills this tradition.

4. **Epiphanic moment for disciples**: Unlike most Hebrew Bible theophanies, which are private encounters, the transfiguration includes witnesses who are overwhelmed by the experience. Peter's confused proposal to build three tabernacles (Mark 9:5-6) reflects the human struggle to comprehend and respond to divine manifestation.

Jürgen Moltmann sees in the transfiguration a revelation of "the eternal glory of God shining through the vulnerability of Jesus' humanity"—a moment that reveals the paradoxical nature of the Incarnation itself.[17]

Post-resurrection Appearances

The post-resurrection appearances of Jesus constitute the final category of Christological theophanies in the New Testament. These narratives present complex portraits of divine manifestation that both affirm and transform traditional theophanic patterns.

---

16   N.T. Wright, *The Resurrection of the Son of God, Christian Origins and the Question of God,* vol. 3 (Minneapolis: Fortress Press, 2003), 654.

17   Jürgen Moltmann, *The Way of Jesus Christ: Christology in Messianic Dimensions,* trans. Margaret Kohl (Minneapolis: Fortress Press, 1993), 149.

Characteristics and Patterns

The gospel accounts present post-resurrection appearances with several distinctive features:

1. **Transformed yet recognizable presence**: Jesus appears in a form that is simultaneously continuous with his pre-crucifixion identity yet somehow transformed. The disciples often fail to recognize him immediately (Luke 24:16; John 20:14), suggesting a transformation that transcends normal human appearance.

2. **Physical yet transcendent**: Jesus invites Thomas to touch his wounds (John 20:27) and eats fish to demonstrate his physicality (Luke 24:42-43), yet also appears suddenly in locked rooms (John 20:19, 26), suggesting a mode of existence that transcends normal physical limitations.

3. **Interpretive function**: Many post-resurrection appearances include significant teaching moments where Jesus interprets scripture (Luke 24:27, 44-47) or provides instruction for the disciples' mission (Matthew 28:18-20; John 21:15-19).

4. **Commissioning elements**: These appearances frequently include elements of commissioning the disciples for their future mission, establishing a connection between divine manifestation and human vocation.

N.T. Wright notes that these appearances "represent neither the resuscitation of a corpse nor merely spiritual visions but rather the emergence of a new form of embodied human existence beyond death—a transformed physicality that becomes the foundation for Christian hope."[18]

Theological Integration

The post-resurrection appearances integrate several theological themes related to divine manifestation:

---

18   Wright, *The Resurrection of the Son of God,* 608-615.

1. **Validation of crucifixion**: By appearing with his wounds still visible, the risen Christ establishes continuity between the crucified Jesus and the exalted Lord, suggesting that divine glory is revealed not despite the cross but through it.

2. **Inauguration of new creation**: Paul's designation of Christ as "the firstfruits of those who have fallen asleep" (1 Corinthians 15:20) positions the resurrection as the inauguration of new creation. The post-resurrection appearances thus function as theophanies that reveal not only God in Christ but also the nature of humanity's eschatological transformation.

3. **Authorization of apostolic witness**: These appearances authenticate the witnesses who will proclaim Christ, establishing a chain of testimony that connects subsequent Christian communities to these foundational theophanic encounters.

4. **Anticipation of parousia**: The ascension narrative in Acts 1:9-11 concludes the post-resurrection appearances with an angelic promise of Christ's return "in the same way," creating an eschatological framework for understanding divine manifestation.

Richard Bauckham suggests that the post-resurrection appearances serve as "bridge events between the historical ministry of Jesus and the ongoing experience of the early church, providing theological authorization for the church's proclamation while also establishing patterns for ongoing encounter with the risen Christ."[19]

Conclusion: Theological Synthesis

This examination of christophanies and incarnation reveals several interconnected theological principles regarding divine manifestation in biblical tradition:

1. **Progressive revelation**: Divine self-disclosure in scripture follows a trajectory of increasing clarity and intimacy,

---

19   Bauckham, *Jesus and the God of Israel,* 265.

culminating in the Incarnation as the definitive revelation of God's nature and purposes.

2. **Embodied revelation**: Throughout biblical tradition, God accommodates human limitations by manifesting in forms accessible to human perception, with the Incarnation representing the ultimate divine accommodation to human experience.

3. **Transformative encounter**: Divine manifestations consistently transform those who experience them, altering their perception, identity, and mission. The post-resurrection appearances particularly demonstrate this transformative impact.

4. **Paradoxical presence**: Biblical theophanies, particularly those associated with Christ, consistently present divine manifestation in paradoxical terms—glory in humility, transcendence in immanence, divinity in humanity.

5. **Community-forming revelation**: Divine manifestations in Christ establish new communities of witness and interpretation, forming the foundation for ongoing theological reflection on divine presence.

As Kathryn Tanner observes, "The Incarnation establishes the pattern for all divine self-communication—God gives God's self without reserve while never ceasing to be God, creating communion without collapsing the distinction between creator and creature."[20] This paradoxical pattern of divine self-disclosure provides the theological foundation for understanding christophanies and incarnation as both the fulfillment of previous divine manifestations and the establishment of a new mode of divine presence that continues in the church through the Holy Spirit.

---

20   Kathryn Tanner, *Jesus, Humanity and the Trinity: A Brief Systematic Theology* (Minneapolis: Fortress Press, 2001), 17.

Part IV

Theological and Interpretive Issues

Chapter 13

The Angel of the Lord

Textual Analysis of Key Passages

The enigmatic figure identified as "the angel of the LORD" *(mal'ak YHWH)* appears in numerous biblical texts, creating significant interpretive challenges through paradoxical presentation as both distinct from and identified with God. These appearances establish theological tension regarding divine presence and mediation that has generated diverse interpretations throughout religious history.

Genesis 16:7-14 presents the angel's encounter with Hagar in the wilderness. Initial identification as "the angel of the LORD" (Genesis 16:7) suggests divine emissary distinct from God himself. However, subsequent narrative blurs this distinction as the angel promises, "I will so greatly multiply your offspring that they cannot be counted" (Genesis 16:10), claiming divine prerogative using first-person declaration. Hagar's response—naming God "El-roi" (God of seeing) and expressing surprise at surviving divine vision—further confuses the distinction between angel and God proper.

This theological ambiguity, according to David Clines, "creates deliberate narrative tension regarding divine representation and presence, establishing theological framework where divine messenger simultaneously represents God while embodying direct divine speech and authority."[1] This pattern recurs throughout angel of the LORD appearances, suggesting intentional theological presentation rather than merely textual confusion.

Genesis 21:17-19 presents another Hagar encounter, where "the angel of God" calls from heaven, identifies himself with God who heard the boy's voice, then performs divine action by opening Hagar's eyes to see water. Genesis 22:11-18 describes the angel stopping Abraham's sacrifice of

---

1   David J.A. Clines, *"Yahweh and the God of Christian Theology,"* Theology 83, no. 695 (1980): 323-30.

Isaac, speaking with direct divine authority, and making covenant promises typically associated with God's direct speech. As Victor Hamilton observes, "These accounts consistently present the angel speaking with unmediated divine authority without qualification, suggesting identity rather than merely agency relationship with God."[2]

Exodus 3:2-6 presents particularly significant ambiguity in the burning bush theophany: "The angel of the LORD appeared to him in a flame of fire out of a bush" (Exodus 3:2), yet immediately afterward "God called to him out of the bush" (Exodus 3:4). This seamless narrative transition, according to Thomas Dozeman, "eliminates clear distinction between the angel's appearance and God's speech, creating theological framework where divine presence manifests through angelic mediation without suggesting ontological separation."[3]

Numbers 22:22-35 presents the angel of the LORD opposing Balaam, physically blocking his path while remaining invisible to him until "the LORD opened the eyes of Balaam" (Numbers 22:31). The angel declares, "I have come out as adversary" *(śāṭān)*, functioning as divine representative enforcing divine boundaries. According to Jacob Milgrom, "This adversarial role establishes the angel not merely as messenger but as executor of divine judgment, exercising divine prerogative to oppose those working against divine purposes."[4]

Judges contains significant angel of the LORD appearances, including commissioning Gideon (Judges 6:11-24) and announcing Samson's birth (Judges 13:2-23). Both narratives feature explicit human recognition of divine encounter following angelic appearance. Gideon exclaims, "Help me, Lord GOD! For I have seen the angel of the LORD face to face" (Judges 6:22). Similarly, Manoah declares to his wife, "We shall surely die, for we have seen God" (Judges 13:22). According to Barry Webb,

---

2 Victor P. Hamilton, *The Book of Genesis: Chapters 18-50,* New International Commentary on the Old Testament (Grand Rapids: Eerdmans, 1995), 14.

3 Thomas B. Dozeman, *Commentary on Exodus* (Grand Rapids: Eerdmans, 2009), 128.

4 Jacob Milgrom, *Numbers,* JPS Torah Commentary (Philadelphia: Jewish Publication Society, 1990), 189.

"These parallel responses indicate theological understanding where angelic encounter constitutes genuine divine manifestation, transcending merely creaturely messenger visitation."[5]

Zechariah presents distinctive angel of the LORD tradition, where the angel functions primarily as interpreting figure explaining prophetic visions. Zechariah 1:12 presents the angel interceding with God on Israel's behalf, creating clearer distinction between angel and God proper than earlier narrative appearances. According to Carol Meyers, "This intercessory role represents theological development where the angel functions as advocate within divine council rather than direct divine manifestation, suggesting increasing conceptual separation while maintaining special mediatorial relationship."[6]

Several textual patterns emerge across these appearances. First, the angel consistently speaks with unmediated divine authority, often using first-person divine declarations without qualification. Second, human recipients typically respond to these appearances as direct divine encounters, expressing fear of death appropriate to theophanic experience. Third, the narratives frequently shift between referring to "the angel of the LORD" and "the LORD" without explanation, suggesting theological identification transcending merely agency relationship. Fourth, the angel exercises divine prerogatives including covenant promises, miraculous actions, and executionary judgment.

This textual complexity, according to Benjamin Sommer, "establishes theological category where divine presence genuinely manifests through particular mediating agent while maintaining essential divine unity, creating conceptual space for divine self-disclosure without compromising divine transcendence."[7] This category would prove significant for subsequent theological reflection regarding divine presence and representation.

---

5   Barry G. Webb, *The Book of Judges,* New International Commentary on the Old Testament (Grand Rapids: Eerdmans, 2012), 222.

6   Carol L. Meyers and Eric M. Meyers, *Haggai, Zechariah 1-8,* Anchor Bible 25B (Garden City, NY: Doubleday, 1987), 113.

7   Benjamin D. Sommer, *The Bodies of God and the World of Ancient Israel* (Cambridge: Cambridge University Press, 2009), 40.

Historical Interpretations

The enigmatic angel of the LORD has generated diverse interpretations throughout religious history, with Jewish and Christian traditions developing distinctive approaches reflecting their theological frameworks and interpretive concerns. These historical interpretations demonstrate both exegetical creativity and theological sophistication in addressing the textual ambiguities.

Early Jewish interpretation increasingly emphasized distinction between the angel and God proper, reflecting developing theological concern for divine transcendence. According to Michael Fishbane, "Post-exilic Jewish interpretation progressively reframed earlier theophanic accounts through mediatorial concepts including angels, creating theological distance between divine essence and divine manifestation."[8] This interpretive trajectory appears in Septuagint translation choices, targum expansions, and rabbinic exegesis.

The Septuagint typically translated the Hebrew *mal'ak YHWH* as *ho angelos kyriou* (the angel of the Lord) rather than creating distinctive designation, maintaining the original's ambiguity. However, James Charlesworth notes that "Septuagint occasionally introduced additional descriptive phrases suggesting mediatorial understanding rather than direct divine appearance, reflecting developing theological caution regarding divine embodiment."[9]

The Aramaic targums frequently replaced direct divine appearance with mediatorial concepts including "angel of the LORD" *(mal'aka daYYY),* "glory of the LORD" *(yeqara daYYY),* and "word of the LORD" *(memra daYYY).* According to Bruce Chilton, "These systematic substitutions represent theological refinement regarding divine manifestation,

---

8   Michael Fishbane, *Biblical Interpretation in Ancient Israel* (Oxford: Clarendon Press, 1985), 209.
9   James H. Charlesworth, *The Old Testament Pseudepigrapha and the New Testament: Prolegomena for the Study of Christian Origins* (Cambridge: Cambridge University Press, 1985), 57.

introducing explicit mediation where Hebrew text presented direct divine appearance."[10] This pattern appears particularly in Genesis 17:1, 18:1, and Exodus 19:20, where Hebrew references to direct divine appearance become mediated manifestations in targum renderings.

The Qumran community's texts reflect particular interest in angelic mediation, developing elaborate angelology while maintaining angels' subordinate status. According to John Collins, "Qumran literature presents intensified focus on angelic beings without elevating them to divine status, maintaining theological balance where angels function as genuine divine agents without becoming independent divine powers."[11]

Rabbinic interpretation generally maintained distinction between the angel and God proper while acknowledging the angel's unique status as primary divine representative. Genesis Rabbah 9:2 states that "generally, dreams come through an angel and visions through a man's thought, but Moses was privileged, and his communications came directly from God." According to Alan Segal, "This distinction establishes hierarchical revelatory framework where direct divine communication represents exceptional privilege rather than normal theophanic pattern."[12]

Later Jewish mystical tradition developed sophisticated angelological systems incorporating the angel of the LORD within elaborate heavenly hierarchies. According to Elliot Wolfson, "Merkabah mysticism and subsequent kabbalah maintained the angel's significance as divine manifestation while integrating this figure within complex intermediary frameworks connecting divine unity with created diversity."[13] This approach preserved the angel's theological significance while subordinating angelic mediation to direct divine experience sought through mystical practices.

---

10   Bruce D. Chilton, *The Glory of Israel: The Theology and Provenience of the Isaiah Targum* (Sheffield: JSOT Press, 1983), 69.

11   John J. Collins, *Apocalypticism in the Dead Sea Scrolls* (London: Routledge, 1997), 47.

12   Alan F. Segal, *Two Powers in Heaven: Early Rabbinic Reports about Christianity and Gnosticism* (Leiden: Brill, 1977), 34.

13   Elliot R. Wolfson, *Through a Speculum That Shines: Vision and Imagination in Medieval Jewish Mysticism* (Princeton: Princeton University Press, 1994), 85.

Early Christian interpretation took radically different approach, identifying the angel of the LORD with the pre-incarnate Christ. Justin Martyr (c. 100-165 CE) provided systematic argument for this identification: "He who is called the Angel of Great Counsel and is God, and Lord, and Christ... appeared in the form of fire from the bush and conversed with Moses."[14] This christological reading, according to Darrell Hannah, "utilized the angel's textual ambiguity to establish theological continuity between Old Testament divine manifestations and New Testament incarnation, creating unified salvation-historical narrative centered on Christ."[15]

Irenaeus (c. 130-202 CE) similarly affirmed christological identification: "The Scripture is full of the Son of God's appearing: sometimes to talk and eat with Abraham, at other times to instruct Noah about the measures of the ark... inquiring after Adam, bringing judgment upon Sodom, directing Jacob on his journey, and speaking with Moses from the bush."[16] According to Robert Wilken, "This christological interpretation established theological continuity across biblical revelation while acknowledging qualitative difference in incarnation's permanent divine embodiment."[17]

Augustine (354-430 CE) developed nuanced approach suggesting the angel of the LORD represented the trinitarian God appearing through angelic mediation while anticipating incarnation: "The angel is understood to be the Savior himself of whom the prophet says, 'The angel of his presence saved them'... not that he is a real angel, but because by being given the title of messenger [angel], he foreshadows his future coming in the flesh, when he would be called the messenger of great counsel."[18] This

---

14   Justin Martyr, *Dialogue with Trypho,* 59, in Ante-Nicene Fathers, vol. 1, ed. Alexander Roberts and James Donaldson (Peabody, MA: Hendrickson, 1994), 227.

15   Darrell D. Hannah, *Michael and Christ: Michael Traditions and Angel Christology in Early Christianity*(Tübingen: Mohr Siebeck, 1999), 151.

16   Irenaeus, *Against Heresies,* 4.10.1, in Ante-Nicene Fathers, vol. 1, 474.

17   Robert L. Wilken, *The Spirit of Early Christian Thought: Seeking the Face of God* (New Haven: Yale University Press, 2003), 83.

18   Augustine, *On the Trinity,* 3.26, in Nicene and Post-Nicene Fathers, vol.

interpretation, according to Lewis Ayres, "integrated christological reading with trinitarian framework while maintaining theological tension between divine unity and particular divine manifestation."[19]

Medieval Jewish interpretation generally continued earlier trajectory emphasizing the angel's distinctness from God while maintaining special mediatorial status. Maimonides (1138-1204 CE) identified the angel of the LORD as created being representing divine presence, explicitly arguing against any suggestion of divine embodiment or actual divine manifestation. According to Menachem Kellner, "Maimonides' approach reflects rationalist emphasis on divine incorporeality and transcendence, rejecting any interpretive tradition suggesting genuine divine embodiment even temporarily."[20]

Medieval Christian interpretation typically maintained christological identification while incorporating increasingly sophisticated theological distinctions. Thomas Aquinas (1225-1274 CE) combined angelophany and christological readings by suggesting the angel of the LORD represented created angelic being manifesting divine presence while anticipating Christ's incarnation. According to Richard Cross, "This nuanced approach maintained theological connection between Old Testament theophanies and incarnation while recognizing qualitative difference between temporary manifestation and permanent divine embodiment."[21]

Reformation interpretations developed different trajectories reflecting distinctive theological concerns. Martin Luther (1483-1546 CE) strongly emphasized christological identification, arguing that angel of the LORD appearances represented direct pre-incarnate Christ manifestations. According to Mickey Mattox, "Luther's christocentric hermeneutic interpreted angel appearances as genuine divine self-disclosure anticipating

---

3, ed. Philip Schaff (Peabody, MA: Hendrickson, 1994), 63.

19   Lewis Ayres, *Nicaea and Its Legacy: An Approach to Fourth-Century Trinitarian Theology* (Oxford: Oxford University Press, 2004), 42.

20   Menachem Kellner, *Maimonides' Confrontation with Mysticism* (Oxford: Littman Library of Jewish Civilization, 2006), 154.

21   Richard Cross, *The Metaphysics of the Incarnation: Thomas Aquinas to Duns Scotus* (Oxford: Oxford University Press, 2002), 67.

incarnation rather than merely created angelic mediation."[22] John Calvin (1509-1564 CE) presented more nuanced approach, suggesting the angel simultaneously represented created being and divine presence, anticipating Christ while maintaining distinction between temporary manifestation and incarnation.

Modern historical-critical scholarship has generally avoided christological readings while exploring various historical-contextual interpretations. Some scholars identify the angel as literary device representing divine presence through narrative personification; others suggest redactional explanation where earlier direct theophany traditions were modified to include angelic mediation reflecting developing theological refinement; still others propose ancient Near Eastern parallel explaining the angel as divine hypostasis similar to Egyptian ba or Mesopotamian zaqiqu representing divine extension. According to James Kugel, "These diverse explanations reflect modern scholarly concern with historical development and comparative religious context rather than theological synthesis or dogmatic consistency."[23]

This interpretive diversity demonstrates the angel of the LORD's theological significance across religious traditions. According to R. Kendall Soulen, "The persistent interpretive attention given this enigmatic figure reflects recognition that these texts address fundamental theological questions regarding divine presence, representation, and self-disclosure that remain significant across divergent religious frameworks."[24] This ongoing engagement suggests the angel traditions provide particularly rich theological resources for understanding divine manifestation.

Christological Implications

The angel of the LORD traditions have particular significance for

---

22   Mickey L. Mattox, *"Defender of the Most Holy Matriarchs": Martin Luther's Interpretation of the Women of Genesis in the Enarrationes in Genesin,* 1535-45 (Leiden: Brill, 2003), 89.

23   James L. Kugel, *The God of Old: Inside the Lost World of the Bible* (New York: Free Press, 2003), 34.

24   R. Kendall Soulen, *The Divine Name(s) and the Holy Trinity, Volume 1: Distinguishing the Voices* (Louisville: Westminster John Knox, 2011), 175.

christological reflection, providing theological antecedent for understanding Christ as simultaneously distinct from and identified with God. This conceptual framework has generated substantial theological development throughout Christian tradition, establishing interpretive continuity between Old Testament theophanies and incarnational theology.

The textual pattern where the angel simultaneously functions as divine representative yet speaks directly as God creates what Larry Hurtado calls "theological space for understanding divine self-disclosure through particular agent who genuinely embodies divine presence while maintaining distinction within divine identity."[25] This pattern provides conceptual vocabulary for later trinitarian formulations regarding Christ's relationship with the Father.

Justin Martyr's explicit identification of the angel with the pre-incarnate Logos established interpretive approach that would become dominant in patristic thought: "He who appeared to Abraham under the oak in Mamre is God, sent with two angels... yet God remains ever in the highest heavens, has been seen by no man, and never converses with anyone except through divine power [the Logos]."[26] This exegetical approach, according to Charles Gieschen, "identified the angel not merely as type or anticipation of Christ but as actual pre-incarnate manifestation, creating explicit continuity between Old Testament divine appearances and incarnation."[27]

This christological interpretation addressed significant theological challenge facing early Christianity: explaining how Christ could be legitimately worshiped within monotheistic framework. By identifying Christ with the angel of the LORD who legitimately received worship as divine manifestation while remaining distinct from the Father, early Christian theology established conceptual category for understanding Christ's divine status without suggesting multiple gods. According to

---

25   Larry W. Hurtado, *One God, One Lord: Early Christian Devotion and Ancient Jewish Monotheism*, 3rd ed. (London: T&T Clark, 2015), 87.

26   Justin Martyr, *Dialogue with Trypho*, 56, in Ante-Nicene Fathers, vol. 1, 223.

27   Charles A. Gieschen, *Angelomorphic Christology: Antecedents and Early Evidence* (Leiden: Brill, 1998), 188.

Alan Segal, "The angel of the LORD traditions provided crucial biblical precedent for explaining how Christ could be simultaneously divine yet distinct from the Father, allowing genuine divine worship without compromising monotheistic commitment."[28]

The angel tradition particularly supported christological understanding of Christ's mediatorial role. Hebrews presents Christ as superior to angels while fulfilling mediatorial functions previously attributed to angelic beings, particularly delivering divine revelation: "Long ago God spoke to our ancestors in many and various ways by the prophets, but in these last days he has spoken to us by a Son" (Hebrews 1:1-2). According to Harold Attridge, "This salvation-historical framework establishes Christ as fulfillment rather than contradiction of previous mediatorial traditions, creating theological continuity while acknowledging incarnation's unprecedented nature."[29]

The angel christology provided theological vocabulary for explaining Christ's pre-existence without requiring Greek philosophical categories potentially foreign to biblical thought. By connecting Christ with the angel of the LORD, early Christian theology established biblical foundation for understanding Christ's activity throughout salvation history rather than beginning merely at incarnation. According to James Dunn, "This exegetical approach created salvation-historical continuity where the same divine person appears through progressive revelation culminating in incarnation, allowing genuine pre-existence within biblical rather than merely philosophical framework."[30]

However, this interpretive approach required careful theological boundaries against subordinationist tendencies that might reduce Christ to merely exalted angel. Various Christian movements including Arianism

---

28   Alan F. Segal, *Two Powers in Heaven: Early Rabbinic Reports about Christianity and Gnosticism,* 208.

29   Harold W. Attridge, *The Epistle to the Hebrews,* Hermeneia (Philadelphia: Fortress Press, 1989), 49.

30   James D.G. Dunn, *Christology in the Making: A New Testament Inquiry into the Origins of the Doctrine of the Incarnation,* 2nd ed. (Grand Rapids: Eerdmans, 1996), 155.

potentially utilized angel christology to suggest Christ's created status, prompting orthodox theologians to emphasize qualitative distinction between Christ and created angels. According to Darrell Hannah, "The Council of Nicaea's 'begotten not made' formulation directly addressed potential misuse of angel christology, establishing clear ontological distinction between Christ and creatures while maintaining Christ's genuine mediatorial function."[31]

This theological tension produced increasingly sophisticated christological formulations distinguishing Christ's unique status from both created angels and the Father. According to Charles Gieschen, "Patristic christology progressively refined understanding of Christ as uncreated divine Word who genuinely manifests through Old Testament theophanies while transcending merely angelic status, creating coherent theological framework connecting biblical angel traditions with trinitarian doctrine."[32]

Modern theological engagement with angel christology typically emphasizes incarnation's unprecedented nature while maintaining conceptual continuity with previous divine self-disclosure. Karl Barth maintained christological connection while emphasizing qualitative difference: "The Old Testament knows nothing of an Incarnation of God... yet we may say that in these representations... there is a prefiguration of what happens definitively in Jesus Christ."[33] This approach, according to Kevin Vanhoozer, "recognizes genuine theological continuity while maintaining incarnation's uniqueness, creating hermeneutical framework where earlier divine manifestations find fulfillment rather than contradiction through incarnation."[34]

---

31   Darrell D. Hannah, *Michael and Christ: Michael Traditions and Angel Christology in Early Christianity,* 163.

32   Charles A. Gieschen, *Angelomorphic Christology: Antecedents and Early Evidence,* 190.

33   Karl Barth, *Church Dogmatics,* ed. G.W. Bromiley and T.F. Torrance, trans. G.W. Bromiley (Edinburgh: T&T Clark, 1936-1977), I/1, 366.

34   Kevin J. Vanhoozer, *Remythologizing Theology: Divine Action, Passion, and Authorship* (Cambridge: Cambridge University Press, 2010), 212.

The angel christology provides particularly valuable theological resource for understanding Christ's revelatory significance. By establishing pattern where divine presence genuinely manifests through particular mediating agent without compromising divine unity, these traditions create conceptual foundation for incarnational theology's central claim that God becomes genuinely present in Christ without ceasing to be transcendent God. According to Thomas Torrance, "The angel of the LORD narratives establish theological paradigm where divine self-disclosure occurs through particular agent who genuinely embodies divine presence while maintaining distinction, creating biblical vocabulary for understanding incarnation as revelation-in-relationship rather than merely divine information."[35]

This revelatory framework transforms understanding of both Old Testament theophanies and incarnation itself. Rather than presenting Christ as radical theological innovation disconnected from previous divine self-disclosure, angel christology establishes incarnation as fulfillment of God's consistent self-revealing character. According to N.T. Wright, "This interpretive continuity presents God as fundamentally self-revealing throughout salvation history rather than remote deity who becomes accessible only through incarnation, creating theological synthesis where incarnation represents supreme expression of God's consistent communicative nature."[36]

Modern Scholarly Perspectives

Contemporary biblical scholarship has developed diverse approaches to the angel of the LORD traditions, reflecting various methodological frameworks and interpretive concerns. These modern perspectives demonstrate both continuing fascination with this enigmatic figure and developing exegetical sophistication in addressing the textual complexities.

---

35   Thomas F. Torrance, *The Christian Doctrine of God: One Being Three Persons* (Edinburgh: T&T Clark, 1996), 95.
36   N.T. Wright, *The New Testament and the People of God* (Minneapolis: Fortress Press, 1992), 259.

Historical-critical approaches typically emphasize diachronic development, suggesting these traditions reflect historical theological evolution rather than consistent conceptual presentation. According to James Kugel, "The textual ambiguities likely represent historical development where earlier direct theophany traditions were modified to include angelic mediation, reflecting evolving theological refinement regarding divine manifestation."[37] This developmental perspective identifies the angel as transitional theological concept mediating between earlier anthropomorphic divine appearances and later emphasis on divine transcendence.

Some scholars propose redactional explanation where different textual layers reflect distinct theological perspectives. According to David Carr, "The tensions between angel as divine messenger and angel as divine manifestation potentially represent different redactional strata, with earlier anthropomorphic traditions subsequently modified to introduce mediating figure while maintaining narrative continuity."[38] This approach explains textual ambiguity through literary historical development rather than theological intention.

Comparative religious approaches examine ancient Near Eastern parallels providing potential contextual background for biblical angel traditions. Mesopotamian concepts including *vuzinu* (divine image) and *salmu* (divine representation) present divine presence manifesting through particular physical form while maintaining divine transcendence. Egyptian religion similarly distinguished between divine *ka* (life force) and *ba* (soul) that could manifest separately from the deity's essential nature. According to Mark Smith, "These conceptual parallels suggest broader ancient Near Eastern theological framework for understanding divine manifestation through particular representation while maintaining divine transcendence, providing cultural context for biblical angel traditions."[39]

---

37   James L. Kugel, *The God of Old: Inside the Lost World of the Bible*, 36.
38   David M. Carr, *Reading the Fractures of Genesis: Historical and Literary Approaches* (Louisville: Westminster John Knox, 1996), 194.
39   Mark S. Smith, *The Origins of Biblical Monotheism: Israel's Polytheistic Background and the Ugaritic Texts* (Oxford: Oxford University Press, 2001), 54.

Some scholars emphasize literary-narrative function, suggesting the angel's ambiguous presentation serves specific storytelling purposes. According to Robert Alter, "The narrative ambiguity creates deliberate theological tension within the text, forcing readers to engage interpretive questions regarding divine presence and representation rather than providing simplistic theological answers."[40] This approach views textual complexity as intentional literary strategy rather than confusion or historical development.

Social-scientific approaches examine how angel traditions functioned within Israel's developing religious identity. According to Susan Niditch, "The angel mediator potentially provided theological resource for maintaining divine accessibility during periods of institutional disruption, particularly exile, when traditional sacred spaces became unavailable."[41] This functional perspective interprets angel traditions as theological adaptation to changing social circumstances rather than merely abstract theological concept.

Some scholars emphasize canonical-theological reading, examining how these traditions function within canonical context regardless of historical development. According to Brevard Childs, "The canonical presentation establishes theological dialectic between divine transcendence and divine accessibility, creating framework for understanding divine self-disclosure that maintains both divine freedom and genuine divine communication."[42] This approach prioritizes final textual form's theological function over hypothetical developmental reconstruction.

Jewish scholarly perspectives typically emphasize the angel as legitimate divine representative while maintaining ontological distinction from God proper. According to Benjamin Sommer, "These traditions demonstrate biblical comfort with divine self-manifestation through particular forms

---

40   Robert Alter, *The Art of Biblical Narrative,* rev. ed. (New York: Basic Books, 2011), 124.

41   Susan Niditch, *Ancient Israelite Religion* (Oxford: Oxford University Press, 1997), 84.

42   Brevard S. Childs, *Introduction to the Old Testament as Scripture* (Philadelphia: Fortress Press, 1979), 132.

without compromising divine unity, establishing theological category where divine presence genuinely appears while transcending any particular manifestation."[43] This interpretive approach maintains traditional Jewish emphasis on divine unity while acknowledging biblical theophanic complexity.

Christian scholarly perspectives increasingly recognize christological interpretation as theological rather than strictly exegetical approach, distinguishing between historical meaning and theological significance. According to Walter Moberly, "While christological readings appropriately connect these traditions with incarnational theology within Christian canonical context, responsible interpretation acknowledges this represents theological development beyond original textual meaning."[44] This nuanced approach respects historical meaning while affirming legitimate theological development within interpretive traditions.

Philosophical hermeneutical approaches emphasize how angel traditions address fundamental theological questions regarding representation and presence. According to Jean-Louis Chrétien, "These narratives engage philosophical problems of mediation and immediacy, presence and distance, representing theological response to fundamental phenomenological questions regarding divine accessibility."[45] This approach connects biblical angel traditions with broader philosophical discourse about representation and presence beyond specifically religious contexts.

These diverse scholarly perspectives collectively demonstrate the angel of the LORD traditions' continuing theological significance. According to Wesley Hill, "The persistent interpretive fascination with these texts reflects recognition that they address fundamental theological questions regarding divine self-disclosure that remain significant across diverse interpretive

---

43   Benjamin D. Sommer, *The Bodies of God and the World of Ancient Israel*, 42.

44   R.W.L. Moberly, *The Bible, Theology, and Faith: A Study of Abraham and Jesus* (Cambridge: Cambridge University Press, 2000), 105.

45   Jean-Louis Chrétien, *The Ark of Speech*, trans. Andrew Brown (London: Routledge, 2004), 47.

frameworks and religious traditions."[46] This ongoing engagement suggests these traditions provide particularly valuable theological resources for contemporary religious thought regarding divine presence and mediation.

Modern scholarship increasingly recognizes legitimate plurality of interpretive approaches rather than seeking single definitive explanation. According to R. Kendall Soulen, "The angel of the LORD traditions invite continuing interpretive engagement precisely because they resist reduction to single conceptual solution, maintaining theological tension between divine presence and divine transcendence that remains fundamentally significant for religious understanding."[47] This interpretive openness allows these traditions to function as ongoing theological resource rather than merely historical religious phenomenon.

---

46   Wesley A. Hill, *Paul and the Trinity: Persons, Relations, and the Pauline Letters* (Grand Rapids: Eerdmans, 2015), 32.
47   R. Kendall Soulen, *The Divine Name(s) and the Holy Trinity, Volume 1: Distinguishing the Voices*, 184.

Chapter 14

Divine Presence and Absence

The dialectic of divine presence and absence represents one of the most profound theological tensions in biblical literature. Throughout the biblical canon, divine manifestations are counterbalanced by experiences of divine hiddenness, creating a complex theological framework that resists simplistic resolution. This chapter examines the various modes of divine presence depicted in biblical texts, the role of intermediary figures in mediating that presence, the theological significance of divine hiddenness, and the implications of this dialectic for spiritual formation. As Samuel Terrien aptly observes, "The elusive presence of God constitutes the central theological problem of the entire Bible."[1]

Modes of Divine Presence

Biblical literature presents divine presence through multiple modalities, each contributing to a nuanced understanding of how the transcendent God becomes accessible to human experience.

Physical Manifestations

The most direct mode of divine presence appears in anthropomorphic theophanies, where God takes on human-like form. Genesis provides several examples: God walks in the garden (Gen 3:8), visits Abraham at Mamre (Gen 18:1-15), and wrestles with Jacob at Peniel (Gen 32:22-32). These narratives present divine presence in remarkably concrete terms, though often with elements that signal divine otherness.

Benjamin Sommer argues that these anthropomorphic appearances reflect an ancient "embodiment theology" wherein "the biblical God has a body, which is not a metaphor but an actual body, with discrete form...

---

1   Samuel Terrien, *The Elusive Presence: Toward a New Biblical Theology* (San Francisco: Harper & Row, 1978), 1.

and yet is nonetheless different from all other bodies."[2] This corporeality of divine presence challenges both traditional philosophical notions of divine incorporeality and contemporary tendencies to demythologize biblical anthropomorphism.

Symbolic Loci of Presence

Beyond anthropomorphic appearances, biblical texts identify specific symbols and locations where divine presence dwells with particular intensity:

1. **The Ark of the Covenant**: Described as the footstool of God and the location "from between the cherubim" where God would speak (Exod 25:22), the Ark represented mobile divine presence. As Menahem Haran notes, "The Ark functioned not merely as a symbol of divine presence but as its actual locus—the place where YHWH's presence 'condensed' for interaction with the human realm."[3]

2. **Tabernacle/Temple**: The mishkan (tabernacle) is explicitly designated as the place where God will "dwell among" the Israelites (Exod 25:8), with the Hebrew root (שכן/shkn) emphasizing the concept of divine indwelling. This presence is later transferred to the Jerusalem temple, which Solomon acknowledges cannot "contain" God yet serves as the focal point of divine-human communion (1 Kgs 8:27-30).

3. **Divine Glory** (kavod YHWH): The visible manifestation of divine presence, typically described as radiant light or fire, appears at pivotal moments in Israel's history: at Sinai (Exod 24:16-17), filling the tabernacle (Exod 40:34-35), and the temple (1 Kgs 8:10-11). Walther Eichrodt describes the kavod

---

2   Benjamin D. Sommer, *The Bodies of God and the World of Ancient Israel* (Cambridge: Cambridge University Press, 2009), 1-2.

3   Menahem Haran, *Temples and Temple-Service in Ancient Israel: An Inquiry into Biblical Cult Phenomena and the Historical Setting of the Priestly School* (Winona Lake, IN: Eisenbrauns, 1985), 246.

as "a mode of revelation in which God's holiness is transmuted into a form accessible to human perception."[4]

4. **Divine Name**: Deuteronomic theology develops the concept of the divine name (שם/shem) as the mode of God's presence in the sanctuary. Rather than God physically dwelling in the temple, God causes the divine name to dwell there (Deut 12:5, 11; 14:23). Sandra Richter suggests this represents "a theological adaptation preserving divine transcendence while maintaining the reality of divine presence in cultic contexts."[5]

5. **Divine Face** (panim): Moses' request to see God's glory results in the partial revelation of God's "back" but not God's "face" (Exod 33:18-23), establishing the face as the most direct mode of divine presence. The priestly blessing invokes God's face shining upon and being lifted toward the people (Num 6:25-26), while the Psalms repeatedly express longing to "seek" and "behold" God's face (Ps 24:6; 27:8-9).

Mediated Presence

Biblical texts also present divine presence as mediated through various phenomena:

1. **Natural Elements**: Divine presence manifests through fire (Exod 3:2-4; 19:18), clouds (Exod 13:21-22; 40:34-38), wind/spirit (1 Kgs 19:11-13), and thunder/lightning (Exod 19:16; Ps 18:7-15), though the texts typically distinguish God from these elements.

2. **Divine Spirit**: The ruach YHWH (spirit/breath of God) represents divine presence extending into creation and human experience. This presence empowers leaders (Judg 3:10; 6:34),

---

4   Walther Eichrodt, *Theology of the Old Testament,* vol. 2, trans. J.A. Baker (Philadelphia: Westminster Press, 1967), 30-31.

5   Sandra L. Richter, *The Deuteronomistic History and the Name Theology: "leškēn šemô šām" in the Bible and the Ancient Near East* (Berlin: Walter de Gruyter, 2002), 95.

inspires prophets (Ezek 2:2; 11:5), and sustains all life (Ps 104:29-30). John Levison observes that "the spirit represents divine presence that penetrates human interiority, creating a genuine indwelling of God within the human person."[6]

3. **Divine Word**: God's dabar (word) functions as an extension of divine presence that actively accomplishes divine purposes (Isa 55:10-11). The prologue to John's Gospel develops this concept by identifying the divine Word (Logos) as both "with God" and divine itself (John 1:1), ultimately becoming incarnate (John 1:14).

4. **Dreams and Visions**: Throughout scripture, divine presence is mediated through dreams (Gen 28:10-17; 1 Kgs 3:5-15) and visionary experiences (Isa 6:1-13; Ezek 1:4-28), creating a mode of divine-human encounter that transcends normal sensory perception.

Covenantal and Communal Presence

Beyond localized manifestations, biblical theology develops the concept of divine presence extended through covenant relationship and within the faith community:

1. **Covenantal Formula**: The recurring promise "I will be your God, and you will be my people" (Lev 26:12; Jer 30:22; Ezek 36:28) establishes divine presence through mutual relationship rather than merely physical manifestation.

2. **Presence with Individuals**: Numerous biblical figures are described as having God "with them" (Gen 21:22; 39:2; Judg 6:12), suggesting divine presence manifested through guidance, blessing, and protection.

3. **Community as Divine Dwelling**: Later biblical and rabbinic traditions develop the concept of the Shekinah (divine presence) dwelling among the people, particularly when they gather for prayer, study, or justice (m. Avot 3:2; Matt 18:20).

---

6   John R. Levison, *Filled with the Spirit* (Grand Rapids: Eerdmans, 2009), 25.

Samuel Balentine notes that these varied modes of divine presence create "an intentional theological dialectic—God is both manifest and hidden, dwelling in particular locations yet transcending spatial limitations, revealing himself through physical forms while remaining fundamentally other."[7]

Intermediary Figures

The tension between divine transcendence and immanence generates various intermediary figures who mediate divine presence while preserving divine otherness.

Angels as Mediators

Angels function as the primary mediators of divine presence throughout biblical literature. The term מַלְאָךְ (*mal'akh*/messenger) designates beings who bridge the divine-human divide:

1. **Messengers**: Angels frequently deliver divine communications (Gen 16:7-12; Judg 13:3-5; Luke 1:26-38; Rev 1:1), embodying divine authority while preserving divine transcendence.

2. **Manifestations of Presence**: Angels sometimes appear to represent divine presence itself, speaking in the first person as God (Gen 16:10; 22:11-12; Exod 3:2-6). This phenomenon raises the theological question of whether such angelic appearances constitute direct divine presence or mediated presence.

3. **Guardians of Divine Space**: Angels mark the boundaries between divine and human spheres (Gen 3:24; Exod 25:18-22; Rev 4:6-8), simultaneously signaling divine presence and its inaccessibility.

Michael Heiser suggests that "the biblical concept of angels developed in part as a theological solution to the problem of divine presence—allowing

---

7   Samuel E. Balentine, *The Hidden God: The Hiding of the Face of God in the Old Testament* (Oxford: Oxford University Press, 1983), 175.

God to interact with the created order while maintaining appropriate ontological distinction."[8]

The Angel of the Lord

The enigmatic "Angel of the Lord" (מלאך יהוה/mal'akh YHWH) represents a special category of intermediary, appearing throughout the Hebrew Bible with remarkable theological ambiguity. This figure simultaneously exhibits distinction from YHWH (being sent by God) and identification with YHWH (speaking as God and receiving worship).

Key appearances include:

- Hagar's encounter in the wilderness (Gen 16:7-14)
- Abraham's near-sacrifice of Isaac (Gen 22:11-18)
- Jacob's blessing of Joseph's sons (Gen 48:15-16)
- Moses at the burning bush (Exod 3:2-6)
- Balaam's confrontation (Num 22:22-35)
- Gideon's commissioning (Judg 6:11-24)
- Samson's parents (Judg 13:3-23)

Stephen Gero identifies three main interpretive approaches to this figure: "(1) the identification theory, seeing the Angel as a manifestation of YHWH himself; (2) the representation theory, viewing the Angel as distinct from but authorized to speak for YHWH; and (3) the interpolation theory, suggesting that references to the Angel represent later theological modifications of direct theophanic accounts."[9]

Jewish interpretation typically emphasized the representation theory, developing concepts like the Metatron in later mystical traditions. Early Christian interpretation tended toward identification, often seeing the Angel of the Lord as pre-incarnate appearances of Christ, though contemporary scholarship is more cautious about such direct Christological identifications.

---

8   Michael S. Heiser, *The Unseen Realm: Recovering the Supernatural Worldview of the Bible* (Bellingham, WA: Lexham Press, 2015), 36.

9   Stephen Gero, *"The Spirit as a Dove at the Baptism of Jesus,"* Novum Testamentum 18, no. 1 (1976): 24.

Wisdom as Divine Mediator

Wisdom literature personifies divine Wisdom (המכח/hokmah) as a mediating figure between God and creation:

1. **Proverbs**: Wisdom appears as a feminine figure present with God at creation who calls humanity to relationship (Prov 1:20-33; 8:1-36), offering herself as the path to knowledge of God.

2. **Sirach**: Wisdom is identified with Torah and described as taking up residence in Jerusalem (Sir 24:1-23), connecting divine presence to both instruction and location.

3. **Wisdom of Solomon**: Wisdom is portrayed as "a pure emanation of the glory of the Almighty" and "a reflection of eternal light" (Wis 7:25-26), language that would influence later Christological and pneumatological formulations.

Roland Murphy observes that "personified Wisdom represents divine immanence within the created order—God's presence and activity made accessible through a mediating figure that is neither fully identified with nor completely separate from God."[10]

Divine Attributes as Mediators

Various divine attributes function as personified mediators of divine presence in biblical and post-biblical Jewish literature:

1. **Word** (Memra): Targum traditions render anthropomorphic descriptions of God with the circumlocution "the Word (Memra) of the Lord," creating a linguistic buffer between divine transcendence and immanence.

2. **Glory** (Kavod): Ezekiel's visions distinguish between the human-like figure on the throne and the surrounding radiance (Ezek 1:26-28), potentially separating God's essence from God's perceptible glory.

---

10   Roland E. Murphy, *The Tree of Life: An Exploration of Biblical Wisdom Literature,* 3rd ed. (Grand Rapids: Eerdmans, 2002), 148.

3. **Spirit** (Ruach): The divine Spirit increasingly takes on personal characteristics in later biblical texts (Isa 63:10-14; Ps 51:11), functioning as the mode of divine presence especially in prophetic inspiration.

4. **Name** (Shem): The divine Name develops from a mode of presence to a hypostasis in some Second Temple traditions, particularly in magical and mystical contexts.

Daniel Boyarin suggests that these hypostatic mediators reveal "a fundamental tension within monotheistic theology—the need to conceptualize God as simultaneously transcendent and immanent generates intermediary figures who paradoxically both protect and compromise strict monotheism."[11]

Hidden and Revealed God

The biblical tension between divine presence and absence creates a profound dialectic of revelation and concealment that shapes theological reflection throughout the canon.

Divine Hiddenness in Hebrew Scripture

Various Hebrew Bible traditions acknowledge and grapple with divine hiddenness:

1. **Sinai Theophany**: Even in this paradigmatic revelation, God remains partially concealed in "thick darkness" (Exod 20:21), establishing a pattern of simultaneous disclosure and concealment.

2. **Moses' Limited Vision**: God's declaration that no one can see the divine face and live, followed by the partial revelation of God's "back" (Exod 33:20-23), establishes the principle that divine revelation always remains partial.

---

11   Daniel Boyarin, *Border Lines: The Partition of Judaeo-Christianity* (Philadelphia: University of Pennsylvania Press, 2004), 112.

3. **Prophetic Lament**: The prophets frequently express anguish over divine absence or hiddenness, particularly in times of national crisis (Isa 45:15; 57:17; 64:7; Ezek 39:23-24).

4. **Psalmic Expressions**: The Psalms contain numerous laments over God's perceived absence (Ps 10:1; 13:1-2; 22:1-2; 44:24; 88:14), creating a liturgical framework for expressing the experience of divine hiddenness.

5. **Wisdom Tradition**: Ecclesiastes and Job particularly wrestle with divine inscrutability, questioning human capacity to comprehend divine purposes or presence (Job 23:8-9; Eccl 8:17).

Samuel Balentine observes that "biblical faith does not deny or minimize the reality of divine hiddenness but rather incorporates it as an essential aspect of authentic relationship with God."[12]

Theological Patterns of Hiddenness

Biblical texts present several theological patterns for understanding divine hiddenness:

1. **Hiddenness as Judgment**: Prophetic traditions often interpret divine absence as divine judgment for covenant unfaithfulness (Deut 31:17-18; Isa 59:2; Mic 3:4), suggesting that broken relationship results in withdrawn presence.

2. **Hiddenness as Protection**: Moses' limited vision (Exod 33:20-23) and Isaiah's temple vision (Isa 6:5) suggest that divine hiddenness protects humans from a presence they cannot fully endure.

3. **Hiddenness as Epistemological Limitation**: Wisdom traditions emphasize the limits of human knowledge in comprehending divine reality (Job 38-41; Eccl 3:11; 8:17), framing divine hiddenness in terms of ontological difference.

---

12   Balentine, *The Hidden God*, 164.

4. **Hiddenness as Pedagogical Strategy**: The Song of Songs portrays the beloved's occasional disappearance as intensifying desire and search (Song 3:1-4; 5:2-8), suggesting divine hiddenness may function to deepen human longing for God.

Theologian Eberhard Jüngel suggests that "divine hiddenness does not contradict divine revelation but rather constitutes its essential counterpart— God reveals precisely as the one who cannot be fully comprehended."[13]

Divine Hiddenness in New Testament

New Testament texts continue to wrestle with the dialectic of divine presence and absence:

1. **Jesus' Cry of Dereliction**: Jesus' quotation of Psalm 22:1 from the cross—"My God, my God, why have you forsaken me?" (Mark 15:34; Matt 27:46)—represents the paradigmatic expression of divine absence within Christian tradition.

2. **Post-Resurrection Absence**: The ascension creates a new theological situation of Christ's simultaneous presence through Spirit and absence in bodily form (John 16:7; Acts 1:9-11), establishing the church between the times of presence.

3. **Pauline "Now/Not Yet"**: Paul's eschatological framework acknowledges the tension between present experience of God "in part" and future knowledge "face to face" (1 Cor 13:12), placing Christian existence within this dialectic.

4. **Johannine Absence/Presence**: John's Gospel presents Jesus as simultaneously departing and coming to his disciples through the Paraclete (John 14:15-29), creating a complex theological account of mediated presence.

5. **Apocalyptic Unveiling**: Revelation's vision of the New Jerusalem, where "the dwelling of God is with mortals" (Rev

---

13   Eberhard Jüngel, *God as the Mystery of the World: On the Foundation of the Theology of the Crucified One in the Dispute between Theism and Atheism*, trans. Darrell L. Guder (Grand Rapids: Eerdmans, 1983), 227.

21:3), represents the eschatological resolution of the presence/absence dialectic.

Rowan Williams observes that "Christianity does not eliminate divine hiddenness but reconfigures it christologically—God is most fully revealed precisely in the moment of greatest apparent absence, the cross."[14]

Deus Absconditus/Deus Revelatus

The theological tradition has formalized this biblical dialectic through the paired concepts of Deus absconditus (the hidden God) and Deus revelatus (the revealed God):

1. **Patristic Formulations**: Early church fathers like Gregory of Nyssa developed the concept of divine darkness (γνόφος/gnophos) as a higher mode of divine presence beyond sensory or conceptual comprehension.[15]

2. **Medieval Mysticism**: The apophatic tradition, exemplified by Pseudo-Dionysius and later developed by figures like Meister Eckhart, embraced divine hiddenness as the pathway to authentic encounter with God beyond limiting concepts.

3. **Reformation Thought**: Luther particularly emphasized the dialectic of the hidden and revealed God, insisting that God is reliably encountered only through the cross, which paradoxically reveals God through apparent abandonment.

4. **Modern Articulations**: Karl Barth's dialectical theology and Jewish thinkers like Martin Buber and Emmanuel Levinas have continued to explore the theological significance of divine presence that never fully surrenders its transcendent hiddenness.

Contemporary theologian Terence Fretheim suggests that "biblical faith does not seek to resolve the tension between divine presence and absence but rather to inhabit it faithfully—recognizing both the genuine

---

14   Rowan Williams, *Christ on Trial: How the Gospel Unsettles Our Judgment* (Grand Rapids: Eerdmans, 2000), 87.

15   Gregory of Nyssa, *The Life of Moses*, II.162-169.

encounters with divine presence and the equally genuine experiences of divine hiddenness as essential elements of relationship with God."[16]

Implications for Spiritual Formation

The biblical dialectic of divine presence and absence has profound implications for spiritual formation, shaping how faith communities understand and practice communion with God.

Liturgical Expressions

Religious rituals across traditions reflect the dialectic of divine presence and absence:

1. **Sacramental Theology**: Christian sacramental theology articulates how material elements mediate divine presence while maintaining appropriate distinction, with Eucharistic controversies often centering on how to understand divine presence in the elements.

2. **Sacred Space**: Architectural and ritual distinctions between sacred and profane space—from the biblical Holy of Holies to contemporary sanctuary design—reflect the theological principle that divine presence is both localized and transcendent.

3. **Prayer Practices**: Liturgical prayers often move between expressions of divine presence ("The Lord be with you") and acknowledgment of divine transcendence ("who art in heaven"), creating a dialectical rhythm that shapes spiritual consciousness.

4. **Seasons of Presence/Absence**: Liturgical calendars incorporate seasons of both celebration (divine presence) and waiting/absence (Advent, Lent), training communities in the rhythm of presence and absence that characterizes spiritual experience.

---

16   Terence E. Fretheim, *The Suffering of God: An Old Testament Perspective* (Philadelphia: Fortress Press, 1984), 137.

Nathan Mitchell suggests that "effective liturgy does not deny the human experience of divine absence but rather creates ritual containers for honestly expressing and faithfully enduring it."[17]

Spiritual Practices

Spiritual practices across traditions engage the dialectic of divine presence and absence:

1. **Contemplative Silence**: Contemplative traditions across religions value silence as the appropriate response to divine mystery that transcends language, embodying the paradox that God is encountered beyond both presence and absence.

2. **Lament and Praise**: The biblical tradition of moving between lament over divine absence and praise for divine presence establishes an emotional range that resists both despair and presumption.

3. **Spiritual Direction**: The practice of spiritual direction often involves helping individuals interpret experiences of both divine presence and absence as potentially meaningful aspects of the spiritual journey.

4. **Desert/Wilderness Spirituality**: From the biblical wilderness narratives to monastic desert traditions, withdrawal into spaces of apparent divine absence has paradoxically become a privileged location for divine encounter.

Barbara Brown Taylor's exploration of "learning to walk in the dark" articulates how "divine absence itself becomes a mode of presence when embraced as part of the spiritual journey rather than rejected as its failure."[18]

---

17   Nathan D. Mitchell, *Meeting Mystery: Liturgy, Worship, Sacraments* (Maryknoll, NY: Orbis Books, 2006), 62.
18   Barbara Brown Taylor, *Learning to Walk in the Dark* (New York: HarperOne, 2014), 15.

Dark Night Traditions

The "dark night" tradition developed by John of the Cross provides a comprehensive framework for understanding divine absence as a purifying stage in spiritual development:

1. Night of Sense: The withdrawal of sensible consolations in prayer represents the beginning of purification from attachment to particular experiences of God.

2. Night of Spirit: The deeper experience of divine absence purifies the will and intellect from conceptual idolatry, creating space for union beyond understanding.

3. Transformative Darkness: The experience of absence ultimately transforms the relationship with God from one based on particular experiences to one founded in naked faith.

Constance FitzGerald observes that "the dark night tradition represents the most developed theological framework for understanding how divine absence itself functions as a mode of presence—not as punishment or abandonment but as invitation to deeper union."[19]

Faith in Absence

Contemporary theological reflection has emphasized how faith specifically operates in the context of experienced divine absence:

1. Bonhoeffer's "World Come of Age": Dietrich Bonhoeffer's prison writings explore how God's absence from the world of human problem-solving creates space for authentic human responsibility and mature faith.

2. Moltmann's Theology of Hope: Jürgen Moltmann's framework interprets divine absence as creating the eschatological tension that generates authentic hope for future divine presence.

3. Weil's "Waiting on God": Simone Weil's concept of "waiting

---

19   Constance FitzGerald, "From Impasse to Prophetic Hope: Crisis of Memory," *Proceedings of the Catholic Theological Society of America 64* (2009): 24.

on God" in the void of divine absence offers a contemplative practice that neither denies absence nor despairs of presence.

4. Spiritual Formation in Secular Age: Charles Taylor's analysis of the "secular age" suggests that the experience of divine absence has become the default backdrop for faith, requiring more intentional practices of discerning divine presence.

Michael Plekon suggests that "mature faith embraces the dialectic of presence and absence rather than seeking to resolve it prematurely— recognizing both experiences as essential to the relationship between transcendent God and finite humanity."[20]

Conclusion

The biblical dialectic of divine presence and absence creates a theological framework that resists simplistic resolution. Throughout scripture, divine self-disclosure appears alongside divine hiddenness, creating a complex pattern that acknowledges both the reality of divine-human communion and its inherent limitations. This tension generates various modes of mediated presence, from cultic objects and sacred spaces to intermediary figures and hypostatic attributes, all attempting to navigate the paradox of a God who is simultaneously revealed and concealed.

Rather than resolving this tension, biblical faith embraces it as constitutive of authentic relationship with God. The dialectic of presence and absence shapes liturgical practices, spiritual disciplines, and theological reflection across traditions, inviting faith communities to dwell faithfully within the tension rather than collapsing it toward either pure transcendence or unmediated immanence.

As contemporary theologian Sarah Coakley observes, "The enduring significance of the biblical witness lies precisely in its refusal to deny either divine presence or divine absence, instead creating a theological vision capacious enough to embrace both as essential dimensions of the God who is neither exhausted by revelation nor completely hidden, but rather

---

20   Michael Plekon, *Hidden Holiness* (Notre Dame, IN: University of Notre Dame Press, 2009), 43.

continually drawing humanity into the transformative tension between revealing and concealing."[21]

---

21   Sarah Coakley, *God, Sexuality, and the Self: An Essay 'On the Trinity'* (Cambridge: Cambridge University Press, 2013), 309.

Chapter 15

Interpretive Challenges

The study of angelophanies and theophanies presents numerous hermeneutical difficulties that have challenged interpreters across centuries and traditions. This chapter examines four primary interpretive challenges: distinguishing between angels and theophanies, understanding anthropomorphism and divine appearance, differentiating between visionary and physical manifestations, and translating these phenomena across cultural contexts. As James Barr aptly observes, "The interpretation of divine manifestation narratives involves not merely exegesis of individual texts but engagement with fundamental theological questions concerning divine transcendence, immanence, and communication."[1] These interpretive challenges reflect broader tensions within biblical theology—between divine transcendence and immanence, between historical particularity and universal significance, and between literal and symbolic modes of understanding sacred texts.

Distinguishing Angels from Theophanies

The Terminological Ambiguity

One of the most fundamental challenges in the study of divine manifestations is determining whether a particular appearance represents an angel (as a distinct created being) or a theophany (a manifestation of God). Several factors contribute to this interpretive difficulty:

1. **Overlapping Terminology**: The Hebrew term מַלְאָךְ (mal'akh) and Greek term ἄγγελος (angelos) primarily denote function ("messenger") rather than ontology, making it difficult to determine whether "the angel of the LORD" represents a distinct being or a manifestation of YHWH himself.

---

1   James Barr, *The Semantics of Biblical Language* (Oxford: Oxford University Press, 1961), 218.

2. **Fluid Narrative Transitions**: Many biblical accounts exhibit remarkable fluidity between references to an angel and to God, often within the same narrative unit. Genesis 16:7-13 begins with "the angel of the LORD" appearing to Hagar but concludes with Hagar addressing "the LORD who spoke to her." Exodus 3:2-6 similarly shifts from "the angel of the LORD" in the burning bush to "God called to him" within a few verses.

3. **Shifting Pronominal References**: In numerous angelic encounters, pronouns shift between first and third person, with the angel sometimes speaking as a representative ("the LORD has heard your affliction," Gen 16:11) and sometimes as God directly ("I am the God of your father," Exod 3:6).

Michael Heiser notes that "this fluidity is not accidental but reflects a sophisticated theological understanding of divine presence—one that allows for God to be simultaneously transcendent and immanent through the mechanism of agency."[2]

Historical Interpretive Approaches

Various interpretive traditions have developed different approaches for distinguishing between angels and theophanies:

1. **Rabbinic Perspectives**: Rabbinic tradition typically maintained a distinction between God and created angels, often interpreting passages with fluid identity as examples of the Jewish legal principle of agency (חיל/shaliach)—"the one sent is as the one who sent him." According to Daniel Boyarin, "This principle allowed rabbis to maintain both divine transcendence and the reality of divine communication through intermediaries."[3]

2. **Patristic Christological Readings**: Early Christian interpreters frequently resolved the ambiguity by identifying "the angel of

---

2   Michael S. Heiser, *The Unseen Realm: Recovering the Supernatural Worldview of the Bible* (Bellingham, WA: Lexham Press, 2015), 42.

3   Daniel Boyarin, *Border Lines: The Partition of Judaeo-Christianity* (Philadelphia: University of Pennsylvania Press, 2004), 117.

the LORD" as pre-incarnate appearances of the Logos/Christ. Justin Martyr's Dialogue with Tryphopresents this interpretation systematically, arguing that the God who appeared to the patriarchs was not the Father but the Son, preserving divine transcendence while explaining anthropomorphic appearances.[4]

3. **Medieval Jewish Rationalism**: Maimonides and other medieval Jewish philosophers typically interpreted theophanies as either prophetic visions or angelic mediators, rejecting any literal anthropomorphism as incompatible with divine incorporeality. According to Maimonides, "Every reference to God speaking, appearing, or acting in physical ways must be understood either as a prophetic vision or as the activity of a created intermediary."[5]

4. **Reformation Perspectives**: Many Reformation theologians returned to identifying "the angel of the LORD" as a manifestation of the pre-incarnate Christ. Calvin, for instance, concluded that "the eternal Son of God, who would later become incarnate, appeared to the patriarchs as the Mediator, under the form of an angel while retaining his full divinity."[6]

5. **Modern Critical Approaches**: Contemporary historical-critical scholarship typically views the fluid identities as evidence of source compilation or redactional activity. According to R.W.L. Moberly, "The tensions between angelic and divine identities may reflect the merging of originally distinct traditions or progressive theological reflection on the nature of divine presence."[7]

---

4   Justin Martyr, *Dialogue with Trypho*, 56-60.

5   Moses Maimonides, *The Guide of the Perplexed,* trans. Shlomo Pines (Chicago: University of Chicago Press, 1963), 1:28.

6   John Calvin, *Institutes of the Christian Religion,* ed. John T. McNeill, trans. Ford Lewis Battles (Philadelphia: Westminster Press, 1960), 1.13.10.

7   R.W.L. Moberly, *The Old Testament of the Old Testament: Patriarchal Narratives and Mosaic Yahwism* (Minneapolis: Fortress Press, 1992), 97.

Contemporary Hermeneutical Frameworks

Recent scholarship has developed several frameworks for addressing this interpretive challenge:

1. **Theological Anthropology**: Benjamin Sommer suggests understanding these texts through the lens of an "embodiment theology" wherein the biblical God possesses multiple embodiments, some more directly representative of divine presence than others. In this view, "the angel of the LORD represents one form of divine embodiment, neither identical with nor entirely separate from God's fullness."[8]

2. **Divine Agency**: Scholars like Larry Hurtado propose understanding these figures through ancient concepts of principal agency, where "the agent is both identified with and distinguished from the one who sends—not through ontological identity but through representational authority."[9]

3. **Narrative Theology**: Some interpreters focus on the narrative function of ambiguity, suggesting that "the text's refusal to clearly distinguish between God and God's messenger serves a theological purpose—communicating the paradox of mediated immediacy in divine-human encounter."[10]

4. **Canonical Approaches**: Canonical readings consider how later biblical texts interpret earlier manifestations. For example, Exodus 23:20-23 emphasizes both the distinction of the "angel" who will guide Israel and the presence of God's "name" within this figure, suggesting a theological framework for understanding mediated divine presence.

---

8   Benjamin D. Sommer, *The Bodies of God and the World of Ancient Israel* (Cambridge: Cambridge University Press, 2009), 40.

9   Larry W. Hurtado, *One God, One Lord: Early Christian Devotion and Ancient Jewish Monotheism,* 2nd ed. (Edinburgh: T&T Clark, 1998), 21.

10   Carol A. Newsom, "Angels," in *The Anchor Bible Dictionary,* ed. David Noel Freedman (New York: Doubleday, 1992), 1:251.

Carol Newsom suggests that "rather than attempting to resolve the ambiguity definitively, interpreters should recognize that the text's fluidity itself communicates something essential about divine presence—namely, that God is encountered through mediation that never entirely eliminates the mystery of divine transcendence."[11]

Anthropomorphism and Divine Appearance

A second major interpretive challenge concerns the significance of anthropomorphic descriptions of God in theophanic accounts and their relationship to ontological claims about divine nature.

Varieties of Biblical Anthropomorphism

Biblical texts present divine anthropomorphism in various forms and degrees:

1. **Physical Anthropomorphism**: Some texts describe God with explicitly human physical features—walking in the garden (Gen 3:8), having a face, back, and hands (Exod 33:20-23), appearing as a man (Gen 18:1-2; 32:24-30).

2. **Emotional Anthropomorphism**: Divine emotions are frequently described in human terms—God experiences regret (Gen 6:6), jealousy (Exod 20:5), anger (Num 11:1), and compassion (Exod 34:6).

3. **Cognitive Anthropomorphism**: Texts attribute human cognitive processes to God—remembering (Gen 8:1), changing his mind (Exod 32:14), testing (Gen 22:1), and not knowing outcomes until they occur (Gen 22:12).

4. **Social Anthropomorphism**: God is portrayed engaging in human social activities—walking, talking, eating meals (Gen 18:1-8), and entering into covenantal relationships.

5. **Metaphorical Anthropomorphism**: Many texts use clearly figurative human imagery for God—rock, fortress, shield,

---

11   Newsom, *"Angels,"* 1:252.

father, judge, king, shepherd—without implying literal physical resemblance.

Interpretive Traditions

Various traditions have developed different approaches to anthropomorphic theophanies:

1. **Literal Interpretations**: Some early interpreters and traditions took anthropomorphic descriptions at face value. Certain strands of rabbinic tradition, particularly those reflected in the Shi'ur Qomah texts, developed elaborate descriptions of God's cosmic body based on biblical anthropomorphisms.[12]

2. **Allegorical Reading**: Philo of Alexandria systematically reinterpreted anthropomorphic theophanies as allegorical expressions of philosophical truths, arguing that "God cannot literally have a human form but is described anthropomorphically to accommodate human understanding."[13]

3. **Accommodation Theory**: Calvin and other Reformed theologians developed the concept of divine accommodation, wherein "God adapts self-revelation to human cognitive limitations without compromising divine transcendence."[14] As Calvin famously stated, God "lisps with us as nurses are accustomed to do with little children."

4. **Form-Critical Approaches**: Modern form criticism typically explains anthropomorphic theophanies as reflecting earlier, more primitive stages of religious development or as literary conventions for expressing divine activity in accessible terms.

5. **Canonical-Literary Approaches**: Some contemporary approaches focus on the literary and theological function of anthropomorphism within the canonical context rather than its historical development or philosophical implications.

---

12   See discussion in Sommer, *The Bodies of God*, 79-83.
13   Philo of Alexandria, *On the Confusion of Tongues*, 27.134-28.146.
14   Calvin, *Institutes*, 1.13.1.

Theological Implications

The interpretation of anthropomorphic theophanies raises profound theological questions:

1. **Imago Dei and Divine Form**: Genesis 1:26-27 suggests humans are made in God's "image" and "likeness," raising the possibility of genuine correspondence between divine and human form. As Wolfhart Pannenberg asks, "Does the imago Dei imply that anthropomorphic language about God contains a kernel of ontological truth rather than mere accommodation?"[15]

2. **Incarnational Theology**: Christian theology affirms God's assumption of human form in Christ, potentially lending retrospective significance to earlier anthropomorphic theophanies. Karl Barth suggests that "all divine self-disclosure occurs with reference to the incarnation, whether prospectively or retrospectively."[16]

3. **Divine Freedom vs. Nature**: The very possibility of theophany raises questions about divine nature. Katherine Sonderegger observes that "if God cannot appear in created form, this would seem to limit divine freedom; yet if God can appear in any form, this seems to render divine nature indeterminate."[17]

4. **Revelatory Paradox**: Anthropomorphic theophanies embody the paradox that divine self-disclosure always involves both revelation and concealment. According to David Aaron, "The anthropomorphic form simultaneously reveals divine presence while concealing divine essence, creating a dialectic of knowing and unknowing."[18]

---

15   Wolfhart Pannenberg, *Systematic Theology*, trans. Geoffrey W. Bromiley (Grand Rapids: Eerdmans, 1991), 1:219.

16   Karl Barth, *Church Dogmatics II/1: The Doctrine of God*, trans. T.H.L. Parker et al. (Edinburgh: T&T Clark, 1957), 260-261.

17   Katherine Sonderegger, *Systematic Theology: Volume 1, The Doctrine of God* (Minneapolis: Fortress Press, 2015), 87.

18   David H. Aaron, *Biblical Ambiguities: Metaphor, Semantics, and Divine Imagery* (Leiden: Brill, 2001), 34.

Michael Wyschogrod offers a provocative contemporary Jewish perspective, suggesting that "the persistent biblical anthropomorphism is not primitive or metaphorical but revelatory—disclosing that God's transcendence does not negate but rather establishes the possibility of genuine divine-human communion in shared form."[19]

Vision vs. Physical Manifestation

A third interpretive challenge involves distinguishing between visionary experiences and physical manifestations—whether divine appearances occur in objective, physical reality or in subjective, visionary experience.

Textual Ambiguities

Biblical theophanic accounts often leave ambiguous whether the manifestation is physical or visionary:

1. **Explicit Visionary Framework**: Some accounts are clearly framed as visions (Isa 6:1-13; Ezek 1:1-28; Dan 7:1-28; Rev 1:9-20), though even these raise questions about the nature of visionary experience in biblical thought.

2. **Ambiguous Phenomenology**: Many accounts describe sensory experiences without clarifying their mode—Jacob's wrestling (Gen 32:22-32), Moses at the burning bush (Exod 3:1-15), and Paul's Damascus road experience (Acts 9:3-9) all involve sensory perception yet remain phenomenologically ambiguous.

3. **Varying Witness Experience**: Some accounts mention that only certain individuals perceive the divine manifestation. At Paul's conversion, his companions "heard the voice but saw no one" (Acts 9:7), while in Daniel 10:7, "only Daniel saw the vision; the men who were with him... did not see the vision."

4. **Physical Effects**: Several accounts describe physical effects of the encounter—Jacob's dislocated hip (Gen 32:25, 31), Moses'

---

19   Michael Wyschogrod, *The Body of Faith: Judaism as Corporeal Election* (New York: Seabury Press, 1983), 76.

radiant face (Exod 34:29-35), or Saul/Paul falling to the ground (Acts 9:4)—suggesting some form of physical interaction.

John Collins notes that "the distinction between vision and physical manifestation may reflect modern categorical assumptions foreign to the biblical worldview, which did not necessarily distinguish sharply between different modes of perception as we do."[20]

Interpretive Approaches

Various interpreters have adopted different approaches to this challenge:

1. **Rationalistic Reduction**: Beginning with Spinoza and developed through the Enlightenment, rationalistic approaches typically reduced all theophanic accounts to either internal psychological experiences or figurative literary descriptions.

2. **Mystical-Experiential Interpretation**: Some interpreters, influenced by mystical traditions, understand theophanies as altered states of consciousness that transcend normal categories of "internal" and "external." According to Bernard McGinn, "Mystical experience typically dissolves the firm boundary between internal and external perception."[21]

3. **Objective-Subjective Integration**: Rudolf Otto and phenomenologists of religion propose understanding religious experience as involving both objective and subjective elements— "the holy" manifests in ways that are simultaneously external to the subject yet internally perceived.

4. **Cultural-Linguistic Approaches**: Some modern interpreters focus on the cultural-linguistic frameworks that shape both experience and its articulation. As George Lindbeck suggests,

---

20   John J. Collins, *The Apocalyptic Imagination: An Introduction to Jewish Apocalyptic Literature,* 2nd ed. (Grand Rapids: Eerdmans, 1998), 16.

21   Bernard McGinn, *The Foundations of Mysticism: Origins to the Fifth Century, The Presence of God: A History of Western Christian Mysticism,* vol. 1 (New York: Crossroad, 1991), xvii.

"Religious experience is always already interpreted through available linguistic and conceptual resources."[22]

5. **Narrative-Theological Reading**: Rather than deciding whether manifestations are "physical" or "visionary," some interpreters focus on their narrative-theological function. J. Richard Middleton suggests that "the text's refusal to clarify the mode of manifestation preserves the mystery of divine presence while affirming its reality."[23]

Contemporary Phenomenological Perspectives

Recent philosophical and scientific perspectives offer additional frameworks for navigating this interpretive challenge:

1. **Constructivist Models**: Constructivist approaches emphasize how perception always involves active construction rather than passive reception, suggesting that all perception (not just religious experience) involves subjective elements.

2. **Embodied Cognition**: Theories of embodied cognition propose that cognitive processes extend beyond the brain to include bodily systems and environmental interactions, challenging sharp distinctions between "internal" and "external" experience.

3. **Participatory Epistemology**: Some scholars propose participatory models of religious knowing, wherein divine manifestation involves the active participation of both God and human percipients, transcending subject-object dichotomies.

4. **Neuro-theological Perspectives**: Some interdisciplinary work explores how religious experiences may involve distinctive neurological patterns without thereby reducing them to "merely" subjective phenomena.

---

22   George A. Lindbeck, *The Nature of Doctrine: Religion and Theology in a Postliberal Age* (Louisville, KY: Westminster John Knox Press, 1984), 33.
23   J. Richard Middleton, *The Liberating Image: The Imago Dei in Genesis 1* (Grand Rapids: Brazos Press, 2005), 25.

William Alston's philosophical work suggests that "mystical perception might function as a genuine mode of cognitive access to divine reality, operating according to its own appropriate doxastic practices rather than those of sensory perception but no less capable of yielding knowledge."[24]

Cross-cultural Translation of Divine Encounter

The fourth interpretive challenge involves translating theophanic accounts across cultural and historical contexts—how these narratives can be meaningfully interpreted in settings far removed from their originating contexts.

Historical-Cultural Embeddedness

Biblical theophanic accounts are thoroughly embedded in their ancient Near Eastern contexts:

1. **Shared Cosmological Assumptions**: Ancient Near Eastern cultures shared certain cosmological frameworks—multiple heavens, divine councils, and the possibility of traffic between divine and human realms—that fundamentally shaped theophanic accounts.

2. **Cultural Literary Conventions**: Many features of biblical theophanies reflect broader literary conventions of the ancient world. John Walton notes that "divine appearances at crucial narrative moments constitute a common literary device across ancient Near Eastern texts."[25]

3. **Changing Metaphysical Frameworks**: The metaphysical assumptions of biblical authors differ significantly from those of later interpreters, creating hermeneutical challenges as these texts are read through evolving philosophical frameworks.

---

24   William P. Alston, *Perceiving God: The Epistemology of Religious Experience* (Ithaca, NY: Cornell University Press, 1991), 223.

25   John H. Walton, *Ancient Near Eastern Thought and the Old Testament: Introducing the Conceptual World of the Hebrew Bible* (Grand Rapids: Baker Academic, 2006), 249.

4. **Phenomenological Vocabularies**: The vocabulary and conceptual resources available for describing extraordinary experiences vary across cultures and historical periods, affecting both expression and interpretation of theophanic accounts.

Catherine Bell observes that "religious symbols and experiences are never culturally neutral but always embedded in specific systems of meaning that shape both their expression and reception."[26]

Translation Across Philosophical Frameworks

The interpretation of theophanies across philosophical frameworks presents particular challenges:

1. **Platonic Dualism**: When biblical texts were read through Platonic and Neo-Platonic frameworks, emphasis shifted from concrete divine manifestations to abstract divine attributes, often downplaying the significance of material theophanies.

2. **Aristotelian Categories**: Medieval scholastic interpretations analyzed theophanies through Aristotelian categories of substance, accident, and causality, raising new questions about the ontological status of divine appearances.

3. **Cartesian Subject-Object Dualism**: Modern interpretations often reflect Cartesian assumptions about the separation of mind and matter, subject and object, raising questions about the "objectivity" of theophanic experiences that biblical authors might not have formulated.

4. **Post-Enlightenment Naturalism**: Contemporary naturalistic assumptions challenge the possibility of divine manifestation altogether, creating interpretive frameworks where theophanies must be explained as either purely natural phenomena or literary fictions.

---

26   Catherine Bell, *Ritual Theory, Ritual Practice* (Oxford: Oxford University Press, 1992), 74.

Charles Taylor suggests that "the modern secular age has created conditions where divine manifestation becomes problematic in ways unimaginable to pre-modern consciousness, requiring new hermeneutical strategies for meaningful interpretation."[27]

Cross-cultural Missionary Translation

The translation of theophanic concepts in missionary contexts illustrates these challenges:

1. **Indigenous Parallels and Distinctions**: Missionaries have often sought indigenous parallel concepts to translate theophanic ideas, sometimes obscuring important distinctions. According to Lamin Sanneh, "The translation of theophanic concepts necessarily involves both cultural continuity and discontinuity, creating complex interpretive dynamics."[28]

2. **Ontological Assumptions**: Differing ontological assumptions about the nature of spirits, ancestors, and divine beings create challenges for translating theophanic accounts across religious contexts.

3. **Phenomenological Continuities**: Despite conceptual differences, phenomenological similarities in extraordinary religious experiences across cultures can provide bridges for meaningful translation of theophanic accounts.

4. **Power Differentials**: The translation of theophanic concepts often occurs within contexts of power imbalance, raising questions about whose interpretive frameworks take precedence in contested readings.

Andrew Walls observes that "the translation of Christian concepts, including divine manifestation, into new cultural contexts inevitably

---

27   Charles Taylor, *A Secular Age* (Cambridge, MA: Harvard University Press, 2007), 25.

28   Lamin Sanneh, *Translating the Message: The Missionary Impact on Culture*, 2nd ed. (Maryknoll, NY: Orbis Books, 2009), 53.

transforms both the receiving culture and the understanding of the concepts themselves—a process of creative mutual influence rather than simple transplantation."[29]

Contemporary Hermeneutical Approaches

Several contemporary approaches offer resources for cross-cultural interpretation of theophanies:

1. **Phenomenological Bracketing**: Phenomenological approaches attempt to temporarily bracket metaphysical assumptions to focus on the structural features of religious experience across cultural contexts.

2. **Ricoeurian Hermeneutics**: Paul Ricoeur's concepts of distanciation and appropriation provide frameworks for understanding how ancient texts can generate new meaning in contemporary contexts while respecting their historical otherness.

3. **Gadamerian Fusion of Horizons**: Hans-Georg Gadamer's concept of the "fusion of horizons" suggests how the historical horizon of the text and the contemporary horizon of the interpreter might engage in productive dialogue.

4. **Postcolonial Hermeneutics**: Postcolonial approaches highlight how power dynamics affect interpretive practices, calling for critical awareness of the political dimensions of cross-cultural biblical interpretation.

5. **Comparative Theological Approaches**: Recent developments in comparative theology offer methods for bringing theophanic accounts into conversation with other religious traditions' accounts of divine manifestation without premature harmonization or reductive comparison.

---

29   Andrew F. Walls, *The Missionary Movement in Christian History: Studies in the Transmission of Faith* (Maryknoll, NY: Orbis Books, 1996), 27.

Kwame Bediako suggests that "African readers bring distinct hermeneutical resources to theophanic texts, often recognizing dimensions of these accounts obscured by Western philosophical frameworks—not because they are 'closer' to the biblical world but because their interpretive traditions engage different questions."[30]

Conclusion: Toward an Integrative Hermeneutic

These four interpretive challenges—distinguishing angels from theophanies, understanding anthropomorphism, differentiating between visionary and physical manifestation, and translating divine encounters across cultures—reflect broader tensions within biblical hermeneutics. Rather than seeking definitive resolution to these tensions, an integrative hermeneutic might embrace them as productive paradoxes that generate ongoing theological reflection.

Such an approach recognizes that divine manifestation narratives function across multiple interpretive registers simultaneously:

1. **Historical-Critical Register**: These texts can be approached as historical sources reflecting the religious experiences and theological reflections of ancient communities, embedded within specific cultural contexts.

2. **Literary-Narrative Register**: The accounts function as literary narratives with specific rhetorical strategies, character development, and plot structures that shape theological meaning.

3. **Canonical-Intertextual Register**: Within their canonical contexts, theophanic accounts establish patterns and typologies that generate meaning through their relationships with other texts.

4. **Philosophical-Theological Register**: These narratives raise enduring philosophical and theological questions about divine-

---

30   Kwame Bediako, *Christianity in Africa: The Renewal of a Non-Western Religion* (Edinburgh: Edinburgh University Press, 1995), 175.

human relationship, transcendence and immanence, and the nature of religious knowledge.

5. **Existential-Spiritual Register**: As accounts of transformative encounters, these texts continue to shape religious imagination and spiritual practice across diverse communities of interpretation.

Walter Brueggemann suggests that "the most faithful interpretation of theophanic texts honors both their historical particularity and their ongoing generative capacity—their ability to disclose new meanings in new contexts precisely because they emerge from and witness to genuine encounters with divine mystery."[31]

The interpretive challenges surrounding divine manifestation narratives ultimately reflect the central paradox these texts communicate: that the transcendent God becomes genuinely present within created reality without surrendering divine otherness. As Karl Rahner observes, "The mystery of divine self-communication constitutes both the content of these narratives and the condition for their ongoing interpretation—God remains both revealed and concealed, manifest yet transcendent, in every act of divine self-disclosure and in every act of faithful interpretation."[32]

---

31   Walter Brueggemann, *Theology of the Old Testament: Testimony, Dispute, Advocacy* (Minneapolis: Fortress Press, 1997), 576.
32   Karl Rahner, *Foundations of Christian Faith: An Introduction to the Idea of Christianity,* trans. William V. Dych (New York: Crossroad, 1978), 137.

Chapter 16

Contemporary Significance

The study of angelophanies and theophanies extends beyond historical analysis and exegetical interpretation into contemporary theological, pastoral, and interdisciplinary domains. This chapter explores the ongoing significance of divine manifestation narratives for contemporary religious thought and practice, examining their theological implications, pastoral and liturgical applications, relevance to modern religious experience, and potential for interreligious dialogue. As Terence Fretheim observes, "The biblical witness to divine manifestation continues to shape religious imagination and practice precisely because it addresses the perennial human longing for divine presence that transcends historical and cultural particularity."[1] These ancient accounts of divine-human encounter remain vital sources for theological reflection and spiritual formation in contemporary contexts characterized by religious pluralism, scientific naturalism, and renewed interest in experiential dimensions of religious life.

Theological Implications for Modern Readers

Reimagining Divine Presence

The biblical accounts of divine manifestation offer resources for reimagining divine presence in contemporary theological thought:

1. **Beyond Deistic Distance**: In contexts where philosophical frameworks have emphasized divine transcendence to the point of practical deism, theophanic traditions provide theological foundations for affirming divine immanence and involvement with creation. According to Elizabeth Johnson, "The biblical witness to God's self-manifestation challenges contemporary

---

1   Terence E. Fretheim, *God and World in the Old Testament: A Relational Theology of Creation* (Nashville: Abingdon Press, 2005), 19.

theological tendencies to locate divine activity exclusively at the cosmic level, reminding us that the God of Israel and Jesus enters into particular historical moments and relationships."[2]

2. **Beyond Pantheistic Collapse**: Simultaneously, the dialectic of presence and absence in biblical theophanies resists the collapse of divine-human distinction found in various forms of pantheism and panentheism. As David Bentley Hart notes, "The God who manifests in biblical theophanies remains irreducibly other even in the moment of self-disclosure, preserving the Creator-creature distinction essential to biblical theology."[3]

3. **Incarnational Particularity**: The biblical pattern of divine manifestation culminating in the Incarnation challenges abstract conceptions of divine presence, grounding theological reflection in concrete historical particularity. Sarah Coakley argues that "the scandal of particularity in Christian incarnational theology derives its intelligibility from the broader biblical pattern of divine self-manifestation in specific times, places, and persons."[4]

4. **Material Mediation**: Theophanic accounts contribute to renewed appreciation for material mediation of divine presence in a cultural context often characterized by spiritual-material dualism. According to Belden Lane, "Biblical theophanies consistently present divine presence mediated through material reality—fire, cloud, temple, human form—providing theological foundations for sacramental and incarnational approaches to spirituality."[5]

---

2   Elizabeth A. Johnson, *Ask the Beasts: Darwin and the God of Love* (London: Bloomsbury, 2014), 143.

3   David Bentley Hart, *The Beauty of the Infinite: The Aesthetics of Christian Truth* (Grand Rapids: Eerdmans, 2003), 177.

4   Sarah Coakley, *God, Sexuality, and the Self: An Essay 'On the Trinity'* (Cambridge: Cambridge University Press, 2013), 87.

5   Belden C. Lane, *The Solace of Fierce Landscapes: Exploring Desert and Mountain Spirituality* (Oxford: Oxford University Press, 1998), 42.

Engaging Contemporary Philosophical Questions

Biblical theophanies contribute to engagement with contemporary philosophical discourse:

1. **Phenomenology of Revelation**: The phenomenological character of theophanic accounts resonates with contemporary philosophical interest in the structures of human experience. Jean-Luc Marion's concept of "saturated phenomena" provides a framework for understanding divine manifestations as experiences that exceed conceptual categories, creating the conditions for genuine encounter with transcendence.[6]

2. **Theological Epistemology**: Theophanic accounts raise questions about religious knowing that engage contemporary epistemological concerns. William Abraham suggests that "divine self-manifestation provides an epistemological foundation for theological knowledge that avoids both the rationalistic reductionism of the Enlightenment project and the subjective relativism of certain postmodern approaches."[7]

3. **Hermeneutics of Testimony**: Paul Ricoeur's philosophical work on testimony offers resources for understanding theophanic accounts as witnesses to events that exceed complete conceptualization yet bear transformative significance. According to Ricoeur, "The hermeneutics of testimony acknowledges both the genuine givenness of revelatory events and the interpretive frameworks through which they are received and transmitted."[8]

4. **Theological Aesthetics**: Divine manifestation narratives contribute to contemporary theological aesthetics through their presentation of divine glory (kabod/doxa) as simultaneously

---

6   Jean-Luc Marion, *God Without Being,* trans. Thomas A. Carlson (Chicago: University of Chicago Press, 1991), 106-110.

7   William J. Abraham, *Divine Revelation and the Limits of Historical Criticism* (Oxford: Oxford University Press, 1982), 24.

8   Paul Ricoeur, *Essays on Biblical Interpretation,* ed. Lewis S. Mudge (Philadelphia: Fortress Press, 1980), 123.

beautiful and overwhelming. David Brown argues that "theophanic accounts present an aesthetic vision of divine glory that transcends conventional categories of beauty through its incorporation of awe, wonder, and even terror, challenging domesticated notions of religious experience."[9]

Theological Anthropology

Theophanic narratives inform contemporary theological anthropology in several ways:

1. **Human Capacity for Divine Encounter**: The persistent biblical witness to divine-human encounter affirms human capacity for relationship with transcendence. As Rowan Williams observes, "The possibility of theophany presupposes a human capacity to perceive and respond to divine reality—a theological anthropology in which human beings are constituted precisely by their orientation toward and potential communion with God."[10]

2. **Transformed Perception**: Theophanic accounts frequently describe the transformation of human perception, suggesting that encounter with divine reality fundamentally alters human understanding and consciousness. According to Sandra Schneiders, "Biblical accounts of divine manifestation present a theological anthropology in which authentic humanity emerges through transformed perception resulting from divine encounter."[11]

3. **Embodied Receptivity**: The bodily dimensions of theophanic encounters challenge disembodied conceptions of spiritual

---

9   David Brown, *God and Enchantment of Place: Reclaiming Human Experience* (Oxford: Oxford University Press, 2004), 56.

10   Rowan Williams, *The Edge of Words: God and the Habits of Language* (London: Bloomsbury, 2014), 132.

11   Sandra M. Schneiders, *The Revelatory Text: Interpreting the New Testament as Sacred Scripture,* 2nd ed. (Collegeville, MN: Liturgical Press, 1999), 43.

experience. Sarah Coakley notes that "biblical theophanies consistently present divine encounter as involving embodied human receptivity, contributing to contemporary efforts to develop theological anthropologies that integrate physicality and spirituality."[12]

4. **Vocational Identity**: Many theophanic accounts involve commissioning and vocational calling, suggesting that authentic human identity emerges through responsive relationship to divine purpose. Walter Brueggemann argues that "the prophetic vocation narratives present a theological anthropology in which human identity is constituted not through autonomous self-determination but through responsive engagement with divine address."[13]

Ecological Theology

Recent theological engagement with ecological concerns has found resources in theophanic traditions:

1. **Creation as Theophanic Space**: Biblical theophanies frequently occur within natural settings—mountains, wilderness, bodies of water—suggesting creation's capacity to mediate divine presence. According to Terence Fretheim, "The natural settings of many biblical theophanies indicate that creation itself functions as a medium of divine self-disclosure, providing biblical foundations for ecological theology."[14]

2. **Material Sacramentality**: The material mediation of divine presence in theophanies supports sacramental approaches to creation. Denis Edwards suggests that "the biblical pattern of divine presence mediated through created reality provides

---

12   Coakley, *God, Sexuality, and the Self,* 114.

13   Walter Brueggemann, *The Prophetic Imagination,* 2nd ed. (Minneapolis: Fortress Press, 2001), 30.

14   Fretheim, *God and World in the Old Testament,* 27.

theological resources for developing ecological spiritualities that recognize creation's capacity to bear divine presence."[15]

3. **Divine Immanence**: Theophanic traditions balance divine transcendence with emphatic divine immanence, challenging theological frameworks that have contributed to ecological exploitation through radical divine-world separation. Elizabeth Johnson argues that "recovering biblical testimony to divine presence within creation contributes to theological foundations for environmental ethics by challenging anthropocentric frameworks built on absolute divine transcendence."[16]

4. **Transfiguring Vision**: The transfiguration narratives particularly suggest the potential transformation of human perception to recognize divine glory within the material world. According to Dorothy Lee, "The transfiguration presents created reality as capable of being permeated by divine glory without losing its created integrity, offering a theological vision of creation's eschatological transformation rather than replacement."[17]

Pastoral and Liturgical Applications

Homiletical Resources

Divine manifestation narratives provide rich resources for contemporary homiletics:

1. **Narrative Proclamation**: Theophanic accounts offer compelling narrative structures for proclamation that engage both cognitive and affective dimensions. Thomas Long suggests that "preaching theophanic texts invites hearers into transformative encounters

---

15   Denis Edwards, *Ecology at the Heart of Faith* (Maryknoll, NY: Orbis Books, 2006), 51.

16   Johnson, *Ask the Beasts*, 159.

17   Dorothy A. Lee, *Transfiguration, New Century Theology* (London: Continuum, 2004), 114.

with divine presence that parallel the encounters described in the text itself."[18]

2. **Tension Between Presence and Absence**: The dialectic of divine presence and absence in biblical theophanies provides homiletical resources for addressing contemporary experiences of God's seeming hiddenness. According to Barbara Brown Taylor, "Effective preaching acknowledges both divine revelation and hiddenness, creating space for honest engagement with experiences of divine absence while witnessing to the possibility of genuine divine presence."[19]

3. **Transformative Encounter**: Many theophanic narratives describe transformative encounters that reshape identity and vocation, providing homiletical paradigms for inviting contemporary transformative engagement with divine reality. David Lose argues that "preaching theophanic texts effectively involves more than explaining historical contexts or extracting moral principles—it requires creating the conditions for transformative encounter with the God who continues to manifest divine presence."[20]

4. **Multisensory Communication**: The multisensory character of biblical theophanies encourages homiletical approaches that engage multiple human faculties beyond purely cognitive processing. Jana Childers notes that "theophanic texts invite multisensory proclamation that engages imagination, emotion, and embodied presence alongside intellectual understanding."[21]

---

18   Thomas G. Long, *The Witness of Preaching,* 2nd ed. (Louisville, KY: Westminster John Knox Press, 2005), 197.

19   Barbara Brown Taylor, *When God is Silent* (Cambridge, MA: Cowley Publications, 1998), 76.

20   David J. Lose, *Preaching at the Crossroads: How the World—and Our Preaching—Is Changing* (Minneapolis: Fortress Press, 2013), 64.

21   Jana Childers, *Performing the Word: Preaching as Theatre* (Nashville: Abingdon Press, 1998), 51.

Liturgical Expressions

Theophanic traditions have shaped liturgical practices across Christian traditions:

1. **Sacred Space**: Architectural and artistic elements in liturgical spaces often draw from theophanic imagery—cloud, fire, light, throne—to create environments that suggest divine presence. According to Richard Kieckhefer, "Church architecture across traditions consistently incorporates theophanic symbols that suggest the building itself functions as a locus of divine manifestation, a contemporary analogue to the biblical tabernacle and temple."[22]

2. **Sacramental Theology**: Sacramental practices reflect theophanic patterns of divine presence mediated through material elements. Alexander Schmemann observes that "the Eucharist functions as an ongoing theophany in which divine presence is genuinely manifested through material elements without being reduced to or contained by them."[23]

3. **Liturgical Drama**: Many liturgical traditions incorporate dramatic elements drawn from theophanic accounts, particularly in high feast celebrations. Nathan Mitchell suggests that "liturgical dramaturgy creates participatory experiences of divine manifestation through symbolic actions, spatial arrangements, and sensory elements that draw participants into the dynamics of divine-human encounter."[24]

4. **Worship Practices**: Contemporary worship practices across denominational boundaries draw from biblical accounts of divine manifestation, albeit with varying emphases. David Peterson

---

22   Richard Kieckhefer, *Theology in Stone: Church Architecture from Byzantium to Berkeley* (Oxford: Oxford University Press, 2004), 97.

23   Alexander Schmemann, *For the Life of the World: Sacraments and Orthodoxy* (Crestwood, NY: St. Vladimir's Seminary Press, 1973), 35.

24   Nathan D. Mitchell, *Meeting Mystery: Liturgy, Worship, Sacraments* (Maryknoll, NY: Orbis Books, 2006), 84.

notes that "worship practices reflect theological assumptions about divine presence—from high liturgical traditions emphasizing mediated presence through ordained ministers and sacramental elements to Pentecostal and charismatic traditions emphasizing immediate divine manifestation through spiritual gifts."[25]

Spiritual Direction and Formation

Theophanic accounts inform approaches to spiritual direction and formation:

1. **Discernment of Experience**: The varied experiences of divine presence in biblical accounts provide frameworks for discerning contemporary spiritual experiences. According to Eugene Peterson, "Biblical narratives of divine-human encounter offer discernment resources for spiritual directors helping others interpret experiences that may indicate divine presence, providing both validation of genuine encounter and criteria for distinguishing authentic from inauthentic experiences."[26]

2. **Expectant Receptivity**: The biblical pattern of divine initiative in manifestation encourages spiritual practices characterized by receptivity rather than technique-driven attempts to manufacture religious experience. David Benner suggests that "spiritual formation grounded in biblical theophanic traditions emphasizes receptive attentiveness to divine self-disclosure rather than manipulative techniques for generating religious experiences."[27]

---

25   David Peterson, *Engaging with God: A Biblical Theology of Worship* (Downers Grove, IL: InterVarsity Press, 1992), 219.

26   Eugene H. Peterson, *The Contemplative Pastor: Returning to the Art of Spiritual Direction* (Grand Rapids: Eerdmans, 1989), 91.

27   David G. Benner, *Sacred Companions: The Gift of Spiritual Friendship and Direction* (Downers Grove, IL: InterVarsity Press, 2002), 163.

3. **Integration of Disturbance**: Theophanic accounts frequently describe disruptive and disorienting divine encounters, providing resources for integrating disturbing spiritual experiences. Janet Ruffing notes that "biblical theophanies legitimate spiritual experiences that disturb and disorient, challenging approaches to spiritual direction that evaluate experiences primarily through the criterion of consolation."[28]

4. **Communal Context**: Many biblical theophanies occur within communal contexts or lead to community formation, suggesting the importance of communal discernment and formation. According to Elizabeth Liebert, "The communal dimension of many biblical theophanies challenges individualistic approaches to spiritual formation, emphasizing the role of community in both discerning and responding to divine manifestation."[29]

Pastoral Care in Suffering

Theophanic traditions provide resources for pastoral care in contexts of suffering:

1. **Divine Presence in Affliction**: Biblical theophanies frequently occur in contexts of distress and displacement, suggesting divine presence within rather than only after suffering. Emmanuel Lartey argues that "the biblical pattern of divine manifestation in wilderness, exile, and persecution provides pastoral resources for affirming divine presence within rather than only beyond experiences of suffering."[30]

2. **Transformative Presence**: Many theophanic accounts describe transformative divine presence that does not immediately

---

28   Janet K. Ruffing, *Spiritual Direction: Beyond the Beginnings* (New York: Paulist Press, 2000), 105.

29   Elizabeth Liebert, *The Way of Discernment: Spiritual Practices for Decision Making* (Louisville, KY: Westminster John Knox Press, 2008), 39.

30   Emmanuel Y. Lartey, *In Living Color: An Intercultural Approach to Pastoral Care and Counseling,* 2nd ed. (London: Jessica Kingsley Publishers, 2003), 68.

remove suffering but provides resources for enduring and finding meaning within it. According to Deborah van Deusen Hunsinger, "Effective pastoral care draws from the biblical witness to divine presence that transforms suffering not primarily by removing it but by entering into it and transfiguring it from within."[31]

3. **Lament as Invocation**: The biblical integration of lament with theophanic traditions suggests the pastoral significance of creating space for honest expression of pain as a context for potential divine manifestation. Walter Brueggemann observes that "biblical lament does not merely express pain but constitutes a liturgical practice that creates the conditions for potential divine manifestation, challenging pastoral approaches that move too quickly from pain to resolution."[32]

4. **Eschatological Hope**: The biblical trajectory culminating in the vision of unmediated divine presence (Rev 21:3-4) provides pastoral resources for eschatological hope amid present suffering. According to Jürgen Moltmann, "The biblical promise of ultimate divine manifestation that will wipe away every tear does not trivialize present suffering but places it within an eschatological horizon that generates authentic hope."[33]

Angels and Theophanies in Contemporary Religious Experience

Phenomenology of Contemporary Encounters

Research on contemporary religious experiences reveals ongoing reports of angelophanies and theophanic encounters:

---

31 Deborah van Deusen Hunsinger, *Bearing the Unbearable: Trauma, Gospel, and Pastoral Care* (Grand Rapids: Eerdmans, 2015), 42.

32 Brueggemann, *The Prophetic Imagination,* 46.

33 Jürgen Moltmann, *The Coming of God: Christian Eschatology,* trans. Margaret Kohl (Minneapolis: Fortress Press, 1996), 302.

1. **Contemporary Angel Encounters**: Surveys indicate widespread reports of angel encounters across demographic categories, suggesting the persistence of this form of religious experience. According to Robert Wuthnow's research, "Approximately 76% of Americans express belief in angels, with nearly half reporting personal experiences interpreted as angelic encounters."[34]

2. **Theophanic Experiences**: Studies of religious experience document accounts of direct divine encounter that parallel biblical theophanic patterns. The research of William James, Alister Hardy, and David Hay has documented numerous reports of experiences interpreted as direct divine manifestation, often characterized by qualities of light, overwhelming presence, and life transformation.[35]

3. **Near-Death Experiences**: Many near-death experience accounts include elements paralleling biblical theophanic features—overwhelming light, encounter with a being of light, life review, and transformation. Carol Zaleski's comparative study suggests "significant phenomenological parallels between contemporary near-death experiences and traditional accounts of divine encounters, raising questions about their relationship to religious traditions of divine manifestation."[36]

4. **Mystical Experiences**: Contemporary mystical experiences often exhibit features paralleling biblical theophanies—sense of direct encounter with ultimate reality, ineffability, noetic quality, and transformative impact. William Alston's philosophical work suggests "potential epistemological continuity between biblical theophanic accounts and contemporary mystical experiences,

---

34   Robert Wuthnow, *After Heaven: Spirituality in America Since the 1950s* (Berkeley: University of California Press, 1998), 123.

35   William James, *The Varieties of Religious Experience: A Study in Human Nature* (New York: Longmans, Green, 1902), 66-67.

36   Carol Zaleski, *Otherworld Journeys: Accounts of Near-Death Experience in Medieval and Modern Times* (Oxford: Oxford University Press, 1987), 184.

challenging reductive approaches that categorically distinguish ancient from modern experiential claims."[37]

Interpretive Frameworks

Various interpretive frameworks have been applied to contemporary accounts of divine manifestation:

1. **Psychological Approaches**: Psychological interpretations range from pathologizing these experiences as hallucinations to recognizing them as authentic psychological phenomena with potential adaptive functions. According to Ralph Hood, "Contemporary psychology of religion has moved beyond purely reductive approaches to religious experiences, developing more nuanced frameworks that recognize their psychological reality and potential adaptive significance without necessarily making metaphysical claims about their referents."[38]

2. **Neuroscientific Research**: Recent neuroscientific studies have identified brain states associated with religious experiences, generating both reductive interpretations (these experiences are "nothing but" brain activity) and non-reductive approaches acknowledging correlation without assuming causation. David Newberg suggests that "identified neural correlates of religious experience demonstrate the embodied nature of these experiences without determining their ultimate ontological status."[39]

3. **Sociological Analysis**: Sociological approaches examine how cultural contexts shape both the content and interpretation of experiences interpreted as divine manifestations. According to Ann Taves, "Experiences deemed 'religious' are constructed

37   William P. Alston, *Perceiving God: The Epistemology of Religious Experience* (Ithaca, NY: Cornell University Press, 1991), 210.

38   Ralph W. Hood Jr., *Dimensions of Mystical Experiences: Empirical Studies and Psychological Links* (Amsterdam: Rodopi, 2001), 147.

39   Andrew B. Newberg, *Principles of Neurotheology* (Farnham, UK: Ashgate, 2010), 151.

through processes of attribution shaped by available cultural schemas, raising important questions about the relationship between experience itself and its subsequent categorization."[40]

4. **Theological Discernment**: Various theological traditions have developed discernment practices for evaluating experiences claiming divine origin. Sandra Schneiders observes that "theological discernment traditions emphasize criteria such as consistency with scripture and tradition, ethical fruits, communal confirmation, and interior freedom as indicators of authenticity in experiences claiming divine source."[41]

Cultural Representations

Contemporary culture continues to engage with angelophanies and theophanies through various media:

1. **Popular Literature**: Angels and divine manifestations feature prominently in popular religious literature, bestselling memoirs of spiritual experience, and fiction. According to Peter Gardella, "The persistence of angels and divine encounters in contemporary popular literature indicates ongoing cultural engagement with the possibility of direct contact between divine and human realms, albeit often in forms considerably removed from traditional theological frameworks."[42]

2. **Visual Arts**: Contemporary visual arts continue to explore the challenge of representing divine manifestation, engaging the tension between presence and absence central to theophanic traditions. According to John Dillenberger, "Contemporary religious art frequently employs abstraction, light effects, and

---

40   Ann Taves, *Religious Experience Reconsidered: A Building-Block Approach to the Study of Religion and Other Special Things* (Princeton, NJ: Princeton University Press, 2009), 62.

41   Schneiders, *The Revelatory Text*, 97.

42   Peter Gardella, *American Angels: Useful Spirits in the Material World* (Lawrence: University Press of Kansas, 2007), 175.

ambiguous forms to suggest divine presence while acknowledging its resistance to direct visual representation."[43]

3. **Film and Television**: Cinema and television frequently incorporate angelic figures and divine manifestation narratives, though often with significant reinterpretation. S. Brent Plate observes that "cinematic representations of divine manifestation engage the visual challenge of depicting the invisible, employing techniques such as extraordinary light, visual distortion, and special effects to suggest transcendent presence breaking into ordinary reality."[44]

4. **Digital Media**: Emerging digital media create new possibilities for representing and experiencing divine manifestation through virtual reality, immersive environments, and interactive narratives. According to Rachel Wagner, "Digital media's capacity to create immersive experiences that transcend ordinary perception creates new possibilities for representing divine manifestation, while raising significant questions about embodiment and mediation in religious experience."[45]

Religious Experience in Secular Contexts

Contemporary discourse on religious experience occurs within increasingly secular contexts:

1. **Contested Epistemological Status**: Claims of divine manifestation occur within cultural contexts where such experiences' epistemic status is fundamentally contested rather than assumed. Charles Taylor observes that "the contemporary 'secular age' is characterized not by the absence of religious belief

---

43   John Dillenberger, *Visual Arts and Christianity in America: From the Colonial Period to the Present* (New York: Crossroad, 1989), 228.

44   S. Brent Plate, *Religion and Film: Cinema and the Re-creation of the World,* 2nd ed. (New York: Columbia University Press, 2017), 74.

45   Rachel Wagner, *Godwired: Religion, Ritual and Virtual Reality* (New York: Routledge, 2012), 93.

but by its contested status, creating new conditions for both experiencing and interpreting potential divine manifestations."[46]

2. **Democratization of Experience**: Contemporary religious experience occurs in contexts of democratized spirituality that emphasize personal experience over institutional authority. According to Robert Wuthnow, "The contemporary spiritual landscape is characterized by emphasis on direct personal experience of transcendence apart from institutional mediation, creating both new possibilities and challenges for discerning authentic divine manifestation."[47]

3. **Therapeutic Framing**: Religious experiences in contemporary contexts are often interpreted through therapeutic rather than traditional theological frameworks. James K.A. Smith notes that "contemporary accounts of divine encounter frequently emphasize psychological healing and self-actualization over traditional theological categories such as holiness, judgment, or commission, reflecting broader cultural therapeutic emphases."[48]

4. **Pluralistic Context**: Claims of divine manifestation now occur within religiously pluralistic contexts that raise questions about particularity and universality. According to Robert Orsi, "Contemporary religious experiences must be interpreted within increasingly pluralistic contexts where multiple religious traditions offer competing interpretive frameworks, creating new challenges for theological discernment."[49]

---

46   Charles Taylor, *A Secular Age* (Cambridge, MA: Harvard University Press, 2007), 3.

47   Wuthnow, *After Heaven*, 168.

48   James K.A. Smith, *Desiring the Kingdom: Worship, Worldview, and Cultural Formation* (Grand Rapids: Baker Academic, 2009), 140.

49   Robert A. Orsi, *Between Heaven and Earth: The Religious Worlds People Make and the Scholars Who Study Them* (Princeton, NJ: Princeton University Press, 2005), 188.

Comparative Religious Perspectives

Cross-cultural Phenomenologies

Comparative study reveals both commonalities and distinctives in how various religious traditions conceptualize divine manifestation:

1. **Manifestation Typologies**: Cross-cultural study suggests certain recurring typologies of manifestation experiences—luminous appearances, auditory messages, overwhelming presence, and transformative encounters. Mircea Eliade's comparative work identifies "recurring phenomenological patterns in hierophanic accounts across cultural and historical contexts, suggesting potentially universal structures in human experiences of sacred manifestation."[50]

2. **Cultural Variations**: Despite phenomenological similarities, the specific content, interpretation, and significance of manifestation experiences vary considerably across traditions. According to William James, "The same types of experience receive radically different interpretations within different religious frameworks, suggesting that while the experiential 'raw material' may contain cross-cultural commonalities, its meaning is inseparable from interpretive traditions."[51]

3. **Mediation Patterns**: Religious traditions develop distinctive patterns for mediating divine presence—through persons (shamans, prophets, gurus), objects (icons, relics, sacred sites), practices (meditation, ritual, prayer), or texts. Ann Taves suggests that "comparative study reveals both similarities and differences in how religious traditions establish certain persons, objects, or practices as particularly efficacious mediators of divine presence."[52]

---

50   Mircea Eliade, *The Sacred and the Profane: The Nature of Religion,* trans. Willard R. Trask (New York: Harcourt, 1959), 21.

51   James, *The Varieties of Religious Experience,* 422.

52   Taves, *Religious Experience Reconsidered,* 89.

4. **Bodily Expression**: Divine manifestation experiences across traditions frequently involve distinctive bodily expressions and somatic experiences. According to Thomas Csordas, "The embodied dimensions of religious experience constitute a potentially universal domain for comparative study, revealing how divine manifestation is experienced and expressed through culturally shaped bodily practices."[53]

Abrahamic Traditions

Judaism, Christianity, and Islam share certain theophanic themes while developing distinctive emphases:

1. **Jewish Developments**: Post-biblical Jewish traditions developed complex angelologies and distinctive approaches to divine manifestation through concepts like the Shekinah (divine presence), Kavod (divine glory), and restrictions on visual representation. According to Elliot Wolfson, "Medieval Jewish mysticism developed sophisticated theoretical frameworks for divine manifestation that negotiated the tension between biblical theophanic accounts and philosophical emphasis on divine incorporeality."[54]

2. **Christian Particularity**: Christianity's distinctive contribution centers on the Incarnation as definitive theophany, with implications for understanding both previous and subsequent divine manifestations. According to Hans Urs von Balthasar, "The Incarnation establishes the normative pattern for authentic theophany in Christian theology—divine self-disclosure through self-giving love that respects creaturely freedom rather than overwhelming it through sheer power."[55]

---

53   Thomas J. Csordas, *Body/Meaning/Healing* (New York: Palgrave Macmillan, 2002), 241.

54   Elliot R. Wolfson, *Through a Speculum That Shines: Vision and Imagination in Medieval Jewish Mysticism* (Princeton, NJ: Princeton University Press, 1994), 324.

55   Hans Urs von Balthasar, *The Glory of the Lord: A Theological Aesthetics,*

3. **Islamic Perspectives**: Islamic tradition emphasizes divine transcendence while acknowledging certain modes of divine self-disclosure, particularly through the Qur'an as divine speech and the concept of God's "signs" (ayat) in creation. Sachiko Murata observes that "Sufi traditions particularly developed approaches to divine self-manifestation (tajalli) that maintain divine transcendence while affirming the possibility of experiential knowledge of divine reality."[56]

4. **Comparative Angelologies**: Angels function differently across Abrahamic traditions—as members of the divine council and occasional mediators in Judaism, witnesses to and servants of Christ in Christianity, and consistently obedient messengers in Islam. David Keck suggests that "comparative study of angelology reveals how each Abrahamic tradition negotiates the theological tension between divine transcendence and accessibility through distinctive understandings of intermediary beings."[57]

Asian Religious Traditions

Asian religious traditions offer different conceptual frameworks for understanding manifestations of ultimate reality:

1. **Buddhist Perspectives**: Buddhist traditions approach manifestation through concepts like Buddha-nature, Dharmakaya (truth body), and Sambhogakaya (enjoyment body) rather than through the personal divine being assumed in Abrahamic theophanic accounts. According to Malcolm David Eckel, "Mahayana Buddhist traditions developed sophisticated frameworks for understanding how ultimate reality manifests in perceivable forms without compromising its ultimate nature,

---

vol. 1, trans. Erasmo Leiva-Merikakis (San Francisco: Ignatius Press, 1982), 432.

56   Sachiko Murata, *The Tao of Islam: A Sourcebook on Gender Relationships in Islamic Thought* (Albany: State University of New York Press, 1992), 267.

57   David Keck, *Angels and Angelology in the Middle Ages* (Oxford: Oxford University Press, 1998), 189.

providing alternative conceptual resources for interpreting manifestation experiences."[58]

2. **Hindu Traditions**: Hindu concepts of divine manifestation include darshan (seeing/being seen by deity), avatars (divine descents), and varied relationships between ultimate reality (Brahman) and personal deities. Diana Eck observes that "Hindu theophanic traditions emphasize the visual dimension of divine-human encounter, developing complex theological understandings of how the invisible becomes visible through divine grace."[59]

3. **Daoist Approaches**: Daoist traditions emphasize the manifestation of Dao through natural processes and inner cultivation rather than through personal divine appearance. According to James Miller, "Daoist approaches to manifestation focus on how the invisible Dao becomes perceptible through natural processes, bodily cultivation, and ritual practice rather than through personalized divine appearances."[60]

4. **Indigenous Traditions**: Indigenous religious traditions often emphasize ongoing communication between human and divine/ spirit realms through various mediators and practices. Vine Deloria Jr. suggests that "Native American religious traditions frequently understand divine manifestation as ongoing communication between human and other-than-human persons through dreams, visions, and natural signs rather than as extraordinary interruptions of normal reality."[61]

---

58   Malcolm David Eckel, *To See the Buddha: A Philosopher's Quest for the Meaning of Emptiness* (Princeton, NJ: Princeton University Press, 1992), 126.

59   Diana L. Eck, *Darśan: Seeing the Divine Image in India,* 3rd ed. (New York: Columbia University Press, 1998), 9.

60   James Miller, *Daoism: A Short Introduction* (Oxford: Oneworld, 2003), 62.

61   Vine Deloria Jr., *God Is Red: A Native View of Religion,* 3rd ed. (Golden, CO: Fulcrum Publishing, 2003), 194.

Interreligious Dialogue

Divine manifestation traditions offer both resources and challenges for interreligious dialogue:

1. **Phenomenological Bridges**: Accounts of extraordinary religious experiences across traditions provide potential phenomenological bridges for dialogue beyond doctrinal formulations. According to Catherine Cornille, "Shared experiential dimensions of religion potentially provide common ground for interreligious dialogue when doctrinal formulations create apparent incommensurability."[62]

2. **Hermeneutical Challenges**: The interpretation of manifestation experiences remains inseparable from broader religious frameworks, creating hermeneutical challenges for dialogue. According to Francis Clooney, "Comparative theology acknowledges both experiential commonalities across traditions and the distinctive interpretive frameworks that give these experiences their specific religious significance."[63]

3. **Multiple Religious Belonging**: Contemporary contexts of multiple religious belonging raise new questions about the relationship between different traditions' understandings of divine manifestation. According to Peter Phan, "Persons who identify with multiple religious traditions navigate complex relationships between different understandings of how ultimate reality manifests, potentially developing integrative approaches that respect distinctive emphases while recognizing commonalities."[64]

---

62   Catherine Cornille, *The Im-Possibility of Interreligious Dialogue* (New York: Crossroad, 2008), 136.

63   Francis X. Clooney, *Comparative Theology: Deep Learning Across Religious Borders* (Malden, MA: Wiley-Blackwell, 2010), 57.

64   Peter C. Phan, *Being Religious Interreligiously: Asian Perspectives on Interfaith Dialogue* (Maryknoll, NY: Orbis Books, 2004), 94.

4. **Universal and Particular**: Divine manifestation traditions raise the fundamental theological question of how universal divine reality relates to particular historical manifestations. According to Jacques Dupuis, "Christian theology of religions must navigate between affirming the universality of divine self-communication and the particularity of its historical manifestations, recognizing both the genuine presence of divine reality in diverse religious traditions and the definitive character of its manifestation in Christ."[65]

Conclusion: Divine Manifestation in a Pluralistic Age

The biblical witness to divine manifestation continues to hold significance in contemporary contexts characterized by religious pluralism, secular critique, and renewed interest in experiential spirituality. The ancient accounts of angelophanies and theophanies provide theological resources for reimagining divine presence beyond both deistic distance and pantheistic collapse, grounding contemporary spiritual formation in the biblical dialectic of divine presence and absence.

These traditions contribute to contemporary theological engagement with philosophical questions concerning religious epistemology, phenomenology of revelation, and theological aesthetics. They provide pastoral and liturgical resources for contemporary religious communities seeking to create contexts for transformative encounter with divine reality while honestly acknowledging experiences of divine hiddenness.

The ongoing reports of angelic and divine encounters in contemporary contexts raise important questions about the relationship between ancient accounts and modern experiences, inviting nuanced engagement beyond both uncritical acceptance and reductive dismissal. Comparative study of divine manifestation across religious traditions reveals both phenomenological similarities and distinctive theological interpretations, creating both possibilities and challenges for interreligious dialogue.

---

65   Jacques Dupuis, *Toward a Christian Theology of Religious Pluralism* (Maryknoll, NY: Orbis Books, 1997), 254.

As Kevin Vanhoozer observes, "The enduring significance of biblical theophanic traditions lies in their witness to divine reality that genuinely communicates itself within history and creation while remaining irreducibly transcendent—a theological vision that continues to challenge both secular naturalism that denies transcendence altogether and religious perspectives that collapse the divine-human distinction."[66] These ancient accounts of divine manifestation continue to invite contemporary readers into the transformative dialectic of divine presence and absence that has shaped religious consciousness across cultures and centuries.

---

66   Kevin J. Vanhoozer, *Remythologizing Theology: Divine Action, Passion, and Authorship* (Cambridge: Cambridge University Press, 2010), 178.

Conclusion

This study has traversed the complex theological terrain of divine manifestations in biblical literature, examining the multifaceted ways in which the transcendent God becomes accessible to human experience through both angelophanies and theophanies. As we conclude this exploration, several key themes emerge that warrant synthesis and reflection: the developmental trajectory of divine manifestation across the biblical canon, the hermeneutical principles that have guided and continue to guide interpretation of these narratives, the enduring theological significance of these accounts, and promising directions for further research in this field.

Synthesis of Biblical Witness

Developmental Trajectory

The biblical record of divine manifestations reveals a discernible trajectory, though one that resists overly simplistic developmental schemes. Several patterns emerge from our study:

1. **From Direct to Mediated Presence**: The earliest biblical narratives often present remarkably direct divine appearances— God walking in the garden (Gen 3:8), visiting Abraham (Gen 18:1-8), wrestling with Jacob (Gen 32:24-30). Later texts increasingly employ mediating elements—the burning bush (Exod 3:1-6), the pillar of cloud and fire (Exod 13:21-22), and angelic messengers. This shift reflects growing theological attention to divine transcendence while maintaining divine accessibility.

2. **From Visual to Verbal Revelation**: While early theophanies frequently emphasize visual manifestation, later biblical tradition increasingly prioritizes verbal revelation. As Walter Moberly observes, "The gradual shift from seeing God to hearing God reflects a deepening theological understanding of divine nature

as transcending visual representation while remaining genuinely communicative through language."[1]

3. **From Individual to Corporate Experience**: Many early theophanies involve individual patriarchal figures in private encounters, while later manifestations—particularly in Exodus—occur in increasingly communal contexts. This shift establishes divine presence as constitutive of community identity rather than merely individual religious experience.

4. **From Limited to Universal Accessibility**: Earlier manifestations typically restrict direct divine encounter to specific individuals (patriarchs, Moses), while later prophetic and apocalyptic traditions envision eschatological divine manifestation that will be universally accessible: "The glory of the LORD shall be revealed, and all flesh shall see it together" (Isa 40:5).

5. **From Transient to Sustained Presence**: The development from momentary theophanies to more enduring divine presence in tabernacle and temple reflects theological concern for ongoing divine-human communion rather than merely occasional divine irruption into human experience.

6. **From Fearsome to Intimate Presence**: While divine manifestations consistently evoke awe, the biblical trajectory moves toward increasingly intimate presentations of divine presence, culminating in the incarnational and indwelling models of the New Testament.

7. **From Multiple Manifestations to Christological Focus**: The New Testament concentrates and reinterprets earlier theophanic traditions through christological focus, presenting Jesus as the definitive divine self-disclosure that fulfills and transcends previous manifestations.

---

1   R.W.L. Moberly, *The Old Testament of the Old Testament: Patriarchal Narratives and Mosaic Yahwism* (Minneapolis: Fortress Press, 1992), 125.

These developmental patterns should not be understood as simple linear progression, as Michael Fishbane notes: "The canonical arrangement of biblical texts creates dialogical relationships between earlier and later theophanic traditions, generating a complex intertextual conversation rather than merely sequential development."[2] The complex canonical interweaving of these traditions resists reductive historical-critical schemes while revealing substantive theological trajectories.

Persistent Tensions

Throughout the biblical canon, several theological tensions persist in divine manifestation accounts:

1. **Transcendence and Immanence**: Biblical theophanic traditions consistently navigate the tension between divine transcendence (God's ontological distinction from creation) and divine immanence (God's genuine presence within creation). This tension generates the various mediating forms of divine presence—angels, glory, name, spirit—that simultaneously manifest and veil divine reality.

2. **Particularity and Universality**: Divine manifestations occur in particular historical contexts to specific individuals and communities while simultaneously claiming universal significance. This tension becomes especially prominent in New Testament christology, where the particular historical person Jesus embodies universal divine reality.

3. **Continuity and Discontinuity**: Each new form of divine manifestation both continues and transforms previous traditions. The tabernacle/temple presence extends wilderness theophanic traditions while institutionalizing them; Christ fulfills previous manifestation patterns while radically reconfiguring them.

4. **Vision and Hiddenness**: Divine manifestations consistently integrate revelation with concealment, disclosure with mystery.

---

2   Michael Fishbane, *Biblical Interpretation in Ancient Israel* (Oxford: Clarendon Press, 1985), 352.

Even the most direct theophanies maintain elements of divine hiddenness—Moses sees God's "back" but not God's "face" (Exod 33:23); Isaiah glimpses the divine throne but with God partially veiled by seraphim (Isa 6:1-3).

5. **Form and Freedom**: Biblical theophanic accounts present recognizable patterns of divine self-disclosure while maintaining divine freedom to manifest in new and unexpected ways. No single manifestation exhausts divine reality or establishes exclusive patterns for future divine presence.

These persistent tensions resist theological resolution precisely because they reflect the fundamental paradox of divine self-disclosure—that the infinite God genuinely communicates with finite humanity without surrendering divine transcendence or overwhelming human freedom. As David Bentley Hart observes, "These tensions constitute not flaws requiring elimination but the generative dynamics of biblical revelation, establishing the conditions for ongoing theological reflection."[3]

Hermeneutical Principles

This study suggests several hermeneutical principles for interpreting divine manifestation narratives:

1. **Historical-Contextual Grounding**: Divine manifestation accounts emerge from specific historical and cultural contexts that shape their form and content. Responsible interpretation requires situating these narratives within their ancient Near Eastern environment while recognizing their distinctive theological contributions.

2. **Literary-Canonical Reading**: These accounts function as literary texts within a canonical context that generates meaning through narrative arrangement, intertextual connections, and theological patterns. Attentiveness to literary features—

---

3   David Bentley Hart, *The Beauty of the Infinite: The Aesthetics of Christian Truth* (Grand Rapids: Eerdmans, 2003), 156.

characterization, plot development, narrative perspective—
reveals theological significance beyond historical referentiality.

3. **Phenomenological Attentiveness**: Divine manifestation
narratives describe extraordinary human experiences that resist
reduction to either purely subjective projections or simple
historical reporting. Phenomenological approaches that attend
to the distinctive structures of religious experience provide
interpretive resources for understanding these accounts.

4. **Theological Integration**: These narratives participate in broader
theological frameworks concerning divine nature, divine-human
relationship, and divine purpose. Their interpretation requires
integration with fundamental theological categories while
allowing these narratives to challenge and reshape theological
assumptions.

5. **Interpretive Humility**: The elusive character of divine
manifestation narratives resists interpretive mastery. As William
Brown notes, "The very nature of theophanic accounts—
describing the appearance of that which transcends appearance—
creates inherent limitations for interpretation that properly
generate interpreting communities rather than interpretive
certainty."[4]

6. **Contemporary Appropriation**: These ancient accounts
continue to shape religious imagination and practice across
diverse contemporary contexts. Their ongoing interpretive
significance emerges through dialogue between their historical
particularity and their capacity to address perennial human
questions about divine presence.

These hermeneutical principles suggest an integrative approach that
respects both the historical particularity of divine manifestation accounts
and their ongoing capacity to generate theological meaning in new
contexts. As Richard Bauckham observes, "Responsible interpretation of

---

4   William P. Brown, *Seeing the Psalms: A Theology of Metaphor* (Louisville,
KY: Westminster John Knox Press, 2002), 83.

theophanic narratives requires methodological plurality—drawing from historical-critical, literary, phenomenological, and theological approaches without allowing any single method to claim interpretive sufficiency."[5]

Theological Significance

Divine Self-Communication

At their core, biblical angelophanies and theophanies witness to divine self-communication as constitutive of both divine nature and human fulfillment. These accounts present God as fundamentally communicative—not merely existing in self-sufficient isolation but actively revealing divine reality to creation. As Karl Barth articulates, "The God who manifests in biblical theophanies is not compelled to self-disclosure by external necessity nor by internal lack, but by the overflowing fullness of divine love seeking communion with creation."[6]

This theological vision challenges both deistic conceptions of divine detachment and pantheistic collapse of divine-human distinction, presenting instead a God who remains transcendent while freely choosing genuine relationship with creation. According to Kathryn Tanner, "The pattern of divine self-manifestation establishes the possibility of non-competitive relationship between Creator and creature—divine presence that enables rather than diminishes authentic creaturely existence."[7]

Human Transformation

Divine manifestation narratives consistently present divine-human encounter as transformative rather than merely informative. Those who experience divine presence emerge with altered identity, vocation, and

---

5   Richard Bauckham, *Jesus and the God of Israel: God Crucified and Other Studies on the New Testament's Christology of Divine Identity* (Grand Rapids: Eerdmans, 2008), 46.

6   Karl Barth, *Church Dogmatics II/1: The Doctrine of God,* trans. T.H.L. Parker et al. (Edinburgh: T&T Clark, 1957), 257.

7   Kathryn Tanner, *Jesus, Humanity and the Trinity: A Brief Systematic Theology* (Minneapolis: Fortress Press, 2001), 17.

perception. According to Sandra Schneiders, "Biblical theophanic accounts suggest that authentic encounter with divine reality fundamentally reshapes human consciousness, revealing both divine mystery and authentic human possibility."[8]

This transformative pattern challenges purely intellectualist approaches to divine revelation that reduce it to propositional content, suggesting instead that genuine knowledge of God involves transformative relationship that engages the whole person. As Rowan Williams observes, "The biblical witness to divine manifestation presents knowing God not primarily as cognitive mastery of divine reality but as transformative participation in divine life through responsive relationship."[9]

Creation as Theophanic Space

Divine manifestation narratives consistently present creation as capable of mediating divine presence—burning bushes, mountain theophanies, temple glory, incarnate Word—challenging dualistic frameworks that radically separate divine and material reality. According to Norman Wirzba, "Biblical theophanies present creation not merely as divine artifact but as potential medium of divine self-disclosure, establishing the theological foundation for sacramental understanding of material reality."[10]

This theological vision provides resources for contemporary ecological theology by affirming creation's capacity to bear divine presence without collapsing the Creator-creature distinction. Elizabeth Johnson suggests that "the biblical pattern of divine self-disclosure through created reality establishes a theophanic understanding of creation that grounds ecological responsibility in theological vision rather than merely utilitarian concerns."[11]

---

8   Sandra M. Schneiders, *The Revelatory Text: Interpreting the New Testament as Sacred Scripture,* 2nd ed. (Collegeville, MN: Liturgical Press, 1999), 105.

9   Rowan Williams, *The Edge of Words: God and the Habits of Language* (London: Bloomsbury, 2014), 187.

10   Norman Wirzba, *From Nature to Creation: A Christian Vision for Understanding and Loving Our World* (Grand Rapids: Baker Academic, 2015), 93.

11   Elizabeth A. Johnson, *Ask the Beasts: Darwin and the God of Love* (London: Bloomsbury, 2014), 267.

Eschatological Horizon

Biblical divine manifestation traditions establish an eschatological horizon of anticipated full divine presence that shapes present experience and practice. According to N.T. Wright, "Biblical eschatology envisions not the elimination of material reality but its transfiguration through unmediated divine presence—'the dwelling of God is with mortals' (Rev 21:3)—fulfilling the trajectory established through previous divine manifestations."[12]

This eschatological vision resists both over-realized eschatologies that claim complete divine presence in present experience and under-realized approaches that postpone divine presence entirely to a future beyond history. Instead, it establishes a dynamic relationship between present mediated divine presence and anticipated unmediated communion. As Jürgen Moltmann observes, "The biblical dialectic of divine presence and absence creates hopeful anticipation that sustains faith during experiences of divine hiddenness while preventing premature claims of eschatological fulfillment."[13]

Directions for Further Research

This study suggests several promising directions for further research:

1. **Interdisciplinary Integration**: Further dialogue between biblical studies, systematic theology, comparative religion, and cognitive science could deepen understanding of divine manifestation narratives. The embodied cognitive dimensions of religious experience provide particularly rich territory for interdisciplinary exploration.

2. **Comparative Theophanies**: More extensive comparative study of theophanic traditions across cultures could illuminate both distinctive biblical emphases and cross-cultural patterns in how

---

12   N.T. Wright, *Surprised by Hope: Rethinking Heaven, the Resurrection, and the Mission of the Church* (New York: HarperOne, 2008), 132.

13   Jürgen Moltmann, *The Coming of God: Christian Eschatology*, trans. Margaret Kohl (Minneapolis: Fortress Press, 1996), 278.

humans conceptualize and experience divine manifestation. Research on indigenous theophanic traditions remains especially underdeveloped.

3. **Gender and Divine Manifestation**: The gendered dimensions of theophanic accounts warrant further exploration, particularly examining how divine manifestation narratives both reflect and challenge gender constructions in their cultural contexts. Female imagery for divine presence in wisdom traditions offers fertile ground for such investigation.

4. **Ecological Hermeneutics**: The natural settings of many biblical theophanies invite deeper ecological readings that explore how these accounts might inform contemporary environmental ethics and theology. The mountain, wilderness, and garden settings of key theophanies particularly invite such analysis.

5. **Reception History**: Though scholarly attention has focused primarily on the historical contexts and literary features of theophanic accounts, their reception history across centuries reveals how these narratives have shaped religious imagination, practice, and theology. This reception history offers rich resources for understanding their ongoing interpretive significance.

6. **Contemporary Religious Experience**: More substantive dialogue between biblical theophanic traditions and contemporary accounts of religious experience could illuminate both continuities and discontinuities in how divine presence is experienced and interpreted across historical contexts. This research requires methodological sophistication that respects both historical particularity and phenomenological patterns.

7. **Liturgical Theology**: The relationship between biblical theophanies and liturgical practices warrants further exploration, examining how worship traditions across confessional boundaries have drawn from these narratives to create contexts for ongoing divine-human communion.

These research directions suggest the continuing vitality of biblical theophanic traditions for contemporary theological reflection, spiritual practice, and interdisciplinary dialogue. As Richard Kearney observes, "The biblical witness to divine manifestation continues to generate new interpretive possibilities precisely because it addresses the perennial human quest for transformative encounter with transcendent mystery."[14]

Conclusion

Biblical angelophanies and theophanies present a theological vision of the God who freely chooses self-disclosure without surrendering divine transcendence—a God who becomes genuinely present within creation while remaining irreducibly other. This vision emerges through diverse manifestation accounts across the biblical canon, reaching its definitive expression in the incarnation of Christ as the ultimate divine self-disclosure that both fulfills and transforms previous theophanic patterns.

These ancient accounts continue to shape religious imagination, theological reflection, and spiritual practice precisely because they address the perennial human longing for divine presence that transcends historical and cultural particularity. Their enduring significance lies not merely in their historical witness to past divine manifestations but in their ongoing capacity to invite contemporary readers into the transformative dialectic of divine presence and absence that constitutes authentic relationship with the living God.

As the twentieth-century Jewish philosopher Abraham Joshua Heschel eloquently expressed, "The God of Israel is a God who reveals, and revelation is not merely the disclosing of a content but the presence of a Person. The essence of prophetic experience is not the essence of reason or contemplation but the consciousness of being nurtured by the divine presence."[15] This consciousness of divine presence—mediated yet genuine, transformative yet freeing, historically particular yet universally significant—constitutes the enduring legacy of biblical theophanic traditions.

---

14   Richard Kearney, *Anatheism: Returning to God After God* (New York: Columbia University Press, 2010), 85.

15   Abraham Joshua Heschel, *The Prophets* (New York: Harper & Row, 1962), 436.

Conclusion

Appendices

Appendix A

Timeline of Significant Angelic and Theophanic Appearances

PATRIARCHAL PERIOD (CA. 2000-1700 BCE)

- Garden of Eden: God walking in the garden (Gen 3:8)
- Abraham at Mamre: Three visitors/LORD appears (Gen 18:1-15)
- Hagar in the wilderness: Angel of the LORD appears (Gen 16:7-14)
- Binding of Isaac: Angel of the LORD intervenes (Gen 22:9-18)
- Jacob's ladder: Angels ascending and descending (Gen 28:10-17)
- Jacob at Peniel: Wrestling with divine/angelic figure (Gen 32:22-32)
- Jacob's blessing of Joseph's sons: Angel who redeemed Jacob (Gen 48:15-16)

EXODUS AND WILDERNESS PERIOD (CA. 1446-1406 BCE)

- Moses and the burning bush: Angel of the LORD/God speaks (Exod 3:1-6)
- Pillar of cloud and fire: Divine guidance in wilderness (Exod 13:21-22)
- Sinai theophany: Divine presence on the mountain (Exod 19:16-20)
- Moses' vision of God's back: Partial divine self-disclosure (Exod 33:18-23)
- Tabernacle glory: Divine presence fills sanctuary (Exod 40:34-38)
- Balaam and the angel: Angel of the LORD blocks path (Num 22:22-35)

PERIOD OF CONQUEST AND JUDGES (CA. 1406-1050 BCE)

- Commander of the LORD's army: Appears to Joshua at Jericho (Josh 5:13-15)
- Angel at Bochim: Rebukes Israel for disobedience (Judg 2:1-5)
- Gideon's call: Angel of the LORD commissions (Judg 6:11-24)
- Manoah and wife: Angel of the LORD announces Samson's birth (Judg 13:2-23)

MONARCHIC PERIOD (CA. 1050-586 BCE)

- Samuel's call: LORD appears at Shiloh (1 Sam 3:1-14)
- David at the threshing floor: Angel of the LORD stays judgment (2 Sam 24:15-17)
- Solomon's temple dedication: Divine glory fills temple (1 Kgs 8:10-11)
- Elijah at Mount Horeb: Divine presence in "sound of sheer silence" (1 Kgs 19:9-18)
- Isaiah's throne vision: Seraphim in the temple (Isa 6:1-8)
- Ezekiel's chariot vision: Divine presence on cherubim throne (Ezek 1:4-28)
- Daniel's vision of the Ancient of Days: Divine throne appearance (Dan 7:9-14)
- Daniel's angelic messenger: Gabriel interprets vision (Dan 8:15-26; 9:20-27)
- Fourth figure in the furnace: Divine/angelic presence with three Hebrews (Dan 3:24-25)

SECOND TEMPLE PERIOD (CA. 515 BCE-70 CE)

- Zechariah's angelic visions: Multiple angelic appearances (Zech 1-6)
- Joshua the high priest: Satan and the Angel of the LORD (Zech 3:1-10)
- Malachi's messenger: Prophesied forerunner of the LORD (Mal 3:1-4)

NEW TESTAMENT PERIOD (CA. 5 BCE-95 CE)

- Annunciation to Zechariah: Gabriel announces John's birth (Luke 1:11-20)

- Annunciation to Mary: Gabriel announces Jesus' birth (Luke 1:26-38)

- Shepherds at Bethlehem: Angelic announcement of Jesus' birth (Luke 2:8-15)

- Joseph's dreams: Angelic guidance regarding Mary and Jesus (Matt 1:20-24; 2:13-23)

- Jesus' temptation: Angels minister to Jesus (Matt 4:11; Mark 1:13)

- Transfiguration: Divine glory revealed in Jesus (Matt 17:1-8; Mark 9:2-8; Luke 9:28-36)

- Gethsemane: Angel strengthens Jesus (Luke 22:43)

- Resurrection: Angels announce empty tomb (Matt 28:2-7; Mark 16:5-7; Luke 24:4-7; John 20:11-13)

- Ascension: Angels interpret Jesus' departure (Acts 1:10-11)

- Peter's prison release: Angel leads apostle from confinement (Acts 12:6-11)

- Cornelius: Angel directs to Peter (Acts 10:3-8, 30-32)

- Paul's conversion: Heavenly light and voice on Damascus road (Acts 9:3-8; 22:6-11; 26:12-18)

- John's apocalyptic visions: Multiple angelic appearances and divine throne visions (Rev 1:12-20; 4-5; 7:1-3; 8-11; 14:6-20; 19:11-16; 21-22)

Appendix B
Glossary of Key Terms in Original Languages

HEBREW/ARAMAIC TERMS

אֱלֹהִים ('elōhîm) - God; gods; divine beings. The primary Hebrew term for deity, typically used as a plural noun with singular verb forms when referring to the God of Israel.

יהוה (YHWH) - The tetragrammaton; the personal name of Israel's God, often rendered as "LORD" in English translations or vocalized as "Yahweh" or "Jehovah" in scholarly contexts.

מַלְאָךְ (mal'āk) - Messenger; angel. Derived from the root meaning "to send," this term designates both human messengers and divine/angelic messengers.

מַלְאַךְ יהוה (mal'ak YHWH) - Angel/messenger of the LORD. A specific figure in Hebrew Bible narratives whose identity is ambiguous, sometimes appearing to be distinct from YHWH while at other times speaking as YHWH.

כְּבוֹד יהוה (kəḇôḏ YHWH) - Glory of the LORD. Visible manifestation of divine presence, typically described as radiant light or fire, associated particularly with tabernacle/temple contexts.

פָּנִים (pānîm) - Face; presence. Used in expressions like "face to face" in theophanic contexts to indicate direct divine encounter.

שֵׁם (šēm) - Name. Deuteronomic theology emphasizes the divine name dwelling in the sanctuary rather than God's direct presence.

רוּחַ (rûaḥ) - Spirit; breath; wind. Represents divine presence extending into creation and human experience.

צֶלֶם (ṣelem) - Image. Used in Genesis 1:26-27 for humans made in God's "image," raising questions about divine form.

דְּמוּת (dəmût) - Likeness; resemblance. Paired with "image" in Genesis 1:26, suggesting correspondence between divine and human form.

כְּרוּב/כְּרוּבִים (kərûḇ/kərûḇîm) - Cherub/cherubim. Composite throne-guardians associated with divine presence in Eden, tabernacle, temple, and Ezekiel's visions.

שָׂרָף/שְׂרָפִים (śārāp̄/śərāp̄îm) - Seraph/seraphim. "Burning ones"; angelic beings in Isaiah's throne vision.

עַמּוּד עָנָן/עַמּוּד אֵשׁ (ʿammûḏ ʿānān/ʿammûḏ ʾēš) - Pillar of cloud/pillar of fire. Visible manifestation of divine presence guiding Israel in wilderness.

הַשְּׁכִינָה (šəḵînāh) - Shekinah. Post-biblical term (from root שׁכן "to dwell") referring to divine presence indwelling the tabernacle/temple or community.

חָזוֹן (ḥāzôn) - Vision. Prophetic perception of divine reality.

הַמַּרְאָה (marʾāh) - Vision; appearance. Visual manifestation or prophetic revelation.

הַתְּמוּנָה (təmûnāh) - Form; likeness. Used for visible representation, particularly in theophanic contexts.

הַמֶּרְכָּבָה (merkāḇāh) - Chariot. Ezekiel's vision of divine throne-chariot (Ezekiel 1); developed into merkabah mysticism in later Jewish tradition.

בַּר אֱנָשׁ (bar ʾĕnāš) - Son of Man (Aramaic). Human-like figure in Daniel 7 who approaches the Ancient of Days, later becoming a messianic title.

עַתִּיק יוֹמִין (ʿattîq yômîn) - Ancient of Days. Divine figure on heavenly throne in Daniel 7.

GREEK TERMS

ἄγγελος (angelos) - Messenger; angel. Greek equivalent of Hebrew malʾāk.

θεοφάνεια (theopháneia) - Theophany. From theos (God) and phainō (to appear); divine manifestation or appearance.

λόγος (logos) - Word; reason. In John's Gospel, the pre-existent divine Word that becomes incarnate in Jesus.

δόξα (doxa) - Glory. Greek equivalent of Hebrew kavod; divine splendor or magnificent presence.

ἐπιφάνεια (epipháneia) - Epiphany; appearance. Divine manifestation or appearance, particularly used for Christ's manifestation.

μορφή (morphē) - Form; shape. Used in Philippians 2:6-7 for Christ existing in "form of God" and taking "form of a servant."

εἰκών (eikōn) - Image. Used for Christ as "image of the invisible God" (Col 1:15).

χαρακτήρ (charaktēr) - Exact representation. Used in Hebrews 1:3 for Christ as "exact imprint" of God's nature.

ἀπαύγασμα (apaúgasma) - Radiance; effulgence. Used in Hebrews 1:3 for Christ as "radiance of God's glory."

πρόσωπον (prosōpon) - Face; presence. Used in expressions about seeing God "face to face."

ὀπτασία (optasía) - Vision; appearance. Supernatural appearance or vision.

ὅραμα (horama) - Vision. Something seen, especially a supernatural vision.

θρόνος (thronos) - Throne. Symbol of divine authority in theophanic and apocalyptic contexts.

παρουσία (parousía) - Presence; coming. Used for eschatological appearance of Christ.

σκηνόω (skēnoō) - To dwell; tabernacle. Used in John 1:14 for the Word "dwelling" among humans.

κύριος (kyrios) - Lord. Greek translation of Hebrew YHWH; also applied to Christ.

υἱὸς τοῦ ἀνθρώπου (huios tou anthrōpou) - Son of Man. Jesus' self-designation, drawing on Daniel 7.

χερουβίμ (cheroubim) - Cherubim. Greek form of Hebrew keruvim.

σεραφίμ (seraphim) - Seraphim. Greek form of Hebrew seraphim.

ἀρχάγγελος (archángelos) - Archangel. Chief or leading angel.

πνεῦμα (pneuma) - Spirit; breath. Greek equivalent of Hebrew ruach.

Appendix C
Comparative Chart of Major Theophanic Texts

PRE-SINAI THEOPHANIES

Passage	Divine Designation	Form of Manifestation	Human Response	Purpose	Key Features
Gen 3:8-24	"LORD God"	Walking in garden	Fear, hiding	Judgment and promise	Divine initiative, mixed with mercy
Gen 15:1-21	"Word of the LORD"	Word, smoking fire pot, flaming torch	Belief, deep sleep	Covenant establishment	Divine self-binding through ritual
Gen 16:7-14	"Angel of the LORD/God"	Humanlike appearance	Recognition, naming	Comfort and promise	Fluid identity between angel and LORD
Gen 18:1-33	"LORD" (with two angels)	Three men	Hospitality, intercession	Judgment announcement and dialogue	Divine accommodation to human form
Gen 28:10-22	"LORD"	Voice from top of ladder with angels	Awe, worship	Promise and revelation	Connection between heaven and earth
Gen 32:22-32	"Man"/"God"	Humanlike wrestler	Struggle, request for blessing	Identity transformation	Physical effect (hip displacement)
Exod 3:1-15	"Angel of the LORD"/"God"/"I AM"	Burning bush	Fear, hiding face, removal of sandals	Commission	Self-revelation of divine name

SINAI/WILDERNESS THEOPHANIES

Passage	Divine Designation	Form of Manifestation	Human Response	Purpose	Key Features
Exodus 13:21-22	Not specified	Pillar of cloud/fire	Following	Guidance	Regular, ongoing manifestation
Exodus 19:16-25	"LORD"	Fire, smoke, trumpet blast	Fear, trembling	Covenant establishment	Boundaries set to protect people
Exodus 24:9-18	"God of Israel"	Pavement of sapphire, consuming fire	Worship, meal	Covenant ratification	Limited visibility, graduated access
Exodus 33:7-23	"LORD"	Cloud, partial visibility	Worship, intercession	Reassurance of presence	Partial revelation ("back" not "face")
Exodus 40:34-38	"Glory of the LORD"	Cloud, fire	Deference (Moses unable to enter)	Indwelling of tabernacle	Institutionalization of presence
Numbers 12:4-10	"LORD"	Pillar of cloud	Fear, intercession	Prophetic authority	Uniqueness of Moses' access

PROPHETIC THEOPHANIES

Passage	Divine Designation	Form of Manifestation	Human Response	Purpose	Key Features
1 Kings 19:9-18	"LORD"	Fire, earthquake, wind, sound of silence	Fear, covering face	Reassurance and commission	Divine presence beyond spectacular phenomena
Isaiah 6:1-13	"LORD" (with seraphim)	Enthroned, temple-filling presence	Unworthiness, willing service	Prophetic commission	Mediated vision (seraphim)
Ezekiel 1:4-28	"Likeness of the glory of the LORD"	Throne-chariot, humanlike form	Falling on face	Prophetic commission	Complex symbolism, graduated revelation
Daniel 7:9-14	"Ancient of Days" and "one like a son of man"	White-haired enthroned figure	Anxiety, questioning	Eschatological revelation	Heavenly court scene
Zech 1-6	"Angel of the LORD" and interpreting angel	Multiple symbolic visions	Questioning, learning	Restoration promises	Mediated revelation through angelic interpreter

NEW TESTAMENT CHRISTOPHANIES AND THEOPHANIES

Passage	Divine Designa-tion	Form of Manifesta-tion	Human Response	Purpose	Key Features
Matthew 17:1-8 (and parallels)	"Beloved Son"	Transfig-ured Jesus, bright cloud	Fear, confusion, falling on face	Revelation of identity	Continuity with Moses/ Elijah, divine endorse-ment
Acts 9:3-9 (and parallels)	"Lord"/ "Jesus"	Blinding light, voice	Falling, blindness, questioning	Conversion and commission	Sensory disruption, selective perception
Revelation 1:12-20	"One like a son of man"	Glorious humanlike figure	Falling as dead	Commis-sioning and revelation	Combining multiple theophanic traditions
Revelation 4-5	"Lord God Almighty" and "Lamb"	Enthroned figure and slain Lamb	Worship	Revelation of heavenly reality	Integration of divine transcen-dence and sacrificial vulnerabil-ity

THEMATIC COMPARISONS

Theme	Hebrew Bible Pattern	New Testament Development
Mode of Revelation	Progressive shift from visual to verbal	Word becomes flesh (John 1:14)
Mediating Figures	Angels, particularly "Angel of the LORD"	Christ as definitive mediator (1 Timothy 2:5)
Human Access	Restricted, graduated (Exodus 19:12-13, 21-24)	New and living way opened (Hebrew 10:19-22)
Divine Form	Descriptions typically partial or veiled	"Whoever has seen Me has seen the Father" (John 14:9)
Community Formation	Individual encounters leading to community identity	Community as continuing locus of divine presence (1 Corinthians 3:16)
Glory Manifestation	External, often threatening radiance	Glory revealed in crucified and risen Christ (John 1:14; 2 Corinthians 4:6)
Response Pattern	Fear, unworthiness, then commission	Same pattern, but emphasis on bold access (Hebrew 4:16)

Appendix D
Select Bibliography for Further Study

PRIMARY SOURCES AND REFERENCE WORKS

Charlesworth, James H., ed. *The Old Testament Pseudepigrapha*. 2 vols. Garden City, NY: Doubleday, 1983-1985.

Elliger, K., and W. Rudolph, eds. *Biblia Hebraica Stuttgartensia*. Stuttgart: Deutsche Bibelgesellschaft, 1997.

Freedman, David Noel, ed. *The Anchor Bible Dictionary*. 6 vols. New York: Doubleday, 1992.

Kittel, Gerhard, and Gerhard Friedrich, eds. *Theological Dictionary of the New Testament*. Translated by Geoffrey W. Bromiley. 10 vols. Grand Rapids: Eerdmans, 1964-1976.

Koehler, Ludwig, Walter Baumgartner, and Johann Jakob Stamm. *The Hebrew and Aramaic Lexicon of the Old Testament*. Translated by M.E.J. Richardson. 5 vols. Leiden: Brill, 1994-2000.

Nestle, Eberhard, Erwin Nestle, Barbara Aland, and Kurt Aland, eds. *Novum Testamentum Graece*. 28th ed. Stuttgart: Deutsche Bibelgesellschaft, 2012.

Pritchard, James B., ed. *Ancient Near Eastern Texts Relating to the Old Testament*. 3rd ed. Princeton: Princeton University Press, 1969.

VanderKam, James C., and Peter W. Flint. *The Meaning of the Dead Sea Scrolls: Their Significance for Understanding the Bible, Judaism, Jesus, and Christianity*. San Francisco: HarperSanFrancisco, 2002.

ANGELOLOGY

Bhayro, Siam, and Gideon Bohak, eds. *Demons and Illness from Antiquity to the Early-Modern Period*. Leiden: Brill, 2017.

Davidson, Maxwell J. *Angels at Qumran: A Comparative Study of 1 Enoch 1-36, 72-108 and Sectarian Writings from Qumran.* Sheffield: Sheffield Academic Press, 1992.

Hannah, Darrell D. *Michael and Christ: Michael Traditions and Angel Christology in Early Christianity.* Tübingen: Mohr Siebeck, 1999.

Heiser, Michael S. Angels: *What the Bible Really Says About God's Heavenly Host.* Bellingham, WA: Lexham Press, 2018.

Jones, David Albert. *Angels: A History.* Oxford: Oxford University Press, 2010.

Keck, David. *Angels and Angelology in the Middle Ages.* Oxford: Oxford University Press, 1998.

Muehlberger, Ellen. *Angels in Late Ancient Christianity.* Oxford: Oxford University Press, 2013.

Newsom, Carol A. *Songs of the Sabbath Sacrifice: A Critical Edition.* Atlanta: Scholars Press, 1985.

Olyan, Saul M. *A Thousand Thousands Served Him: Exegesis and the Naming of Angels in Ancient Judaism.* Tübingen: Mohr Siebeck, 1993.

Schwartz, Howard. *Tree of Souls: The Mythology of Judaism.* Oxford: Oxford University Press, 2004.

Stuckenbruck, Loren T. *Angel Veneration and Christology: A Study in Early Judaism and in the Christology of the Apocalypse of John.* Tübingen: Mohr Siebeck, 1995.

Sullivan, Kevin P. *Wrestling with Angels: A Study of the Relationship between Angels and Humans in Ancient Jewish Literature and the New Testament.* Leiden: Brill, 2004.

Tuschling, R.M.M. *Angels and Orthodoxy: A Study in Their Development in Syria and Palestine from the Qumran Texts to Ephrem the Syrian.* Tübingen: Mohr Siebeck, 2007.

DIVINE MANIFESTATION IN HEBREW BIBLE

Barr, James. *The Semantics of Biblical Language.* Oxford: Oxford University Press, 1961.

Baruch Levine. *In the Presence of the Lord: A Study of Cult and Some Cultic Terms in Ancient Israel.* Leiden: Brill, 1974.

Friedman, Richard Elliott. *The Disappearance of God: A Divine Mystery.* Boston: Little, Brown, 1995.

Fretheim, Terence E. *The Suffering of God: An Old Testament Perspective.* Philadelphia: Fortress Press, 1984.

Gentry, Peter J., and Stephen J. Wellum. *Kingdom through Covenant: A Biblical-Theological Understanding of the Covenants.* Wheaton, IL: Crossway, 2012.

Hamori, Esther J. *"When Gods Were Men": The Embodied God in Biblical and Near Eastern Literature.* Berlin: de Gruyter, 2008.

Mettinger, Tryggve N.D. *The Dethronement of Sabaoth: Studies in the Shem and Kabod Theologies.* Lund: Gleerup, 1982.

Miller, Patrick D. *The Divine Warrior in Early Israel.* Cambridge, MA: Harvard University Press, 1973.

Moberly, R.W.L. *The Old Testament of the Old Testament: Patriarchal Narratives and Mosaic Yahwism.* Minneapolis: Fortress Press, 1992.

Savran, George W. *Encountering the Divine: Theophany in Biblical Narrative.* London: T&T Clark, 2005.

Sommer, Benjamin D. *The Bodies of God and the World of Ancient Israel.* Cambridge: Cambridge University Press, 2009.

Terrien, Samuel. *The Elusive Presence: Toward a New Biblical Theology.* San Francisco: Harper & Row, 1978.

von Rad, Gerhard. *Old Testament Theology.* Translated by D.M.G. Stalker. 2 vols. New York: Harper & Row, 1962-1965.

NEW TESTAMENT CHRISTOLOGY AND THEOPHANY

Bauckham, Richard. *God Crucified: Monotheism and Christology in the New Testament.* Grand Rapids: Eerdmans, 1999.

Bauckham, Richard. *Jesus and the God of Israel: God Crucified and Other Studies on the New Testament's Christology of Divine Identity.* Grand Rapids: Eerdmans, 2008.

Bockmuehl, Markus. *The Epistle to the Philippians. Black's New Testament Commentary.* London: A&C Black, 1997.

Dunn, James D.G. *Christology in the Making: A New Testament Inquiry into the Origins of the Doctrine of the Incarnation.* 2nd ed. Grand Rapids: Eerdmans, 1996.

Gathercole, Simon J. *The Pre-existent Son: Recovering the Christologies of Matthew, Mark, and Luke.* Grand Rapids: Eerdmans, 2006.

Hengel, Martin. *The Son of God: The Origin of Christology and the History of Jewish-Hellenistic Religion.* Translated by John Bowden. Philadelphia: Fortress Press, 1976.

Hurtado, Larry W. *Lord Jesus Christ: Devotion to Jesus in Earliest Christianity.* Grand Rapids: Eerdmans, 2003.

Lee, Dorothy A. *Transfiguration. New Century Theology.* London: Continuum, 2004.

McGrath, James F. *The Only True God: Early Christian Monotheism in Its Jewish Context.* Urbana: University of Illinois Press, 2009.

Tilling, Chris. *Paul's Divine Christology.* Tübingen: Mohr Siebeck, 2012.

Wright, N.T. *The Climax of the Covenant: Christ and the Law in Pauline Theology.* Minneapolis: Fortress Press, 1992.

ANCIENT NEAR EASTERN AND MEDITERRANEAN CONTEXT

Clifford, Richard J. *The Cosmic Mountain in Canaan and the Old Testament.* Cambridge, MA: Harvard University Press, 1972.

Collins, John J. *The Apocalyptic Imagination: An Introduction to Jewish Apocalyptic Literature.* 2nd ed. Grand Rapids: Eerdmans, 1998.

Keel, Othmar. *The Symbolism of the Biblical World: Ancient Near Eastern Iconography and the Book of Psalms.* Translated by Timothy J. Hallett. New York: Seabury Press, 1978.

Knohl, Israel. *The Divine Symphony: The Bible's Many Voices.* Philadelphia: Jewish Publication Society, 2003.

Kuemmerlin-McLean, Joanne K. *Magic: Old Testament.* In The Anchor Bible Dictionary, edited by David Noel Freedman, 4:468-471. New York: Doubleday, 1992.

Nissinen, Martti. *Prophets and Prophecy in the Ancient Near East. Writings from the Ancient World 12.* Atlanta: Society of Biblical Literature, 2003.

Orlov, Andrei A. *The Enoch-Metatron Tradition.* Tübingen: Mohr Siebeck, 2005.

Orlov, Andrei A. *Divine Scapegoats: Demonic Mimesis in Early Jewish Mysticism.* Albany: State University of New York Press, 2015.

Walton, John H. *Ancient Near Eastern Thought and the Old Testament: Introducing the Conceptual World of the Hebrew Bible.* Grand Rapids: Baker Academic, 2006.

THEOLOGICAL AND PHILOSOPHICAL PERSPECTIVES

Barth, Karl. *Church Dogmatics II/1: The Doctrine of God.* Translated by T.H.L. Parker, W.B. Johnston, Harold Knight, and J.L.M. Haire. Edinburgh: T&T Clark, 1957.

Basil the Great. *On the Holy Spirit.* Translated by David Anderson. Crestwood, NY: St. Vladimir's Seminary Press, 1980.

Coakley, Sarah. *God, Sexuality, and the Self: An Essay 'On the Trinity'.* Cambridge: Cambridge University Press, 2013.

Gregory of Nyssa. *The Life of Moses.* Translated by Abraham J. Malherbe and Everett Ferguson. New York: Paulist Press, 1978.

Jenson, Robert W. *Systematic Theology: Volume 1, The Triune God.* Oxford: Oxford University Press, 1997.

Jüngel, Eberhard. *God as the Mystery of the World: On the Foundation of the Theology of the Crucified One in the Dispute between Theism and Atheism.* Translated by Darrell L. Guder. Grand Rapids: Eerdmans, 1983.

Marion, Jean-Luc. *God Without Being.* Translated by Thomas A. Carlson. Chicago: University of Chicago Press, 1991.

Moltmann, Jürgen. *The Crucified God: The Cross of Christ as the Foundation and Criticism of Christian Theology.* Translated by R.A. Wilson and John Bowden. New York: Harper & Row, 1974.

Pannenberg, Wolfhart. *Systematic Theology.* Translated by Geoffrey W. Bromiley. 3 vols. Grand Rapids: Eerdmans, 1991-1998.

Rahner, Karl. *Foundations of Christian Faith: An Introduction to the Idea of Christianity.* Translated by William V. Dych. New York: Crossroad, 1978.

von Balthasar, Hans Urs. *The Glory of the Lord: A Theological Aesthetics.* 7 vols. Translated by Erasmo Leiva-Merikakis, Joseph Fessio, and John Riches. San Francisco: Ignatius Press, 1982-1989.

SPIRITUAL AND PASTORAL PERSPECTIVES

Brown, David. *God and Enchantment of Place: Reclaiming Human Experience.* Oxford: Oxford University Press, 2004.

Lane, Belden C. *The Solace of Fierce Landscapes: Exploring Desert and Mountain Spirituality.* Oxford: Oxford University Press, 1998.

Merton, Thomas. *New Seeds of Contemplation.* New York: New Directions, 1972.

Peterson, Eugene H. *The Contemplative Pastor: Returning to the Art of Spiritual Direction.* Grand Rapids: Eerdmans, 1989.

Seamands, Stephen. *Ministry in the Image of God: The Trinitarian Shape of Christian Service.* Downers Grove, IL: InterVarsity Press, 2005.

Underhill, Evelyn. *Mysticism: A Study in the Nature and Development of Spiritual Consciousness.* 12th ed. New York: E.P. Dutton, 1930.

Williams, Rowan. *The Edge of Words: God and the Habits of Language.* London: Bloomsbury, 2014.

Dedicated to all who had divine encounters and experienced the presence of the God of the Bible—YHWH.
You are not strange, and you are not alone.

About the Author

Bishop Antonio M. Palmer is the Senior Pastor of Kingdom Celebration Center and the Presiding Bishop of Kingdom Alliance of Churches International, providing apostolic covering to a global network of 74 churches. With a ministry rooted in the Gospel since 1993, he planted his first church in Annapolis, Maryland, in 1995 and became a beacon of leadership, service, and transformation.

A passionate advocate for missions, Bishop Palmer leads leadership conferences, plants churches, and provides humanitarian aid to thousands of children in need across the globe. His work includes substantial financial support for orphanages in India and East Africa, demonstrating a steadfast commitment to serving the underserved.

Bishop Palmer, a respected community leader, is celebrated for fostering unity and collaboration among diverse groups. His efforts address critical issues, promote meaningful dialogue, and inspire transformative change. He holds a Bachelor of Divinity and a Master's in Pastoral Counseling. He has been recognized with numerous accolades, including two Governor Citations, two County Executive Citations, and the prestigious Martin Luther King Jr. Drum Major Award.

As an entrepreneur, Bishop Palmer owns Kingdom Publishing LLC, Antonio Marlin Art, and Kingdom Kare, Inc., a thriving nonprofit organization. He is also the author of seven impactful books: *Living By the Spirit, Love Thyself: Empowering Men for Healthy Living, God's Rest Revealed: A Life Flowing with Milk and Honey, Building an Effective Prayer Life, Mark the Perfect Man: How to Find a Model of Maturity, Revival: God Will Come Where You Are, Rooted and Grounded in Love,* and *Little Kairo Takes on the World* (Children's Book).

www.ingramcontent.com/pod-product-compliance
Lightning Source LLC
Chambersburg PA
CBHW071720120626
46550CB00001B/310